The Middle East and American National Security

The Middle East and American National Security

Forever Wars and Conflicts?

Donald M. Snow

ROWMAN & LITTLEFIELD
Lanham • Boulder • New York • London

Published by Rowman & Littlefield
An imprint of The Rowman & Littlefield Publishing Group, Inc.
4501 Forbes Boulevard, Suite 200, Lanham, Maryland 20706
www.rowman.com

6 Tinworth Street, London SE11 5AL, United Kingdom

Copyright © 2021 by The Rowman & Littlefield Publishing Group, Inc.

All rights reserved. No part of this book may be reproduced in any form or by any electronic or mechanical means, including information storage and retrieval systems, without written permission from the publisher, except by a reviewer who may quote passages in a review.

British Library Cataloguing in Publication Information Available

Library of Congress Cataloging-in-Publication Data

ISBN: 978-1-5381-5468-7 (cloth)
ISBN: 978-1-5381-5469-4 (paperback)
ISBN: 978-1-5381-5470-0 (electronic)

Contents

Preface		vii
1	National Interests and American Involvement in the Middle East	1
2	The Contentious Middle East	17
3	The Special Relationship: Israel	35
4	The Tragedy and Dilemma of Stateless Peoples: Palestine	59
5	The Tragic Fate of Stateless People II: Kurdistan	79
6	The Syrian Pivot after the Civil War	101
7	The Chaotic Shiite Crescent: Iran, Iraq, Syria, Lebanon	121
8	The Mini Cold War Struggle: Iran and Saudi Arabia	141
9	The Forever Wars: Iraq and Afghanistan	161
10	Navigating the Geopolitical Spider's Web	179
11	Challenges for the New Administration	197
Index		213
About the Author		227

Preface

Since it finally extricated itself from what was to that point the country's longest and least successful war in Vietnam in 1975, the physical, if not necessarily intellectual, emphasis of American national security policy has moved into the Middle East. With the exception of minor involvements in Kosovo and Haiti in the 1990s, almost all the actual applications of American military force have been in Middle Eastern states, from landing the Marines in Lebanon in the early 1980s to the ongoing and seemingly perpetual deployment of American forces into war zones in Iraq and Afghanistan and the seemingly bottomless pit of American military sales and grants of equipment to places like Saudi Arabia and Israel.

These experiences share three major characteristics. The first is that most of them have flown under the radar of political discourse and debate in the United States. Most Americans, for instance, are entirely unaware of American assistance and complicity in one of the world's currently most vicious proxy wars between the government of Yemen and the rebel Houthis, but it has caused enormous suffering and controversy in the region. The United States has been involved in conflict and combat in Afghanistan since 2001. Although there have been multiple calls to bring the troops home from presidents Obama and Trump, they were not compelling enough to accomplish that end. Could that be because as of mid-2019, there had been "only" 2,400 American combat deaths (less than 150 per year) in Afghanistan during the country's longest war? Are the costs of American adventures in the Middle East small enough to be tolerable?

The Syrian misadventure revealed a second characteristic of American military and geopolitical involvement in the region, a tendency to misunderstand (or underestimate) the depth and complexity of events and actions in the region. Trump was apparently motivated by a desire to reduce greatly American physical exposure in the region when he ordered the evacuation of U.S. personnel from Syria in late 2019, a goal urged upon him by erstwhile NATO ally Turkey. It also, however, contained the complex of intrigues, moves, and countermoves that marks the area. The Kurds, whose story is chronicled in Chapter 5, were particularly adversely affected, including another of the periodical setbacks for Kurdish nationalism and self-determination (which virtually all regional states join Turkey in opposing). In turn, the backlash included an indirect boost for Syria's rogue leader, Bashar al-Assad, and increased influence for Assad's chief regional ally, Russia, and for expansionist Iran. None of these effects serve visible American interests. It is not clear Trump and company realized this when the fateful decisions were reached. Rather, it is frequently true, as Gordon asserts, that "U.S. policymakers often lack a deep understanding of the countries in question."

The third shared characteristic is the relative lack of success of American arms in the region. The only unarguable triumphs at arms for the United States since it militarily became an active part of the pattern of Middle Eastern violence was the Operation Desert Storm eviction of Iraq from Kuwait in 1990–1991. The irony of that encounter was that it was the only time the United States employed its conventional forces in traditional, European-style against Iraqi armed forces that organized and fought the same way but were not as good at it as the Americans. The experience taught a valuable lesson to Middle Easterners (including the Iraqis): do not fight the Americans the way they want to fight, or you will lose. The lesson was that the only way to frustrate the Americans is by fighting asymmetrically. The Iraqis mounted only a token traditional defense in 2003 and then organized an unconventional, asymmetrical defense aimed at getting rid of the Americans. Others, from the Afghan Taliban to ISIS, also learned the lesson. More recently, an American presence has kept the lid on other simmering conflicts like Syrian Kurdistan before the withdrawal. There have been more attempted uses that have not gone so well.

These adjustments reflect that the political nature of war has changed. Through World War II, the pattern and norm for fighting was warfare between conventional armed forces, the purpose and outcome was the capitulation or exhaustion of the enemy, after which a formal surrender and peace treaty were negotiated. World War II was the last conflict where those characteristics held; they no longer do. When the enemy surrendered, it was easy to determine who had "won." No one surrenders and lays down their arms anymore; assessing victory and defeat are not so easy. (See Snow and Drew for a more complete discussion.)

Contemporary situations, including those in which the United States finds itself, are more difficult, and so is their resolution. Most have some domestic component, pitting elements within a country (which is often an artificial political contrivance anyway) against one another for control of government. Such conflicts are often more furtive and desperate than traditional conflicts, and in many places (notably the Middle East) one or both sides are assisted by outsiders who complicate both the fighting and the politics of the situation. These wars rarely ever end with a negotiated conclusion; instead one side or the other quits the field for a time, vowing to return. Nobody admits defeat; assessing who "won" is virtually impossible. What is common is the degree of desperation on both (or all) sides, and this makes the situations extremely difficult both to assess and influence.

These wars also tend to occur in the developing world, where the style of warfare is markedly different than the European-style fighting associated with the West from the Thirty Years' War in 1648 through World War II. Asymmetrical warfare is an approach to fighting that has evolved as an effective means to negate and prevail over the heavy armies that marked the world wars, and it has proven effective against those kinds of forces a large part of the time. The upshot is that the United States has not prevailed in military involvements since Desert Storm thirty years ago, and this raises the question of whether it should commit itself to involvement in violent situations in Middle East situations where its most important interests are not clearly engaged and where post-Vietnam experience has shown it is not likely to "win" in any decisive way that clearly advances or buttresses American regional or global interests.

In the current national security milieu, the situation in the Middle East has clearly commanded the most American attention of any global region, a status that arguably overly inflates its importance in a world in which its petroleum does not command the fealty it historically has. Malley, in a November/December 2019 *Foreign Affairs* article, underscores the geopolitical importance it has assumed. "The conditions for an all-out war in the Middle East are riper than at any time in recent memory," he writes. "A conflict could break in any number of places for any one of a number of reasons."

This is not an entirely new problem. Writing in 2014, for instance, Bacevich listed all the countries where American arms had been employed since 2014. Other than the Balkans and Haiti, they were all Middle Eastern, and they are all places that would be on any list of countries where the United States is still involved at one level or another. This grim set of scenarios that could explode raises serious questions of whether the United States should become involved in these conflicts, at what levels and how, and what the United States can and should do to defuse or try otherwise to help manage them. Many are complex and interactive, "geopolitical spider webs," as depicted in the title of the final chapter. Examining the possibilities will be the direct subject of the seven central chapters of this book. If Malley and others like him are correct, it is an important, compelling enterprise on which all citizens should have an informed opinion. The reader of this book will not leave with an encyclopedic understanding of this region, but will hopefully know enough about the region and its most explosive problems to reach some judgment about what policy is, what it should be, and the gap between the two.

This manuscript represents a departure, but not an abandonment, of sorts from my recent efforts in writing casebooks for International Relations and National Security. As its title suggests, it moves away from the pattern established in *Cases in International Relations* (eighth edition, December 2019) and *Cases in U.S. National Security*, a textbook published in January 2019 that was modeled on and reflected the content of *Cases in International Relations*. What has been distinctive about the *CIR* series, the first edition of which was published in 2003, was the fact that, unlike many other similar efforts, it was composed entirely of original chapters that I wrote, on the premise that such a mode of presentation would promote both timeliness and uniformity that would add to reader satisfaction and comprehension. That commitment has been continued in more subsequent editions. It has evolved into a format that emphasizes principles of the operation of the international system, generic and geographically based sources of concern, and ongoing dynamics and trends. All are useful and important subjects for a supplementary primer in the international system, and they are all emphasized in the newest edition. The format for the cases in that effort combines the articulation of generic dynamics and problem areas, accompanied by illustrative examples of world problems. Inevitably, these substantive discussions are brief and cannot reflect the subtleties or depth of the situations described. This philosophy was reflected in the first *Cases in U.S. National Security* (*CUSNS*). This volume continues the tradition of original essays; its contents are less encyclopedic; they all concentrate on a single part of the world.

What is different about this volume is its substantive focus. The other book that forms part of the foundation for the effort is *The Middle East, Oil, and the U.S. National Security Policy*. This book was published in 2016 and reflected what I considered to be a national security crisis for the United States, much of which centered on the Middle East region. It was, of course, a presidential election year, and as I described the situation in the preface of that volume, "the United States found itself in what seems to be one of its perpetual crises over national security policy." Another election cycle has been upon us virtually since the inauguration of Donald J. Trump, and the description of the 2016 environment has not changed markedly since: the Middle

East–based national security crisis continues to dominate a great deal of American foreign policy concern—the evolution of especially tight relations that has resulted in American embrace of Israeli sway over Jerusalem and the Golan Heights and the burlesque naming of a small enclave on the Golan after the sitting American president—Trump Heights. As Indyk points out in a 2019 article, the basic dynamics predate the present: "the second intifada dashed hopes for Israeli-Palestinian reconciliation, the Iraq war empowered revolutionary Iran, and the Arab Spring destabilized the region and triggered the rise of the Islamic State." In a strictly national security vein, there has been grumbling in Washington circles about the possibility of war between the United States and Iran, a head-scratching prospect that, like so much of Trump policy, quickly dissipated.

The influence of these two volumes blends to form the rationale and contents of this new volume. National security, after all, is very serious and potentially consequential business for all Americans (and people everywhere else): ultimately, it deals with the circumstances and means by which the country will resort to the use of force in defense of its interests. In a nuclear-armed world, the probabilities that such calculations will degenerate into levels of violence that might endanger individual Americans may be relatively small, but they cannot be dismissed altogether. It is important that Americans (and others) understand the circumstances that could unleash "the dogs of war." It is the central thesis here that most Americans do not have an adequate level of comprehension of those circumstances in the Middle East and that they are forced to rely on the partial, often misleading and misinformed bloviations of public officials and commentators often too uninformed to voice coherent descriptions on the subjects on which they opine. Moreover, most discussions tend to be biased by the preconceived views of the verbal combatants. The large purpose of this volume is to provide information and perspectives that will reduce the misunderstanding and level of knowledge of those who read it. It will not solve highly heated and complex situations to perfect understanding; hopefully it will reduce misunderstanding somewhat.

It will probably not produce analyses that please all readers. National security matters are inherently contentious and politically divisive. The genesis of national security situations is the existence, or at least perception, of threat by some hostile other that includes violent, military potential that can put some or all people in danger. The stakes, in other words, are at least arguably high. Americans tend to view these matters more abstractly than they did a half century ago. The "shadow of the mushroom-shaped cloud" (the title of a monograph I authored in the 1970s) of potential nuclear war with the Soviet Union has faded (but not disappeared entirely) since the implosion of the USSR and the end of the Cold War, and the danger of personal jeopardy has become closer to optional for Americans since selective service (involuntary military service or the draft) was suspended in 1972. Military forces and preparations are still very large, and there are many conflicts, mostly in the developing world, that tempt American participation—including with armed forces. The United States has succumbed to participation, generally with less than clear success, in some of these situations. Whether these adventures should have been entertained or undertaken is debatable, and thorough pre-engagement debate over them has been hampered by the abysmal ignorance of most of the population and many decision-makers about what they might be getting into. The absolute debacle of decision-making leading to the American invasion of Iraq in 2003 is a caricature of the problem.

Many of the problems surrounding thoughtful, informed discussions and understandings of national security problems center on the Middle East, which is a major reason it is the global focus of this book. From an American national security viewpoint, it is where the United States has been principally engaged militarily since the Vietnam War ended for the country in 1975. Since that time, the United States has engaged Iraq twice: in Kuwait in Operation Desert Storm in 1990–1991 and again with the invasion and long, protracted, off-and-on occupation and intrusions since the Iraq War began in 2003. Afghanistan has become the longest war in U.S. history; supporting (and partially financing) Israeli security is a time-consuming commitment, as is selling weapons to countries like Saudi Arabia (including controversial support for Saudi actions in Yemen) and the Gulf States. In addition, the United States has been on peripheries of the Syrian civil war, including support for the Kurds and the strain that has put on American relations with NATO ally Turkey. The American Middle East plate is indeed full in the region.

Although it is a controversial assertion that will be examined in the text, the region is also arguably the part of the world where the outbreak of large-scale, systemic violence is most likely (or least improbable). There are multiple sources of deeply held conflicts in the area based in religion (e.g., Sunni-Shia and Judaism), imperialism (e.g., Iranian assertion of a return to its historical regional role, Israeli aggressiveness in asserting its perpetual control of territories occupied in 1967), weapons balances with incendiary possibilities (most notably the Israeli nuclear arsenal), and historical hatreds (Kurds and Turks, for example). The situation is exacerbated by the overlapping, mutually exclusive nature of solutions to some of these problems and how efforts to solve one problem often make others more intractable. The geopolitical traps involved in operating in the region are ubiquitous and confusing. Hopefully, the discussions that follow will make them somewhat easier to understand. Indyk argues Trump has made them worse. "His policies have fueled the conflict between Iran and Israel, alienated the Palestinians, supported an unending war and a humanitarian crisis in Yemen, and split the Gulf Cooperation Council."

A word about what this book is and is not is appropriate. It is an introduction to some of the most important problems facing the Middle East and American policy and actions toward the region and those problems. It introduces and tries to make some sense of these problems primarily from an American national security vantage point. The rejoinder is necessary. Any of the cases examined could be and have been the subject of numerous extensive, book-length treatments, some of which are listed in the bibliography at the end of each chapter. The reader will not emerge from this book as a certified expert in any of the problems or their management. Hopefully, he or she will have a better understanding that will allow for the development and articulation of more informed and valuable opinions than are possible in the absence of reading it. If I accomplish that, I will feel vindicated for the effort.

The major thrusts of these examination are twofold. First, they are complex and interrelated. The incursion in northern Syria, for instance, is related to more than Turkish concern with Kurdish "terrorists" for instance. It had immediate impacts on parts of the regional balance that will reverberate for some time. The point is not a detailed cataloguing of long-standing conflicts and complexities; it is that they exist and must be taken into account. The second thrust is that things are changing constantly in the region, and this complicates the direction and national security content of American policy and the achievement of American interests. That complexity is present in policy toward any geographic region; it is especially true for the Middle East.

The Middle Eastern geopolitical emphasis occupies most of the contents of this volume. Its bookends are a pair on introductory and summary chapters. Chapter 1 lays out basic national security concepts that recur in the substantive chapters: ideas like the role of nuclear weapons and the criteria for national security thinking, for instance. The purpose is to create a framework useful for thinking about the Middle Eastern chapters without having to interrupt those discussions within the substantive chapters. This chapter concentrates on international rather than domestic American political dimensions, which are covered admirably in other texts and to which I have contributed in the various editions of *National Security* and *Thinking about National Security*. The next seven chapters form the heart of the book, providing case studies of seven different aspects of Middle Eastern conflict and American efforts to achieve its goals within that complex. Following an overview of regional instabilities (Chapter 2), its cases include the dynamics of Israel's role in the area (Chapter 3); the fate of the stateless nations of the region; Palestine (Chapter 4) and Kurdistan (Chapter 5); the central importance of Syria as exemplified by the Syrian civil war and its offspring affecting

Russia, Turkey, and Kurdistan (Chapter 6); the evolving geopolitical balance in the "Shiite crescent" encompassing Iran, Iraq, Syria, and Lebanon (Chapter 7); the mini-cold war competition between Iran and Saudi Arabia (Chapter 8), and the longest morasses for the United States in Iraq and Afghanistan (Chapter 9). The book concludes with a discussion of the complex web of geopolitical interconnections between all these sources of conflict and the difficulties for the Biden administration (Chapters 10 and 11).

The most controversial chapters deal with Israel (Chapters 3 and 4). They are critical of Israeli regional policies, especially the growing permanence of Israeli presence in the 1967 occupied territories, the aggressive emergence of a nuclear-armed Israel as the virtual military hegemon in the region (Chapter 3), and Israeli treatment of the Palestinians (Chapter 4), both pillars of Benjamin Netanyahu's vision of a "greater Israel." Both trends were noted critically by Mearsheimer and Walt in their 2007 book that asserted "Israel has become a strategic liability for the United States." That conviction was widely characterized as anti-Israeli, but the trends the authors identified have accelerated under Netanyahu and are truer now than they were before. Much of the Mearsheimer/Walt critique remains relevant and underlies some arguments made here.

Finally, a word about style seems appropriate. This is a book written for students who are neither experts in international relations nor in social science vocabulary. I have tried (as I have in all my books) to keep the text conversational, nontechnical, and readable for the nonexpert. I have always believed that the formalistic nature of much political science writing is stiff, overly jargonistic, and, as a result, off-putting to the lay reader. My purpose has been to create a text that is readable and, hopefully, engaging—something the student will enjoy reading. My contention is that students either skim or do not even read some of their texts partly because of the way they are written. A text that is either unread or only glanced at does not teach much. My hope is that the student reader will find the text here engaging enough to read attentively. If he or she does, I have succeeded. If not, at least I tried.

BIBLIOGRAPHY

Bacevich, Andrew J. "Even If We Defeat the Islamic State, We'll Still Lose the Bigger War." *Washington Post* (online), October 3, 2014.

Gordon, Philip H. "The False Promise of Regime Change: Why Washington Keeps Failing in the Middle East." *Foreign Affairs* (online), October 7, 2020.

Indyk, Martin. "Disaster in the Desert: Why Trump's Middle Eastern Plan Can't Work." *Foreign Affairs* 98, 6 (November/December 2019), 10–20.

Malley, Robert. "The Unwanted Wars: Why the Middle East Is More Combustible than Ever." *Foreign Affairs* 98, 6 (November/December 2019), 38–47.

Mearsheimer, John J., and Stephen M. Walt. *The Israel Lobby and U.S. Foreign Policy.* New York: Farrar, Straus and Giroux, 2007.

Snow, Donald M. *Cases in International Relations: Principles and Applications.* Eighth Ed. Lanham, MD: Rowman & Littlefield, 2020.

———. *Cases in U.S. National Security: Concepts and Policies.* Lanham, MD: Rowman & Littlefield, 2019.

———. *The Middle East, Oil, and the U.S. National Security Policy: Intractable Conflicts, Impossible Solutions.* Lanham, MD: Rowman & Littlefield, 2016.

———. *National Security.* Seventh Ed. New York and London: Routledge, 2020.

———. *Regional Cases in U.S. Foreign Policy.* Lanham, MD: Rowman & Littlefield, 2018.

———. *The Shadow of the Mushroom-Shaped Cloud.* Columbus, OH: Consortium for International Studies Education, 1978.

———. *Thinking about National Security: Strategy, Policy, and Issues.* New York: Routledge, 2016.

———, and Dennis M. Drew. *From Lexington to Desert Storm and Beyond: War and Politics in the American Experience.* Third Ed. Armonk, NY: M. E. Sharpe, 2010.

1

National Interests and American Involvement in the Middle East

The purpose of this volume is to examine American national security involvement in the Middle East and its seemingly endless conflicts and wars. Especially since around 1980 (the immediate aftermath of the Iranian Revolution of 1979), the region has been the arguable epicenter of U.S. national security policy and efforts to ensure American interests. The complex entanglements in which the United States has been caught up ever since include the country's two longest wars, which are the starkest evidence of the byzantine nature of Middle East politics. There is relatively little evidence the United States was prepared for this immersion either in terms of comprehending the dizzying pace of regional politics or in clearly delineating and sorting out American regional interests.

These concerns form the core of what follows. The journey begins by trying to lay out the framework in which the United States, or any other country, organizes why it is involved in different countries and regions and what it is prepared to do to realize those goals. The key concept is national interests, a notion that states (or countries) typically use to assess why and what they want to accomplish in different places and how they will to go about achieving those goals. The concept of interests is foundational in determining national security priorities and is thus the basis of this chapter.

The other concern is the geopolitical, economic, political, and historical context of the region in which American interests are devised, including the obstacles and complexities in the region. The remaining chapters are devoted to examining some of the most important and perplexing problems that challenge American pursuit of those objectives. The United States is a relative neophyte in dealing with this physical and human landscape, making the examination more contentious than it might otherwise be.

American regional interest is largely a twentieth-century phenomenon originally associated with the industrialization of the United States and its resultant voracious need for energy, including Middle East oil. In the first century of the American Republic, the most memorable American interaction was with the Barbary pirates (or corsairs), which included attacks on American vessels in the Mediterranean Sea by Tripoli-based pirates and resulted in two minor conflagrations with the U.S. Navy, which was formed in 1794 largely to counter the Barbary threat. The most memorable artifact of that experience is a line in the Marine Hymn citing the "shores of Tripoli" as part of the Corp's legacy. That threat ended in 1830 when France conquered and colonized Algeria.

Different influences have shaped U.S. policy since 1945, with oil security always a major agenda item. The first major postwar event was the establishment of the state of Israel in 1948, and protecting the Jewish state rapidly became a primary American goal coequal—and sometimes in conflict—with secure access to oil since many of the of the oil producers opposed the existence of Israel and its treatment of the Palestinians. Cold War posturing with the Soviet Union over influence was part of the mix. There was a stable and workable environment as long as the United States and the government of the Shah of Iran cooperated to keep the oil flowing (except during the oil boycott of 1967).

The year 1979 was the watershed. The Iranian Revolution overthrew the Shah, and he was replaced by a militantly anti-American, fundamentalist Shiite regime that rejected the U.S.-Iranian bargain and was opposed by the fundamentalist Sunni governments of the Gulf States. These events unsettled the region and left the order that had supported American policy in tatters. After international terrorism was added to the mix, the reconstruction of American interests and policies has been a work in progress ever since.

There has been some congealing around that change in the 2010s. Haass summarizes: "President Barack Obama oversaw a pullback from Afghanistan and the Middle East. President Donald Trump has employed mostly economic power to confront foes. But he has essentially ended the U.S. presence in Syria, and he seeks to do the same in Afghanistan." These are sizable trends that reflect a changed assessment of American interests and how to realize them. The journey to understanding these changes and their effects begins by constructing an interest-driven framework in which to analyze events and trends.

NATIONAL INTERESTS AND SECURITY

National security policy and strategy is one of the most fundamental components of politics within any country. Some people within and outside the national security community would argue it is the most consequential area of public discourse. The essence of security is the safety it provides to whatever group to which it is extended (the terms *security* and *safety* are virtual synonyms). In a world community in which individual states are the basic units, the essence of that security is what keeps a country's people and territory safe from physical harm or, in the worst case, destruction. A country that cannot perform that function has put its freedom and identity at risk, and thus does not meet its most basic mandate. In an international system composed of sovereign states, a satisfactory national security strategy is a sine qua non (without this nothing) for national independence, existence, and an acceptable, satisfactory life condition.

The concept is both important and controversial. The reason is that security interests are often nonintersubjective, a concept from the philosophy of science that means conditions of security are not viewed in the same way by everyone, and different observers can reach different conclusions about whether a situation is dangerous to American (or anyone else's) safety. Not all people, for instance, can agree whether (or how much) the challenge posed by illegal crossing of the Mexican-American border represents a threat to the United States. The judgment is not intersubjective.

The basic distinction enshrined in the subjectivity question is whether all observers can and do view a physical or mental phenomenon in the same way. Some national security questions achieve virtual objective status because they are so obvious there is virtual unanimity that certain acts or situations threaten the most basic national interest—the safety and survival of the United States as a sovereign state. Most situations are not so consensual: on those, people disagree.

While threats are a constant part of international existence, how much and what kind of a threat individual problems pose are not entirely matters of agreement in most cases. Virtually everyone agreed there was a major Soviet threat during most of the second half of the twentieth century. During his term in office, President Trump essentially asserted that the successor Russian threat is minimal. Other Americans disagree, as the ongoing controversy over alleged Russian meddling in American elections is evidence. Clarity in threat assessment has been the victim, reflecting a tongue-in-cheek lament by Soviet foreign policy official Georgi Arbatov to his American counterparts as the Soviet Union was dissolving in 1991: "We have done a terrible thing," he said. "We have deprived you of an enemy."

INTERESTS

Although the depiction is oversimplified (for a complete discussion, see Snow, *National Security*, Seventh Edition), one can think of interests along two dimensions. One is the question of who has interests and, among those who have interests, which are controlling. In the relations among states, countries have premier interests, which is why the national interest is the central security concern of international relations most of the time. The second is how important interests are to whoever possesses them, which is a question of priorities. These concepts are, of course, related both in theory and practice.

LEVEL OF INTEREST

Who has interests? In most conventional discussions, there are generally considered to be three candidates. They overlap and occasionally coalesce or come into conflict. These contradictory possibilities make generalization and applications to concrete situations contentious.

The most basic level is individual interests. What conditions of existence are part of the fundamental human endowment and form the cornerstone for all other conditions of human existence? In political democracies, the interests of individuals are considered paramount, and the primacy of those interests are imbedded in basic documents like the American Constitution and Bill of Rights. The protection of "life, liberty, and the pursuit of happiness" forms the basic rationale for the political system in a political democracy. Adherence to this primacy, of course, varies greatly from country to country, and whether those rights are always honored is always a matter of debate, as is the question of what happens when individual rights collide with other levels of interest.

The second level of interests are national interests, conditions that contribute to the state's ability to pursue its interests. These interests, of course, are the basic concern of national security. Especially in political democracies, the rationale for national interests is to promote and protect the individual interests of the citizens, but the realm of national interests is about what challenges to those abilities emanate from broader forces, principally those associated with other states.

The third level consists of international interests, conditions that transcend both the interests of individuals and even the interests of the states. Such interests create or are the result of factors that go beyond national jurisdictions, spanning both individual and state bounds. Typically, they are considered as problems, the solution or management of which can only be successfully managed internationally. On the surface, international interests would seem to be at the pinnacle of the triangle of interests and command the greatest attention, but they do not.

There are numerous reasons for this seeming anomaly. One reason flows from the problem of nonintersubjectivity. Not all observers have the same feelings about conditions and problems on which they disagree, and gaining consensus on the hierarchy and composition of the most important interests of humanity is a very difficult, probably impossible effort. Second, since primary loyalties are toward national interests, the lens through which problems is viewed is that of the state. Different states have conflicting interests in different things. In the competitive, even suspicious nature of interstate relations, the motives of those promoting universal interests at the expanse of national interests thus is always suspect to some.

This discussion may seem abstract, even ironic, but it is not. Global climate change and what to do about it is an excellent case in point. It affects interests at all levels. Individuals living in low-lying places certainly have an interest in arresting the rising of sea levels short of their personal inundation. International interest clearly dictates finding and implementing strategies and programs that will reverse adverse effects on global climate. At the same time, some countries view climate control initiatives as virtual assaults on their national interests—seeing attempts to lower carbon emissions as a way to decrease their energy consumption and thus as a way to disadvantage national economies dependent on energy for prosperity. As well, nonintersubjectivity also enters the calculus: although there is virtual unanimity about the climate change problem and actions needed to vitiate it among members of the scientific community, there are other people who continue not to believe in the problem or to see it as a plot to weaken their country's security position. Intersubjectivity enters the picture: although there is virtual unanimity about the climate change problem among scientists, there are also people who continue not to believe the problem or see it as a plot to weaken their national security position.

INTENSITY OF INTERESTS

The vitality of different interests differ among people and states: some are clearly more important than others, and there are greater or lesser consequences of their realization. No state has the capability to promote or realize all their interests fully, so some ways must be devised to prioritize which are more important. Predictably, different people disagree both on the importance of values and how to realize them.

Various ways have been proposed to create some ordinal ranking of interests. For national security analytical purposes, the most common differentiation is in terms of how important various interests are to the basic security of the country and its inhabitants. The most general distinction is between so-called vital and less-than-vital (LTV) interests. It is a determination about the tolerability of realizing or failing to realize certain conditions necessary for the country's safety and well-being, and it helps dictate the kinds of policies and actions one may contemplate in different situations.

The definitions of the two concepts are largely intuitive, but with very different implications in the national security arena. A vital interest (VI) is a condition a country deems so important to its existence or well-being that it will not willingly compromise on its achievement. An LTV is a condition a country values but would not necessarily endanger its most important values if unrealized. There are gradations of importance within each category. Threats to trade relations, for instance, affect a country's vital interest in promoting the economic prosperity and well-being of its citizens, but not to the extent and vitality of an imminent, credible threat of a nuclear attack on the country. Ordinal distinctions also apply to LTVs.

The basic distinction applies directly to national security matters. One distinction is that VIs involve conditions over which a country might use military force, whereas LTVs are interests where the use of force is excessive. This distinction reflects the traditional realist, Cold War–oriented view of force. Many contemporary analysts have relaxed this criterion, feeling that force can be threatened or applied to a broader range of situations than do the realists.

There are two critical qualifications about vital interests and their role. The first comes from the qualification "willingly" in the definition of a VI. The notion of vitality suggests that states will contemplate or use force whenever they feel their most important interests are threatened, and that is not always true. Using force is a meaningful choice for those who have adequate and appropriate force to invoke it successfully. Some states are too weak or small to qualify, in which case employing force would be decidedly quixotic. Such states may not willingly accept compromising their VIs, but their certainty of failure may force them to do so. The weak, it is sometimes said, "suffer what they must."

The other qualification is that the criteria for situations where force is appropriate are not universally agreed upon. The question may be framed in terms of the intolerability of outcomes: different people disagree about how important and intolerable different outcomes to situations may be. The January 2020 assassination of Iranian General Qasem Soleimani in an American airstrike is a case in point. In terms of tolerability, the action was probably unjustified. Few Americans believed the world was not a better place without the general, but was his role so intolerable as to justify assassinating him? There was no public evidence that the question of vitality entered the calculus of decisions in a White House that typically does not justify its actions in traditional VI–LTV terms. Why did the United States do it? According to Friedman, Trump "watched, fuming, as television reports showed Iranian-backed attacks on the American Embassy in Baghdad," and this caused him to authorize the air strike that killed the Iranian general.

This kind of rejoinder in mind, situations where force may be justified to achieve interests are a basic part of international political practice, and these situations will always be controversial. They are always difficult and contentious, and this is especially true in the Middle East, where situations arguably threatening interests abound and constantly shift. The problem is that saying force may be appropriate does not answer the question of what kinds and amounts of force should be applied to produce desired results. The United States has applied force frequently in the Middle East with arguably little positive lasting impact on American interests. Why? One possibility is that the force applied may not be effective for the situations it is invoked to achieve. Defining interests and applying solutions, after all, assumes what actions work and why.

THREATS AND RESPONSES

The ability to realize state interests varies significantly. This is largely the consequence of the structural nature of the relations among countries being among sovereign states. Sovereignty is defined as supreme authority, and in the international system, the states are sovereign. That means they are the highest authority on what goes on in their sovereign realms. There is no authority superior to that of the state, meaning the relations among states is a state of anarchy (the absence of government). This condition has major implications for how conflicting interests between states are resolved.

In domestic society, state sovereignty answers this dilemma. Since the state is the supreme authority, when conflicts arise between individuals or groups, the state (the supreme authority) can adjudicate claims and render and enforce judgments; the justice system can and does impose order. In international relations, the contestants themselves are the sovereigns, and there is no higher authority that can impose and enforce settlements against them. This situation exists because of vital interests, which are so important to the states that they will not willingly compromise them. This dynamic is the fundamental difference between domestic and international resolution of conflicts. In domestic society, sovereign dictates the subservience of individual and group interests to the state; in the international realm, the state relinquishes its absolute authority only where it chooses to do so. It rarely does so in matters it considers vital. Operationally, this means that achieving national goals is a matter of strength or power. The operative principle is self-help: the state achieves what it has the power to achieve.

The operational means by which occurs is through the application of the instruments of power. In a general sense, these instruments refer to the various categories of hostile action a country may contemplate when it feels its interests are endangered. Conventional descriptions divide those instruments into three categories: diplomatic, economic, and military actions (in generally ascending order of consideration and consequences). The basic distinctions are intuitive. The diplomatic (or political) instrument refers to the use of diplomatic persuasion to convince other states to honor one's interests. This instrument is normally the province and preferred method of members of the diplomatic corps within each country. The economic instruments refer to the use of economic incentives (or carrots) or penalties (or sticks) to gain compliance with interest-based demands. In traditional terms, the military instrument, consisting of threats or actual use of armed force to gain compliance with demands, has been the ultimate method to accomplish policy ends. In an age of burgeoning technology, additional instruments like cyber warfare have become available.

The operational application of the instruments is the issuance and actual carrying out of threats. A threat is a promise to an opponent to do something harmful to someone in the event of noncompliance with a demand. Effective threats need to possess two qualities. First, the threatening state must have the physical capability to carry out the threatened action. This may sound self-evident, but leaders sometimes issue outlandish threats that they could not or would not carry out. North Korea's Kim Jung Un often threatens military actions for which North Korea lacks the capability, and if the DPRK did possess it, its use could result in national destruction, making implementation suicidal. Such threats are said to be bluffs, and they are normally ineffectual.

The second characteristic is the willingness to carry out a threat. If a threatened state does not believe the threatening state would in fact carry out its threat, that declaration is hollow and can only be made believable by carrying it. Making extravagant threats was a frequent accusation against President Trump.

The effectiveness of different threats is also specific to situations. Novices tend to view force as if it is a static commodity, but that is often misleading in specific situations. In the wake of the 2020 Soleimani assassination in Iraq, for instance, President Trump warned Iran not to retaliate because the

United States might unleash its forces and subdue Iran if it did. By virtually any static method of comparison, the United States has more powerful forces than Iran. Whether it would or could employ those forces to bring Iran to its knees is debatable given the distance between Iran and the United States. The simple comparison may be overly simplistic because both the problem and possible solutions are more complex than a simple analysis may reveal. In a January 2020 *Time* story, Sadjadpour illustrates the complexity and multi-faceted calculation regarding Soleimani that had existed in the United States expert community. "When previous Administrations discussed assassinating Soleimani, two questions were usually contemplated: Does he deserve to die? And, was it worth the potential risks?" the author writes, adding "the answer to the first question tended to be affirmative. The answer to the second was always inconclusive."

In the Middle East, the complexity problem is especially constraining, particularly when assessing the use of military force to realize strategic interests. Traditional models work unevenly, and usually not very well. The United States launched a traditional Western-style operation to drive Iraq out of Kuwait in 1991, but that very success was misleading and made subsequent applications of force seem easier than they were. The regional lesson of Operation Desert Storm was the futility of trying to conduct a traditional, Western-style defense against the Americans, and all parties in the region instead now prepare to face the Americans with some sort of asymmetrical option for which massive American force is not especially appropriate. Most Middle Eastern conflicts are relatively small in military terms, often involving relatively small military forces fighting asymmetrically, and American massed force is not particularly appropriate. Special forces are something of an exception. Efforts in Afghanistan have faced this problem.

The reaction to the Soleimani assassination provides a mini-portrait of employing force in the region. The Iranian general was the acknowledged commander of Quds revolutionary militia, which trained and dispatched irregular forces against governments opposed by Iran. The targets of Quds-trained forces, most prominent of which has been Israel, labeled him a terrorist, a designation that was accepted by the Trump administration in authorizing his assassination. The United States proudly announced that it had killed the general at the Baghdad airport, and no other country or force acknowledged a role in the operation, although many regional parties like the Israelis gained far more than the United States by the action. It is virtually impossible to imagine the action did not involve some outside help in its planning, intelligence gathering, or other participation in the action.

Reaction to the killing had immediate ripple effects: it has for instance, redoubled Iraqi displeasure with the American military presence there and increased demands by the government to remove those forces from Iraqi soil. That result, in turn, could make suppression of ISIS (the large reason for a continuing American presence) more difficult and an attempted rebirth of the Caliphate more likely. The killing probably benefited Israel more than anyone else since Soleimani's portfolio included the recruitment and direction of Quds forces that harass the Israeli occupation of territories acquired in 1967. Israel's interests were at least arguably served by the assassination; it is hard to specify how American interests are.

INTERESTS AND THE REALM OF ENDLESS WAR

Since the end of the Vietnam War, the Middle East has been the part of the world where virtually all the applications of force by American troops have occurred. The tragic 1983 bombing of a U.S. Marine installation at the Beirut, Lebanon airport in which 283 Americans perished was a premonition, and America's first major post-Vietnam application of force occurred in 1990, when, the United States responded to the Iraqi invasion of Kuwait and led a coalition of states in Operation Desert Storm to reverse that conquest and restore Kuwaiti sovereignty. Except for relatively minor excursions into the Balkans (Kosovo) and the Caribbean (Haiti) in the 1990s, America's use of force has centered on the Middle East since. As Bacevich summarized in a 2016 book, "From World War II to 1980, virtually no American soldiers were killed in action in the region. Since 1990, virtually no American soldiers have been killed in action anywhere except in the Middle East." The battlegrounds of American endless war have migrated to the sands of the Middle East. Conditions in the region have provided the opportunities. The result has been to make the Middle East, in Malley's words, "the world's most volatile region."

The evidence abounds. In 2017, Wikipedia compiled a list of what it calls "modern" wars in the region. Between 1945 and 2017, it recorded 72 wars in the region. Fully 43 of those conflicts have taken place since 1990. The statistics need not be exact, but collectively they suggest the ubiquity of Middle East conflict. The conflicts have varied from minor clashes between nomadic tribes to large conflicts with high casualty figures. The largest was the Iran-Iraq War of 1980–1988, in which 1 million to 1.25 million perished, followed by the ongoing Syrian Civil War (250–500 thousand casualties), to the 110–165,000 killed in fighting in Iraq between 2003 and 2011. No other region comes close in terms of carnage.

Some countries and areas have been more violence prone than others. Tallying participations from the Wikipedia list, Iraq has been involved in the most conflicts since 1945 (14), followed by Yemen (10), Iran (7), and Syria and Saudi Arabia (5 each), and these are all countries (Yemen being a possible exception) in which the United States has had extensive interactions, including interventions with armed force. They are thus all countries featured in one or more of the case studies in the chapters that follow.

The countries of the region are remarkably fractious and diverse, and this makes it difficult for the United States (or anybody else) to develop an overall regional strategy that reconciles their conflicting interests. In some cases, possible interests are at direct odds; it is difficult to imagine an evenhanded policy that simultaneously encompasses how the United States should deal with Iran and Saudi Arabia, for instance, and friendship with and protection of Israel has placed the country at some odds with the Islamic powers and their public opposition to the Israelis—a problem largely associated with the occupied territories since 1967.

The seeming omnipresence of the American armed forces in the region over the last 30-plus years has been expensive economically and, in terms of human costs, a burden accentuated by the absence of clear success in ending violence or demonstrably achieving opaque objectives. Hence, there has been a growing aversion to the "endless wars" in which the United States finds itself mired. At that, even before President Trump had declared his intention to send an additional 3,000 troops into Iraq at the end of 2019, the United States had roughly 65,000 service members in a variety of regional states conducting various duties, from training troops and guarding facilities to engaging in combat. The public increasingly asks why. Beginning to unravel this problem and thus to deal with the problem of seemingly endless war requires first looking at American interests in the Middle East, a topic introduced in the Choosing Policy (CP) exercise.

CHOOSING POLICY (CP): DETERMINING U.S. INTERESTS AND ALTERNATIVES IN THE MIDDLE EAST

American opposition to involvement in Middle Eastern conflicts grew in the 2010s. Terminating "endless wars" has been the rallying cry. The rigors and sacrifices these conflicts impose have not affected the public uniformly; because of the suspension of conscription in 1972, they have been fought by volunteers who have chosen to serve and sacrifice. The process leading to the endless war depiction began when American forces invaded and occupied Afghanistan in 2001 to capture Osama bin Laden and the Al Qaeda terrorists who had carried out the 9/11 terrorist attacks. The effort failed, and Al Qaeda escaped to Pakistan, but the United States is still in Afghanistan in the twentieth year of the country's longest war. No successful end is in sight.

The United States invaded and conquered Iraq in 2003 and negotiated a withdrawal in 2011. Thanks largely to the threat posed by the Islamic State, the Americans are back, with neither "victory" nor the prospect of an outcome favorable to American interests visible. It is the second longest American war. The forces in Afghanistan and Iraq are included in the over 65,000 American service personnel in the region today. Many are in harm's way.

These two conflicts form the core of the endless war controversy. Underlying policy discussions is the question of interests: what about these various places in the region that is sufficiently important for the country to shed American blood? It is not a new question. It became a central issue over a half century ago regarding the then longest American war in Vietnam between 1965 and 1973. That war ended poorly for the United States. Its lessons may be instructive for framing the question of what to do about today's endless wars.

Comparing analogies is never a precise exercise. Vietnam occurred during the Cold War and was justified in communist–anticommunist terms, and it was much larger and bloodier than Afghanistan and Iraq for Americans; over 58,000 American service personnel died there, and at its peak, over a half million Americans were deployed in the country. It was the first U.S. conflict in which it was impossible to argue convincingly the Americans had won. Many believe we lost. There are parallels relevant to the present. Two are particularly important. One is that the war was long and indeterminate, became very unpopular, and put great pressure on the U.S. government to stop it. The sentiment was strongest among those who might be forced to fight a conflict they never understood or supported, and that created much more citizen pressure than is currently present. The longer the war dragged on, the more unpopular it became, and the mantra of the opponents was "No More Vietnams!" The Nixon administration, after moving glacially toward a settlement during its first term, finally began serious negotiations that allowed the United States to withdraw in March 1973. The memory, however, was a factor in the relatively few deployments of U.S. forces between 1973 and the 1990s, when it was reignited in the Middle East. "No more Vietnams" inhibited American pursuit of its interests with force for nearly two decades. Will the cry against "Endless Wars" have the same effect?

The end of the Vietnam War also ignited a debate in the United States about the use of force that has parallels in the present situation. The Vietnam controversy provided three basic alternative answers to the question of when to use force to promote policy ends. When the United States decided to come to the military aid of the Republic of Vietnam (South Vietnam) in the early 1960s, it implicitly invoked the so-called realist paradigm (see Snow, *National Security*, for a full discussion) to justify the action. The heart of the paradigm was that force should be used only to defend VIs, and that as such, vitality of outcome justified using as much force as seemed required. In Vietnam, that turned out to be a sizable force, which, in retrospect, was arguably excessive to the level and intensity of U.S. interests in the outcome.

The other end of the spectrum of interests was the complete withholding of American force from the conflict. The implicit assumption underlying such a solution was that there were virtually no important American interests in what many considered a civil war in a faraway place and thus did not justify putting Americans at physical risk. This option depicted Vietnam in strictly LTV terms, which suggests that the use of force is unjustified. When the United States withdrew completely in 1973, this was the implicit assessment. Calls for total withdrawal from endless wars in places like Afghanistan and Iraq are arguably examples of this solution. In Vietnam, the American withdrawal included the failure of the United States to accomplish any of its objectives or to realize any of the interests that had justified its initial decision to intervene. Would the same outcome be the result of total withdrawal from the endless wars in the Middle East?

There is a third option intermediate between the extreme: limited engagement. This option addresses situations at or near the boundary between VIs and LTVs, and it suggests that in situations of ambiguity of interest level, there should be a limited option to pursue situations where the worthiness of outcomes might be debatable or ambiguous and in which the commitment of American forces in direct (and especially large-scale) combat role might be difficult or impossible to justify but where interest is sufficient for some limited form of action.

This kind of formulation was proposed at the end of the Nixon administration and became known as the Nixon Doctrine. Its explicit formulation was directed at future situations where American military assistance might be requested but where the public reluctance (sometimes called the "Vietnam hangover") dictated the public would not accept the dispatch of American force. The heart of the doctrine was an admonition to those seeking American help: it said, in essence, that if a threat was sufficient (involved some American interest) the United States would be willing to come to aid of the beleaguered party with military aid, training, and economic assistance, but not with combat force. This option (which is really a continuum of options) is attractive in the abstract but difficult to define and implement in concrete situations. It is also a choice that may be better suited (or less unsuited) to the kinds of situations the country faces in the Middle East.

The central problem with the option is the balance between doing enough to influence situations sufficiently to promote interests without acting so massively that one slips into the danger of involvement in new "endless wars." Some variant of this option is the normal policy the country has to most places, and it is the heart of current policy discussions. The "zero involvement" option, which is implicit in the cry to end endless wars, creates the impression the country has no interests in a given country or region, and despite how low a place may reside in the hierarchy of national priorities, a global power like the United States cannot make such an admission. Why? To do so implicitly admits America is really not a totally global power, and doing so invites other countries (notably Russia or China) to become involved and thus potentially to create an American interest, even if it is limited to countering traditional adversaries.

The other extreme of total involvement is generally unacceptable as well. The obvious consequence of a policy of major involvement is a willingness to employ armed force—including in sizable amounts—to situations where those interests may seem endangered. The problem with this predilection is that it potentially creates a "slippery slope" of gradually increasing involvement from which the country has had a difficult time extricating itself. The danger, of course, is that tendency can become self-perpetuating, as in places like Iraq and Afghanistan, and thus lead to the endless wars that are the current object of criticism and reaction. The gradual buildup to a force of over 500,000 in Vietnam is the prototype of this danger.

That leaves the "middle range of options," and if chosen, begs the question of how much involvement in specific places? Is a given location important but not vital to the United States (somewhere around the divide between VIs and the most important LTVs) suggest an activist level of involvement? If the interest arguably teeters to the LTV side, it may militate toward a less activist approach.

A variant of the middle option is the de facto policy in places like Iraq, where the United States maintains a small force primarily composed of special forces training and equipping local fighters to act as American surrogates in the event of an Islamic State (IS) resurgence—an event deemed likely should the United States withdraw. It offers no decisive result like destroying IS unless the Americans greatly increase their presence, but it probably also offers the reasonable prospects that the return of the Caliphate in full force can be avoided and that an expansion of Russian influence will be avoided.

Is that enough? What do you think? There are advocates of all three options in the political debate. Those who would greatly increase U.S. presence are muted by the cries to terminate endless wars to the point of virtual silence. At the same time, majority expert opinion probably backs some form of the middle option. Recognize that your judgments are tentative and that they may change as you proceed. When you have finished the book, you may want to compare your view then with what it is now.

BIBLIOGRAPHY

Allison, Graham T., and Dimitri K. Simes. "The National Interest." *The National Interest*, 2017.

Art, Robert, and Kenneth A. Waltz (eds.). *The Use of Force: Military Power and International Relations*. Seventh Ed. Lanham, MD: Rowman & Littlefield, 2009.

Bacevich, Andrew. *America's War for the Greater Middle East: A Military History*. New York: Random House, 2016.

Fontaine, Richard. "The Nonintervention Delusion: What War Is Good For." *Foreign Affairs* 98, 6 (November/December 2019), 84–98.

Friedman, Thomas L. "Trump's Choice of Killing Stunned Defense Officials." *New York Times* (online), January 5, 2020.

Fromkin, David. *The Independence of Nations*. New York: Praeger Special Studies, 1981.

Gelvin, James. *The Modern Middle East: A History*. Fourth Ed. Oxford, UK: Oxford University Press, 2015.

Liddell Hart, B. H. *Strategy*. New York: Meridian Press, 1991.

Lissner, Rebecca Friedman. "The National Strategy Is Not a Strategy: Trump's Incoherence Is a Reminder of Why a New Strategy Is Needed." *Foreign Affairs Snapshot* (online), December 19, 2017.

"List of Modern Conflicts in the Middle East." Wikipedia 2017.

London, Joshua E. *Victory in Tripoli: How America's War with the Barbary Pirates Established the U.S. Navy and Shaped a Nation*. New York: Wiley, 2005.

Lynch, Mark. *The New Arab Wars: Uprisings and Anarchy in the Middle East*. Reprint Ed. New York: Public Affairs, 2017.

Malley, Robert. "The Unwanted Wars: Why the Middle East Is More Combustible than Ever." *Foreign Affairs* 98, 6 (November/December 2019), 38–47.

McDougal, Walter A. *The Tragedy of U.S. Foreign Policy: How America's Civil Religion Betrayed the National Interest*. New Haven, CT: Yale University Press, 2016.

McGurk, Brett. "The Cost of an Incoherent Foreign Policy: Trump's Iran Imbroglio Undermines U.S. Priorities Everywhere." *Foreign Affairs* (online), January 20, 2020.

Mearsheimer, John J., and Stephen M. Walt. *The Israel Lobby and U.S. Foreign Policy*. New York: Farrar, Straus and Giroux, 2007.

Megsamen, Kelly. "How to Avoid Another War in the Middle East: De-Escalating after the Soleimani Strike." *Foreign Affairs* (online), January 4, 2020.

Melamed, Avi. *Inside the Middle East: Making Sense of the Most Dangerous and Complicated Region on Earth*. Washington, DC: Skyhorse, 2016.

Nuechterlein, Donald. *America Recommitted: United States National Interests in a Reconstructed World*. Lexington: University of Kentucky Press, 1991.

Peters, Ralph. *Endless War: Middle Eastern Islam versus Western Civilization*. Mechanicsburg, PA: Stackpole Books, 2010.

Sadjadpour, Karim. "On the Brink: How 40 Years of Enmity between Iran and the U.S. Collided in an Assassination." *Time*, January 20, 2020, 16–22.

Schelling, Thomas G. *Arms and Influence.* New Haven, CT: Yale University Press, 1966.

Sky, Emma. "The Death of the U.S.-Iraqi Relationship: Soleimani Wasn't the Only Casualty of the U.S. Strike in Baghdad." *Foreign Affairs* (online), January 3, 2020.

Snow, Donald M. *Cases in U.S. National Security: Concepts and Processes.* Lanham, MD: Rowman & Littlefield, 2019.

———. *The Middle East, Oil, and the U.S. National Security Policy: Intractable Conflicts, Impossible Solutions.* Lanham, MD: Roman & Littlefield, 2016.

———. *National Security.* Seventh Ed. New York: Routledge, 2020.

Stares, Paul B. *Preventive Engagement: How America Can Avoid War, Stay Strong, and Keep the Peace.* New York: Columbia University Press, 2018.

Summers, Harry G. Jr. *On Strategy: A Critical Analysis of the Vietnam War.* Novato, CA: Presidio Press, 1982.

Waltz, Kenneth. *Theory of International Politics.* Revised Ed. Long Grove, IL: Waveland Press, 2010.

2

The Contentious Middle East

As already suggested, the Middle East is the most unstable, violence-prone part of the world, with multiple, overlapping conflicts occurring almost constantly. Conflict is compressed in a relatively small geographic area bounded by the Mediterranean Sea to the west, Afghanistan in the east, the Turkish southern border on the north, and the southern edge of the Arabian Peninsula. The definition is not physically inclusive: northern Africa from Egypt westward and central Asia could be included but have not been because they are relatively tranquil at the moment or because their problems in places like Kashmir are serious but not generally thought of as part of Middle Eastern disorders.

The birthplace of the world's three most prominent monotheistic religions also contains some of the most violent and deeply held antagonisms in the world. The result is an enigma: the Middle East region is simultaneously the birthplace of most Western and other civilizations and, in terms of its contemporary politics and violence, the most uncivilized part of the world. The tribes of the Old Testament, often with different names, are still alive and actively fighting one another in ways reminiscent of the history on which the Bible was based. The overlapping, shifting bases of animosity include ethnicity, language, history and tradition, territorial claims, and, most important, religion. Moreover, the mix of those factors differs from one sub-area to another; all are subject to change as events occur; and problems, actions, and outcomes in one can and usually do affect the structure of interaction in others. At the bottom line, the countries of the region cannot find durable ways to establish or enforce peace among them. Outsiders (including the United States) have not done any better solving the problem.

Beyond a recitation of the factors that are part of the regional mix of instability, there is little agreement about either the overall dynamics, direction, or trajectory of regional instability. One intriguing hypothesis is developmental and parallel to Western evolution. Owen (2015) asserts that "the Muslim world is going through religious turmoil similar to that which raged across northwestern Europe 450 years ago." That process culminated in the Thirty Years' War and the Peace of Westphalia, which has been the cornerstone of modern European politics. Maloney suggests this process is relevant to the Middle East today, asserting "Westphalia has something to teach us," because that history may provide a blueprint for the region. The process leading to Westphalia was bloody and traumatic. Owen concludes, "To aid clear thinking about the contemporary Middle East, it would be useful to look back at the West's own history of ideological strife."

Although it is dangerous and misleading to describe any Middle Eastern situation as "typical" or "illustrative," the volatile situation of the Kurds and Turks in Turkey and northern Syria (discussed in detail in Chapter 5) does show some of the ferocity and complexity of the region especially well and demonstrates vividly Western misunderstanding of the region. Three thousand American troops (mostly Special Forces trainers) trained Kurdish forces in the area and had acted as a tripwire restraining a Turkish invasion and occupation of the area along the Turkish-Syrian border. Turkey sought to convert the area into a secure Turkish barrier between themselves and the Syrian Kurds, who consider the area (they call it Rojava) part of Kurdistan and which they have effectively governed since the rise and decline of the Islamic State. That area, and the adjacent Kurdish Autonomous Region of Iraq have been under such effective Kurdish rule that they could easily declare and enforce it as the beginning of a sovereign Kurdistan, the long-held Kurdish ambition. Enter the Turks.

Ethnic Kurds and the Turks are longtime enemies who have been fighting at least since nearly 20 million Kurds were consigned to Turkey as part of the peace treaty ending World War I. An active Kurdish insurgency against the central government in Ankara is long-standing, although the Kurds are also prominent actors in the Turkish political system. Turks have gained some international support over the years because the Kurdish resistance was led by the arguably communist Kurdish Workers Party (PKK), creating notoriety during the Cold War. Moreover, most of the roughly 20 million Kurds in Turkey live in the Anatolia, which supplies a large portion of Turkish electricity and water and is home to much of the country's tourist trade. Turkish hatred of the Kurds is thus compounded by the economic consequences of Kurdish secession, which the Turks rightfully fear.

Kurdistan would be a geopolitical wild card. Its citizens are not Arabs and do not speak Arabic, and they practice a moderate form of Sunni Islam. As such, they could become a major new and possibly uniquely democratic force in that part of the Middle East, and almost all adjacent states fear the prospect of a united, free Kurdistan (especially the states from which it would be carved). Policy discussions in the United States have emphasized the Kurds' role in defeating ISIS (when they were actually evicting them from areas they considered part of Kurdistan) and have largely ignored the regional consequences of an independent Kurdistan with interests close to those of the Americans. The American abandonment of the Kurds in Syria has damaged that possibility enormously. It was doubtful that many in the Trump administration (especially the president) were aware of any of this when he ordered the withdrawal of U.S. forces.

In *The Middle East, Oil, and the U.S. National Security*, I described the region's affairs as "in a constant crisis state, with multiple violent conflicts going on in different locations with different competitors over different issues" in a chapter titled "The Vexatious Middle East." It is a discouraging assessment. Retired general and former CIA director David Petraeus described the enigma for American policy: "The Middle East is exceedingly complex, and the various conflicts and challenges often seem intractable; we have seen, however, what happens when the United States and its allies withdraw prematurely from situations there and when they seek to avoid engagement in others." Involvement, in other words, is difficult and frustrating; the consequences of trying to avoid involvement are often worse.

The problem is how an outside power like the United States deals with such an enigmatic region in which it was hardly involved before World War II. The inquiry first requires examining the "landscape" of generally unstable, violent Middle Eastern politics, what American Middle Eastern interests are in the region, what outcomes the United States prefers to conflicts that affect those interests, and what, if anything, the United States can do to realize its interests without exacerbating problems with other interests. Like other countries, the United States has struggled to reconcile the contradictions the region presents; it has not been entirely successful in an endeavor where grand success is elusive. As Madawi al-Rasheed puts it in reply to Petraeus, "success was in short supply" in most situations.

THE LANDSCAPE OF MIDDLE EAST VIOLENCE

The Middle East's political instability and violence make it the most pregnant "laboratory" in the world for studying national security problems. It is an area in which the United States has a developed set of national interests, many of which are controversial, and these create a stake for American foreign policy that requires attention and action for the American national security community. This confluence of activity and interest creates a solid rationale for emphasizing the region in a book examining U.S. national security policy.

The richness and thus complexity of Middle Eastern instability can be viewed along two dimensions that interact in different ways in specific situations and create different challenges for interested parties like the United States. These dimensions are contextual and political. The contextual element emphasizes underlying factors that define the political life of the region and its members, and the political component refers to the variation in contents and objectives between states on specific issues.

CONTEXT

The tragic context of the region begins from imperfections with its map. With a relatively few exceptions like Iran and Egypt, there are virtually no regional states with long continuous histories as political units and in which an overriding nationalism has bound the members together. In addition to the ancient civilizations of Persia and Egypt, there have been times when empires have arisen and perished (the Ottomans most recently), and there are current instances where nationalism has developed; Israel and arguably Saudi Arabia and Jordan are examples. Most of the rest of the countries are classically artificial, either of recent vintage or the result of poorly drawn maps during the period between the world wars like Iraq and Syria.

The resulting political mix consists of countries that are either multinational or irredentist. Multinationalism describes the situation where members of more than one self-identified national group have primary loyalty to their subgroup rather than to the state. Virtually all Middle Eastern states are multinational to some degree. Irredentism, on the other hand, refers to the situation where national boundaries separate members of a nationally self-described group (or nationality) and where those members seek to be reunited in a single nationally defined state of their own. The Palestinians and Kurds (the subjects of Chapters 4 and 5) demonstrate the clearest examples in the region. It is no accident that they are also the clearest examples of stateless nations (either multinationalist of irredentist) areas in the region and the world (the Kurds are the globe's largest stateless nationality). Both desire national self-determination that would come at the expense of other inhabitants of their states and especially other countries in the Middle East. The battle over Syrian Kurdistan is exemplary, drawing Syria and Russia into its vortex. The two (Kurds and Palestinians) have similar situations. As Fishman points out, both are "ethnic minorities who make up approximately 20 percent of each country." Moreover, he adds, neither country from which they seek to secede is a "liberal democracy in which the majority recognizes the equal rights of minorities."

Within many of these artificial states, tribally based animosities infect the political atmosphere and exacerbate their violent politics. Tribalism (see Chua) is part of the fabric of multinationalism, and when tribal rivalries and hatreds are deep and long-standing, they can be the source of considerable instability. In numerous cases, poorly drawn political maps have aggregated tribal enemies in states (once again, Syria and Iraq are prime examples), and in others (Afghanistan, for instance) tribal divisions ensure the absence of viable, stable internal politics.

POLITICAL

Ethnic divisions overlay and interact with other indicators of political discord. The majority of Islamic Middle Easterners are, or at least view themselves, as Arabs, although more people make the claim than meet any genetic definition (technically, an Arab is someone who can trace his or her ethnic origin to the Arabian Peninsula). The next largest ethnic group are the Persians, who constitute most of the population of Iran but are found and their language (Farsi) is used in other surrounding countries. Other notable ethnicities include the Turks, whose habitation in Turkey puts them on the fringe of the region and historically of its politics. Smaller, but politically significant ethnicities include the Alawites of Syria and the Houthis of Yemen. These ethnic differences overlap and intermix with sectarian differences within Islam. Most Muslims (about 85 percent worldwide) are Sunni, which is the dominant faith on the Arabian Peninsula, among other places. Shiism is the faith of most other Muslims, with majorities in Iran, Iraq, and Bahrain and among groups such as the ruling Alawites and the rebellious Houthis.

Religious differences are thus multifaceted and account for a great deal of inter-Muslim regional conflict. Both sects have militant and fundamentalist subgroups, and these are often the cause of considerable division and instability. Religious fundamentalists share a belief in literal interpretations of the seventh-century beginnings of the Muslim faith, including a very strict interpretation of how to practice that faith and harsh means of punishment for those who deviate from norms that more moderate Muslims find primitive and objectionable. The most militant Sunni conservatives are the Wahhabi of Saudi Arabia, who share many common beliefs with Salafists like the Islamic

State (IS). Under both their belief systems, even less extreme Muslims are considered apostate, and if they fail to renounce their heretical beliefs, are subject to summary execution. The suicide bombing of a Shiite wedding reception in Afghanistan by an IS militant in August 2019 is an example. Members of Hamas and Hezbollah are accused of similar Shiite fanaticism.

There are also demographic differences. Economically, the Muslim Middle East tends to be divided into the very rich and the poor. The basis of distinction, of course, has been oil possession. The countries that have large oil deposits tend to be very rich; the Persian Gulf states, including states like Iran and Iraq, possess large amounts of petroleum and the cash that accompanies it. The oil producers tend to use their wealth to gain leverage and influence, dispensing riches to those regimes that accord them fealty and withholding that assistance from those who do not. Most are also armed to the teeth with advanced foreign (often American) weaponry bought with oil revenues. Many are also conservative absolute or limited monarchies who also adhere to very traditional (conservative) sects of Sunni or Shiite Islam and insist on traditional forms of sharia law that are offensive both to the West and to more moderate Muslims.

This confluence of oil wealth and reactionary (arguably anachronistic) regimes is often alleged to extend to relations between the oil-rich regimes and terrorist organizations like Al Qaeda (AQ) and IS. This factor further complicates numerous aspects of regional relations. As a primary example, Persian Gulf states led by Saudi Arabia, on the basis of resources, would seem to be natural candidates to provide the funding to rebuild Syria after the civil war ends, but the government of Syria is Shiite, and the Sunni majority is generally much less conservative than the preferences of the Wahhabist rulers of the oil-rich states. Most groups in Syria are considered apostate by very fundamentalist groups like IS. It is not clear how the changing geopolitical and economic dynamics of global energy may affect this relationship, but it remains a source of political complication in the region. No one is sure who, if anyone, will come to the aid of Syria or whatever successor forms it may break into after the fighting ends. It will likely be a fractious and probably highly conflictual, possibly violent, process.

ENTER THE UNITED STATES

Since the United States became the leading world power after World War II, the Middle East has occupied increasing importance in American foreign and defense concerns. Since the end of the Cold War, geopolitics have stabilized in most places, but not in the Middle East. The inherent chaos of its politics and geopolitics has been intensified by the emergence of regionally based terrorism. These have combined with the ongoing American concern—some would say obsession—with the security of the state of Israel. The two factors are not unrelated.

In some measure, however, policy makers have difficulty articulating exactly what it is about the region that engages the United States to the considerable extent that it does or how involved the United States should be. Some of the analysis amounts to little more than the rhetorical assertion that the Middle East is important to the United States because it is. A short article by Robert Satloff in the July/August 2019 issue of *Foreign Affairs* illustrates the point. In its three pages, the article asserts that "the Middle East's tendency is to export insecurity," and that it "has been a persistent source of threats to U.S. vital interests" (the content of which is not specified). He concludes that "the Middle East is just another part of the world where the United States has flawed allies, vicious adversaries, and enduring interests." One way to interpret these assertions is that the Middle East is an important place that should be avoided at all costs. Instead, the region has, especially in the twenty-first century, become the virtual epicenter of U.S. national security policy. President Trump implicitly subscribed to this position in October 2019 when he decided to remove U.S. forces from Syrian Kurdistan to reduce American presence in the region's "endless wars."

Historically, the interests of most countries—including the United States—did not focus on the Middle East. There was early European colonial activity along the African Mediterranean coastal region. Britain has had a colonial relationship with Egypt, and Italy and Spain colonized parts of the African Saharan coast. Most of the heart of the contemporary Middle East, however, was under the effective control of the Ottoman Empire, meaning the Ottoman Turks were the dominant power over a region where others had little interest beyond the symbolism of protecting access to religious sites and artifacts. The only member of the European balance of power that had direct physical contact was Imperial Russia, whose principal interest was in gaining warm water access from the Black Sea into the Mediterranean, over which Ottoman Turkey exercised control.

Two things changed the Middle East and its role in international politics. The first was the sequential impact of the two world wars of the past century. The Ottoman Empire, which had been teetering and crumbling before the Great War (as World War I was euphemistically known), aligned itself with the Central Powers, and when they lost, what remained of Ottoman authority collapsed with it. During the war, there was intense European intrigue in the area led by Britain and France, and their efforts yielded, in the form of the flawed Sykes-Picot agreement, the outline of how the territorial boundaries of the region would be redrawn in the interwar period (see the discussion in *Lawrence in Arabia* for an overview). In retrospect the boundaries that were drawn after World War I and the countries that were created were terribly flawed and created a political map that has led to much subsequent instability in the region. Syria and Iraq are often cited as primary examples of this imperfection, and the fact that these countries are most often mentioned as candidates for partition is not coincidental. The agreement also denied self-determination to the Kurds, which is a growing part of regional instability today. The burgeoning Western interest in Middle Eastern oil underlay most of the geopolitical interest in the area in the early twentieth century.

The Second World War's conduct and outcomes accentuated oil's importance. Much of the wartime competition between the Soviet Union and Germany was over who would control Middle Eastern oil. After the war, the Soviets moved to consolidate a position of dominance, which was frustrated by American resolution in opposing Soviet annexation of Iranian Azerbaijan, an action that demonstrated American activism and created the precedent for the convoluted, volatile U.S.-Iranian relationship that has been so important ever since. More emotionally and arguably importantly for American interests and policy, the German Holocaust accelerated the immigration of Jews out of Europe to Palestine, where they established the state of Israel in 1948 with the blessing of guilt-ridden countries like the United States. Israeli security has been a primary tenet of American policy ever since.

Oil, of course, was the other factor. One consequence of World War II was that much of the power grid in Europe was destroyed or degraded to the point that major structural postwar rebuilding would be necessary. Before the war, the primary power source in Europe was coal, but decisions heavily influenced by the Americans determined that rebuilding would occur with the use of petroleum as the primary energy source. Part of the reason arose from the abundance of oil in the nearby Middle East and the control of much of that resource by Western oil countries that could manipulate both price and supply to recovering allies (as well as maximizing profits for themselves). This arrangement worked well until the Middle East states on top of which the oil rested determined that they could make more money if they nationalized their precious asset and founded the Organization of Petroleum Exporting Countries (OPEC) to gain control of supply and price.

These two factors created the region's transformation into a central international focus and shaped the interests of major powers, including the United States, in contemporary Middle Eastern affairs. The process through which change has occurred has been tortuous, reflecting the nature of the region.

CHANGING U.S. INTERESTS IN THE REGION

Two distinct periods in postwar history directly bear on the interests Americans have in the Middle East region. The first was the Cold War competition. That competition was universal, and the Middle East was one of its principal venues. The region's importance was its physical location as a junction and jumping off point for interaction in Europe, Asia, and Africa, and most importantly during the Cold War because of the continuing struggle for control of Middle Eastern petroleum. This influence was particularly intense in the 1950s and 1960s when the prominence of Middle East oil was greatest: global reserves elsewhere were less well known or developed, making Gulf reserves more crucial than they are now. The demise of the Soviet Union reduced that geopolitical divide, although Russia has reestablished a power base in the area with its relationship with Syria and its emergence as the world's second leading petroleum producer and exporter.

The second period, evolving since 1991, has been the rise of international terrorism. Much of this problem is Middle Eastern and has philosophical roots grounded in more extreme, conservative offshoots of Islam. The philosophical bases of terrorism advocacy and especially funding for terrorist organizations and recruitment are related to oil. Much of the philosophical base comes from fundamentalist Muslims in the Persian Gulf region, and especially the Persian Gulf littoral, where most of the oil is located. Saudi Arabia is particularly exemplary. The state religion of the kingdom is Wahhabism, an especially fundamentalist, anti-Western and anti-secular sect whose members allegedly provided much of the funding and personnel for the September 11 attacks (17 of the 21 terrorists on the mission were Saudi). The founder of Al Qaeda, Osama bin Laden, was the son of a wealthy Saudi with family roots in Yemen, and one of the pillars of his campaign was the expulsion of the United States from the Arabian Peninsula as an act of religious purification.

COLD WAR PRIORITIES

American interests have changed as regional geopolitics has evolved. During the Cold War, American interests and policies were guided by three underlying principles: protection of the state of Israel, guaranteed access to Persian Gulf oil at a reasonable cost, and the exclusion (or minimization) of Soviet influence in the region.

These three pillars of policy are related, if not entirely compatible. Given the structure of postwar international politics, each was important. Sponsorship and protection of the new Jewish state reflected the deep and abiding shame most Western countries—and certainly the United States—felt over their failure to stop the Holocaust well short of its hideous proportions. This sentiment was widely shared within the international system (the United States and the Soviet Union cosponsored the UN resolution in 1948 that created Israel as a sovereign state), and sentiment was especially strong in the United States, the population of which contained the largest Jewish diaspora outside Israel. While the American commitment to Israeli security and survival was strong, there was disagreement within Washington circles (reflected in a similar debate in Israel) about how best to achieve that security, which centered on the fate of the Palestinian state, discussed in Chapter 4.

Secure access to reasonably priced petroleum from the Persian Gulf was the second major pillar. Oil had fueled much international interest in the region before the war, and the Allied decision to rebuild war-torn Europe's power grid based on petroleum energy reinforced this predilection. In addition to the geopolitics of energy and its effects on national well-being, this interest had a commercial aspect. During the first half of the twentieth century, much Western interest in Middle Eastern oil was in controlling that resource, and thus its security and affordability. It also meant that Middle Eastern governments, which did not control the prices the oil companies paid for oil, did not maximize their benefits from that oil. Iran, whose output was controlled by the Anglo-Iranian Oil Company, was the first to react forcefully to this situation, nationalizing the company as part of the Mossadegh revolution of 1951, which began the contentious relationship between the United States and Iran that continues to this day.

During much of the Cold War period, these two objectives were at odds. The reason was straightforward. Most Islamic states in the region were at least rhetorically opposed to the state of Israel and their treatment of the Palestinians (mainly their displacement from Israel). More militant Muslim regimes, including the fundamentalist oil-producing monarchies of the Persian Gulf, voiced this sentiment particularly strongly and included calls for the destruction of Israel. This cry has virtually disappeared from regional political discourse but remains a rallying cry for some Israelis. Such sentiments were expressed most obviously during the series of wars the Arabs waged against Israel, and especially the conflicts in 1967 and 1973, when it appeared that an Arab victory might even occur, causing Israel to arm its nascent but unacknowledged nuclear force (see Chapter 3). The residue of mistrust and animosity from this period created a conflict for the United States, simultaneously committed to Israeli security and commodious relations with the oil-producing states. Reconciling the two priorities created a delicate balancing act for American diplomacy that has largely disappeared with the decline of oil as a central factor in world politics and the recession of Islamic rhetorical obsession with destroying an Israeli state they cannot defeat militarily.

The third pillar of U.S. policy was opposition to Soviet regional influence. One aspect of the Middle East geopolitics was an extension of the Cold War global competition between communism and anticommunism. It centered on the Soviet communist desire to extend its global reach and its historic desire to gain access and to control Middle Eastern petroleum. Communist ideology hindered the Soviet efforts since "godless" (atheistic) communism was fundamentally incompatible with highly theistic Islam. Most Soviet success came from providing military assistance to the Arab states in their crusade against Israel, but the effectiveness of these efforts was ameliorated by the endemic ineffectiveness of Islamic armed forces (see Pollack) and ideological/religious incompatibility. One place where the Russians gained an enduring foothold was Syria, a position they have reinforced with their aid to the Assad regime during the Syrian civil war. McGurk maintains this has left the situation where "Russia is now the main power broker in Syria."

POST–COLD WAR PRIORITIES

American priorities have changed since 1991. At the most obvious level, there is no need to contain a Soviet communist threat that no longer exists, and the successor problem caused by Russian influence in Damascus is more limited depending on the outcome of the Syrian civil war. Since the revolution of 1979, Iran has emerged as a major power apparently intent on regaining some of its historic Persian role as a major power in the region. Especially since the 2016 American election, the United States has moved closer to Israel and its controversial positions on annexation of territories occupied since 1967. The result is an evolving power balance in which Israel and Iran are the two most powerful, influential participants. Overshadowing and influencing all the interactions has been the rise of militant religious terrorism. Terrorism has effectively replaced opposition to communism within the troika of U.S. interests.

The result is an altered set of strategic and policy concerns for the United States. If broad policy pronouncements (e.g., recognizing Jerusalem as the Israeli capital and Israeli sovereignty over the Golan Heights) or actions ($3.8 billion in military assistance to Israel in 2019) are any indication (and they are), Israeli security has moved unequivocally into the top U.S. priority. This position reinforces Israeli military dominance of the region and was reflected in Trump's 2020 policy proposal regarding Palestine. Middle Eastern oil remains part of the hierarchy of U.S. interests, but in different ways than before.

The United States need for that energy supply has drastically declined due to increased American production of shale oil and gas, greater availability of oil from elsewhere, and conservation. The interest now is to protect the access of Persian Gulf petroleum for allies and friends, to deny undue penetration by competitor states like China, and to maintain access to oil supplies the quality and nature of which (e.g., light, low carbon deposits) it still needs.

Terrorism is the wild card. The United States has been physically involved using military force to oppose terrorism since the immediate aftermath of 9/11 and a U.S. led military occupation of Afghanistan. Allegations of Iraqi terrorism support were a major part of justifying invading Iraq in 2003. The IS menace provided the rationale for a U.S. engagement and continued presence in the Syrian civil war. The U.S. has even become an indirect participant in Saudi terrorism in Yemen by selling arms to the Saudis in their campaign against the rebel Houthis.

There is one further factor that is infrequently raised and hardly ever emphasized in the context of security interests in the region. That factor is the potential consequences of regional nuclearization. Israel is the only nuclear weapons state in the region, and it uses that status to anchor its position as the current prime regional military force. Only Iran poses a threat to this Israeli position since it is the only state that physically could create its own arsenal and thus negate or reverse the Israeli advantage in a short period of time. Animosity between the two countries arises from Israeli fear of losing that monopoly and the leverage it provides by accusing the Iranians of being supporters of terror. Iran has consistently denied any intent of "going nuclear," but it is also the primary sponsor (arguably the only active one) of the Palestinian cause, and much of the physical case against Iran stems from support of Palestinian statehood. Promoting that statehood was a primary mission of the assassinated Iranian general Qasem Soleimani. A further deterioration of Israeli-Iranian relations to military conflict poses the ugliest and most dangerous prospects for the region.

THE MESSY MENU OF MIDDLE EASTERN CONFLICT

The plethora of conflicts in the Middle East can be exemplified by cases in point: situations that either are, have been, or may be sources of conflict and violence that draw outsiders into a spider's web they do not fully understand. The cast of participants changes from conflict to conflict, and the possible outcomes to one conflict may have varying, often pernicious effects on others. Nothing geopolitical is ever simple in the Middle East. Problems change, morph into different forms, or emerge in a different configuration.

The purpose of the next six chapters is to present summaries of some of the most important of current problems in the region. It does not present a definitive analysis and solutions; doing so would be pretentious. Rather, it seeks to strip away the sense of simplicity that often seems to inform public discourse and to illustrate the old saying that "for every complex, complicated problem there is an answer that is simple, straightforward and wrong."

The journey begins with the perennial problem of Israel and the Palestinians in Chapters 3 and 4. Chapter 3 is foundational, focusing on the changing status of Israel. No longer the "David" of the region, Israel's nuclear weapons have made the Israelis the most powerful military force in the region. They are "Goliath," and that status allows them to pursue an expansionist policy they could probably not sustain otherwise. The Palestinians are the most obvious victims. Historically, the conflict has been viewed as primarily a real estate dispute between the Israelis and the Palestinians over rightful control of the West Bank, but it has become much more. American policy since 2016 is partly responsible since the Trump administration rejected American historical efforts at neutrality and came down squarely behind the expansionist policies of the Netanyahu regime. That "tilt" placed the United States outside mainstream world positions. Iran has emerged as the chief regional champion of the Palestinians. When the Syrian civil war ends, the Syrians will be drawn in because of Israeli annexation of parts of the Golan Heights. This conflict has been so pervasive and far-reaching that it is also part of Chapter 3.

The next step (Chapter 5) centers on the fate of the region's other stateless people, the Kurds. The desire for Kurdish self-determination is strong, but as the aftermath of American abandonment of Syrian Kurdistan in 2019 demonstrated, it is also subject to the vicissitudes of regional geopolitics. It is an ironic situation. Kurdish nationalism is strong, and the territories that would constitute Kurdistan would likely form a strong, viable state. Kurdistan would be landlocked by less viable states and have no secure access to the outside world except through the countries from which it would be carved—none of which would be predisposed to grant transit to a potential dominant rival.

The outcome of the Syrian civil war vitally affects the fate of that country and others like the Kurds and Palestinians and is the subject of Chapter 6. The civil war itself is winding down, with the Assad regime likely to prevail. The government of Bashar Assad is dominated by Shiite Alawites from the northern coast of the country, who have been aided by Iran (the world's largest Shiite state), who see their role both as promoting Iranian influence in the region and as a launch point in their attempt to force Israel to cede the West Bank to Palestine. It is unclear whether Syria as now constituted will survive the war experience, and speculation abounds about the outcome of partition both on Syria and other regional activists.

These effects extend to several other Middle Eastern actors in the Shiite Crescent, the subject of Chapter 7. The Syrians (in whatever form) will almost certainly demand the return of Golan from Israel, which has invested heavily in transforming their occupation zone into a luxury resort area for Israelis and have, with Trump's blessing, annexed it. Iran will be active attempting to ensure the Syrians retain, even expand, their influence zone, and Russia has a strong interest in the Alawites because they are tied to the naval base at Tartus and because that relationship forms the base for much of Russian regional influence. Part of any partition will almost certainly be independence for the northeastern part of Syria (Rojava), which forms part of the Kurdish state. The outcome in Syria could even extend to the creation of a Kurdish corridor through Syria to the Mediterranean Sea and thus relieve the land-locked Kurdish problem. This latter prospect enrages Turkey, the most adamant opponent of Kurdish self-determination since they fear the Kurds could use northern Syria as a vehicle to aid uniting part of Turkey to Kurdistan. These dynamics were an important part of Turkish determination to occupy Rojava. In the background is the question of who will pay to rebuild postwar Syria. The disposition of Syria thus becomes a central, pivotal part of the regional politics of the Mediterranean Middle East, a problem examined in Chapter 7.

A new power struggle has emerged in the region. It represents a miniature version of the Cold War, and it may prove to be the most difficult and intractable aspect of regional geopolitics. It is the subject of Chapter 8. The focal points of this new competition are Iran and an otherwise incongruous growing relationship between Israel and Saudi Arabia. The Israeli-Iranian aspect centers on regional geopolitical dominance. Its clearest manifestations are in Iranian efforts to expand its regional influence in the Muslim world and Israel's nuclear weapons–based military hegemony. Its symbols include Israeli saber-rattling about the prospects of Iranian nuclear weapons and complaints about Iranian asymmetrical military sponsorship of the Palestinian cause. The Iranian-Saudi competition has a religious (Sunni-Shia) veneer, but it is really a power struggle over hegemony in the Persian Gulf littoral. The struggle over Yemen is its symbol. Widening Israeli-Saudi animosities demonstrate the unconventional dimensions these regional conflicts can develop.

The United States has already found itself ensnared in the endemic complexity and insolubility of two Middle East situations that are examined in Chapter 9. The trigger for the American involvement in both Afghanistan and Iraq was real or alleged ties to terrorism. Within weeks of 9/11, the United States had demanded that the Taliban government of Afghanistan remand

AQ fighters to U.S control since the bin Laden organization had planned the attack there under the Taliban's protective wing. The Afghans refused the demand, and the United States intervened to capture the perpetrators. It failed, but the effort enmeshed the United States in the civil power struggle that was ongoing in Afghanistan. The United States has not extricated itself over 18 years later. In Iraq, the 2003 invasion was advertised as a crusade against terrorists allegedly supported by the Saddam Hussein government. Instead, the United States found itself entangled in a classic asymmetrical resistance against its occupation from which it partially escaped by withdrawal in 2011. The U.S. retains a military presence in a country that, like Syria, is a prime candidate for dismemberment into at least three successor states in the future. Chapter 10 tries to organize the twisted web of relations into as coherent a whole as seems possible. Chapter 11 adds the Biden tough quote.

CHOOSING POLICY: AMERICAN POLICY AND ENDLESS WAR

Determining how the United States can and should attempt to influence the multiple sources of regional conflict, the extent to which different forms of pressure will be effective or ineffective, and what unforeseen spinoff difficulties are created by solving one problem or another is a major undertaking. Moreover, in volatile areas like the Middle East, the only constant surrounding policy seems to be change. The result is a confusing environment in which to fashion and try to implement policy.

As the preceding pages have attempted to detail, American policy toward the area has been changing since the end of the Cold War altered global geopolitical and national security boundaries. For the decade of the 1990s, the United States basically stood astride the international system as a virtual hegemon, and the sources of challenge to that status were limited in scope and danger. The rise of international terrorism symbolized by the 9/11 attacks changed that circumstance and reoriented and refocused American national security priorities and actions. Before the 1990s, as Bacevich pointed out, the United States was not involved greatly in Middle Eastern turmoil and violence; since 9/11, that has been the overwhelming focus of policy.

Numerical representations are staggering, although their exact dimensions are probably unknown or shrouded in classification. Estimates of what the United States has spent on military commitments to the region since 2001 vary but seem to congregate in the $6–$7 trillion dollar range. The largest concentration has been on the wars in Afghanistan and Iraq. The figures do not include peripheral expenditures such as the amount of nominal U.S. foreign assistance to the largest recipient in the world, Israel, virtually all of which is used to augment Israeli military budgets. Over 65,000 American troops are present in at least ten states. The largest concentrations are in Afghanistan (14,000), followed by Kuwait and Qatar (13,000 each) down to 600 in Oman, according to January 2020 figures quoted in *Newsweek*. Should we be spending that much? Should we have so many troops assigned to Middle Eastern states? The numbers may be wrong at the margins or subject to some change. The reality of the priorities they reflect is not wrong. In a broader context, Fontaine cites in a 2019 Foreign Affairs Congressional Research Service (CRS) study that asserts "the United States has employed force over 200 times since the end of the Cold War." Most deployments are in the Middle East.

Regardless of their detailed sagacity, these figures suggest a fundamental characteristic of operational American national security policy since the end of the Cold War. The United States spent large amounts of money in the competition with the Soviet Union and deployed large numbers of troops on the territory of Cold War allies in Europe and Asia, but there was virtually universal agreement these were places where truly vital American interests were engaged. The nuclear balance between the superpowers also meant a slippage into military conflict could have catastrophic, even civilization threatening, consequences.

The situation is clearly different today. The United States has insinuated itself into a deep level of commitment in an area that is arguably important to the country, but is it vital to a degree that the Soviet threat was? International terrorism is routinely portrayed as an equivalent, but Middle East terrorists pose no convincing threat to American existence, the ultimate vital interest. The threat today is more defined somewhere on the boundary between VIs and LTVs, not clearly VIs.

If you accept that construction—and you may not—what does that mean for operational national security policy and more specifically for the deployment and employment of American forces in the Middle East? There are two ways to look at the problem. The first has to do with the strength and vitality of Middle Eastern conflicts to the United States and the salience of those threats to American interests and the ability to remedy those problems at acceptable costs. In Syria, the original assessment of these factors was negative, and the United States eschewed direct involvement. In Afghanistan, the opposite assessment was made, and the Americans are still there. In Iraq, the United States essentially invented reasons for attack (e.g., alleged weapons of mass destruction, unproven ties to terrorism). Again, Americans are still there and have created the endless war reaction in the process.

Should the United States rethink the importance of the region and specific places in terms of both interests and the ability to use force to resolve them in

America's favor? This is the second way to look at the problem. One reason for American endless commitments is because we have devised no successful military strategy for realizing the interests to be served. The Taliban are alive and functioning in Afghanistan, and there is still resistance to American presence in Iraq. In other places where American forces are deployed, their function is to frustrate Iranian expansionism. Are we doing the right thing? Is our policy wrongheaded or is it quixotic? What can we do to improve our success rate? Recognize your answer is tentative and may change as you examine specific situations in Chapters 3–9. That rejoinder in mind, what can we do to begin reducing or eliminating endless wars in the Middle East?

BIBLIOGRAPHY

Anderson, Scott. *Lawrence in Arabia: War, Deceit, Imperial Folly and the Making of the Modern Middle East.* New York: Anchor Books, 2013.

Bacevich, Andrew J. "Even If We Defeat the Islamic State, We'll Still Lose the Bigger War." *Washington Post* (online), October 3, 2014.

Betts, Richard K. "Ending America's Era of Permanent War." *Foreign Affairs* 93, 6 (November/December 2014), 15–24.

Bremmer, Ian. "What Does America Stand For?" *Time* 185, 20 (June 1, 2015), 26–31.

Chua, Amy. *Political Tribes: Group Instincts and the Fate of Nations.* New York: Penguin, 2018.

The CIA World Factbook, 2019–2020. New York: Skyhorse, 2019.

Eland, Ivan. *No War for Oil: U.S. Dependency and the Middle East.* Oakland, CA: Independent Institute, 2011.

Fawcett, Louise. *International Relations of the Middle East.* Fifth Ed. Oxford, UK: Oxford University Press, 2019.

Fishman, Louis. "Pushing for a Political Breakthrough: Kurds in Turkey and Palestinians in Israel." *Current History* 118, 812 (December 2019), 355–360.

Fontaine, Richard. "The Nonintervention Delusion: What War Is Good For." *Foreign Affairs* 98, 6 (November/December 2019), 84–98.

Frantzman, Seth. *After ISIS: America, Iran, and the Struggle for the Middle East.* Jerusalem: Gefen Publishing House, 2019.

Gerges, Fawaz A. *Making the Arab World: Nasser, Qtub, and the Clash That Shaped the Middle East.* Princeton, NJ: Princeton University Press, 2018.

Haass, Richard N. "The Unravelling: How to Respond to a Disordered World." *Foreign Affairs* 93, 6 (November/December 2014), 70–79.

Held, Colbert C., and John Thomas Cummings. *Middle East Patterns: Places, People, and Politics.* Sixth Ed. Boulder, CO: Westview Press, 2014.

Khalidi, Rashid. *Brokers of Deceit: How the U.S. Has Undermined Peace in the Middle East.* Boston, MA: Beacon Books, 2014.

Kuru, Ahmet. *Islam, Authoritarianism, and Underdevelopment: A Global and Historical Comparison.* Cambridge, UK: Cambridge University Press, 2019.

Lesch, David W., and Mark L. Haas. *The Middle East and the United States: History, Politics and Ideologies.* Updated Sixth Ed. New York: Routledge, 2018.

Lewis, Bernard. *The Crisis of Islam: Holy War and Unholy Terror.* New York: Random House, 2004.

———. *What Went Wrong? The Clash between Islam and Modernity in the Middle East.* New York: HarperPerennials, 2003.

Louer, Lawrence (Translated by Ethan Rundell). *Sunnis and Shi'a: A Political History.* Princeton, NJ: Princeton University Press, 2019.

Lynch, Marc. *The New Arab Wars: Anarchy and Uprising in the Middle East.* New York: Public Affairs, 2016.

Malley, Robert. "The Unwanted Wars: Why the Middle East Is More Combustible than Ever." *Foreign Affairs* 98, 6 (November/December 2019), 38–47.

Maloney, Suzanne. "Dreams of Westphalia: Can a Brand Bargain Solve the Middle East Problem?" *Foreign Affairs* 99, 1 (January/February 2020), 148–53.

McGurk, Brett. "Hard Truths in Syria: America Can't Do More with Less, and It Shouldn't Try." *Foreign Affairs* 98, 3 (May/June 2019), 69–84.

Melamed, Avi. *Inside the Middle East: Making Sense of the Most Dangerous and Complicated Region on Earth.* New York: Skyhorse, 2016.

Milton, Patrick, Michael Axworthy, and Brendan Sims. *Toward a Westphalia for the Middle East.* Oxford, UK: Oxford University Press, 2018.

Owen, John M. IV. *Confronting Political Islam: Six Lessons from the West's Past.* Princeton, NJ: Princeton University Press, 2014.

———. "From Calvin to the Caliphate: What Europe's Religious Wars Tell Us about the Modern Middle East." *Foreign Affairs* 94, 3 (May/June 2015), 77–89.

Petras, James. *The Politics of Empire: The U.S., Israel, and the Middle East.* Atlanta, GA: Clarity Press, 2014.

Petraeus, David, and Madawi al-Rasheed. "The Wrong Middle East Strategy." *Foreign Affairs* 98, 1 (January/February 2019), 220.

Pollack, Kenneth A. *Armies of Sand: The Past, Present, and Future of Arab Military Effectiveness.* Oxford, UK: Oxford University Press, 2018.

Provence, Michael. *The Last Ottoman Generation and the Making of the Modern Middle East.* Cambridge, UK: Cambridge University Press, 2017.

Satloff, Robert. "Don't Pull Back." *Foreign Affairs* 98, 4 (July/August 2019), 88–90.

Snow, Donald M. *The Middle East, Oil, and the U.S. National Security Policy: Intractable Conflicts, Impossible Solutions.* Lanham, MD: Rowman & Littlefield, 2016.

———. *What after Iraq.* New York: Pearson Longman, 2009.

Stern, Jessica, and M. Berger. *ISIS: The State of Terror.* New York: ECCO Books, 2015.

Trenin, Dmitri. *What Is Russia Up to in the Middle East?* First Ed. London: Polity, 2017.

Uzi, Rabi. *Civil War and Unification.* Library of Modern Middle Eastern Studies. London: IB Tauris, 2015.

"Where Are American Troops Near Iran? Tens of Thousands of American Soldiers Are in the Middle East, Afghanistan." *Newsweek*, January 6, 2020.

3

The Special Relationship
Israel

The examination of substantive conflict begins with Israel. The state of Israel was established in 1948 to accommodate Jews displaced and often homeless in postwar Europe, and they joined Zionists who had been emigrating to Palestine since the nineteenth century. Ripped from their former homes, these immigrants constituted a stateless nation who sought the safety and protection in a physical area their religion told them was their rightful home, and they ended their "exodus" by founding their own state in the "promised land." The Palestinian Arabs who had inhabited the land previously fled in a dark period of their history they call the nakbah (disaster, cataclysm). The result was to transfer statelessness from the new state of Israel to the Palestinians. Their statelessness remains a central dynamic of regional conflict and is examined in the next chapter.

Israel is important as a starting point for examining the region for at least three reasons. The first is that religiously based hatred and conflict between the Muslims of the region and the Israelis has been a recurrent theme of the region's violent politics for most of the time since Israel became a state. For most of the period between 1948 and the early 1970s, driving the Israelis into the sea in an act of genocide was a rhetorical goal of the "Arab" states, adding to Jewish apprehension from the Holocaust years. Although the calls for Jewish extinction have lessened and are mostly advocated by small groups of Muslim extremists, these cries retain salience for many Israelis and have created the basis for an understandable obsession with security and increasing and consolidating the security of Israelis. This concern underlies much of the political dialog in Israel and the sometimes very controversial actions Israel has taken to enhance its sense of security.

Those actions form the second reason for beginning the examination of regional conflict in Israel. As discussed later in the chapter, solving the security problem has resulted in two broad policy emphases that have become foundational factors in the ongoing fabric of Middle Eastern conflict and the nature and shape of its violence. The first has been territorial. A major problem for Israeli security is its small size and shape (it is long and narrow) and thus its geographically based vulnerability to attack and potential dissection. This has resulted in a policy to enlarge the physical state in ways that would make a successful invasion distinctly less likely to succeed. Its manifestation, as the centerpiece of Netanyahu's drive to create Greater Israel, is the policy of occupation and, in some cases, annexation of territories on Israel's boundaries. Palestine and the Syrian Golan Heights are the most prominent examples.

The second initiative has been Israel's development and deployment of nuclear weapons. It is less thoroughly discussed in the literature because Israel neither confirms nor denies being the regional nuclear power, and its principal patron, the United States, refuses to raise questions about it. The simple fact, however, is that an operational Israeli nuclear capability has existed since 1968, that it probably numbers slightly less than 100 deployed weapons today (making it slightly smaller than the Pakistani arsenal), and that it gives Israel a regional monopoly that is the bedrock of Israel's regional physical security. No Middle Eastern state can contemplate attacking Israel without the credible prospect of an Israeli nuclear retaliation that would destroy the attacker's state. The monopoly has secured Israel, and it is the primary (if publicly unstated) reason for Israeli opposition to an Iranian nuclear weapon.

The third reason for starting with Israel is a recognition of the geopolitical consequences of a second factor. In a strictly military sense, Israel is now the major military power in the region. Its possession of nuclear weapons makes it "Goliath" rather than "David," although many Israelis are reluctant to abandon the sympathy associated with being a beleaguered underdog. The Arab states do not necessarily like the Israelis any more than they ever did, but they recognize there is nothing they can do about them. Israel is now aloof from much of the regional instability with which they have had to deal.

Finally, there is the importance of Israel to the United States. To many Americans, Israel is the most important state in the Middle East. The attachment is primarily emotional in content, spurred by the American sense of shame after World War II at not having intervened sooner and more forcefully than it did to stop the genocide inflicted on Jewish and Roma victims of the Nazi death camps and extending to the Jewish "exodus" to Palestine after the war, and leadership in helping to create the Jewish state of Israel. The U.S. government and American citizens have contributed enormous amounts of resources to Israel and Israelis, and Israel today is the largest recipient of U.S. developmental assistance (primarily military aid) in the world.

The U.S. government considers itself the guarantor of Israeli security. "We have Israel's back." Israel accepts this guarantee's sincerity, but does so conditionally. Israel believes the United States believes it would do anything to save Israel, including putting itself at risk, but it joins the French (who helped develop the Israeli nuclear program) in wondering if that commitment might not be as strong with the possibility that honoring it could result in nuclear war. The two countries have no formal security treaty, and the Israelis feel the need to hedge against the possibility the United States might not come to their aid in a crunch, leaving them to fend for themselves. In the end, the Israelis feel they can depend on only themselves, justifying both nuclear weapons and physical expansion of the Jewish state.

The problem is that these two emphases are each controversial and that their continuation as the chief thrusts of Israeli security policy is at odds with many in the United States and among some Israelis. The Netanyahu government views the two elements as both complementary and reinforcing. Territorial expansion both serves security interests by lowering vulnerabilities to attack and also provides scarce land on which to settle immigrants as part of Greater Israel. As Netanyahu has said, "I want every Jew to feel at home in Israel." The emphasis is self-reinforcing since most of the immigrants settle in the occupied territories and support the government.

Nuclear weapons possession reinforces these predilections. The arsenal's existence is universally known (if unacknowledged). Everyone knows they exist and that the Israelis would use them rather than suffer another Masada. The only physical revelation of their existence came in 1986 when an Israeli "whistle blower" who worked at the nuclear facility announced—complete with photographs—their existence, an act that got him convicted of treason and sentenced to 18 years in prison. The arsenal's existence and belief the Israelis would use them under some circumstances thus becomes the backdrop against which Israeli-Muslim politics is played out. Although no one publicly admits it, this dynamic helps explain why most Islamic states (Iran is the exception) do not volubly denounce Israeli expansionism and intransigence on the Palestinian question.

These positions and their combination are controversial. Both policies contribute to Israel's status as a lawless pariah state in parts of the world since both violate and even flaunt international legal regimes. Within Israel, the opposition to Netanyahu's hardline policies argues for negotiated settlements to territorial questions, especially regarding Palestine (see Chapter 4). These opponents are currently a minority of about 40 percent of the electorate. This policy divide also exists in the United States. President Trump was in a virtual lock-step agreement with Netanyahu, which was reflected in the 2020 proposed Palestinian settlement authored by Trump's son-in-law, Jared Kushner. More liberal Americans agree with their Israeli counterparts and advocate a two-state solution to the Palestinian-Israeli dispute. Both elements in both states and their governments avoid the nuclear question altogether, effectively pretending it does not exist.

The Israeli obsession with security forms the basis of their policy. Unlike virtually any other country in the world, Israelis worry constantly about their belief that not only do their enemies seek to defeat and subjugate the Jewish people to a humiliating existence that has been a recurring theme of their history, but that those enemies want to complete the genocide started by Hitler. The destruction of Israel would be an artifact of that process. One can question the veracity of this obsession and whether it is sometimes overstated to promote Israeli security initiatives and policies. One cannot question whether it is deeply held, virtually universal concern among Israelis and other members of world Jewry.

The current manifestations of the Israeli response to these threats emerged in the late 1960s to form Israel's posture toward the world. The two enabling events were the smashing Israeli victory over its antagonists in the Six-Day War of 1967 and the development of nuclear weapons. The war ended with Israeli occupation of territory that belonged to several of its defeated foes, including Egypt, Syria, Jordan, and Lebanon. Much of this occupied territory remains in Israeli hands, although some (notably Egyptian) was returned as part of the 1982 peace agreement between the two states. The territory the Israelis kept has formed the basis for implementing various aspects of the Greater Israel policy, including the establishment of what some Israelis consider more secure, defensible boundaries. The second enabling event was the successful fabrication of its first nuclear weapons. The Israelis have never physically acknowledged this accomplishment, but it has been chronicled by several authors, notably Hersh and Cohen. As the Israeli arsenal has grown, its existence has solidified Israel's position as the dominant geopolitical actor in the region and reduced Arab calls to destroy Israel to empty rhetoric.

The implications of these two phenomena are central to the question of Israel's place in the Middle East, its security and long-term future as a regional power, and the U.S. attitude and actions toward the country with which it has a "special relationship." They are controversial and form critical elements on American security concerns that form major elements of what follows.

The discussion begins with the enigma of the Israeli nuclear force. These weapons are rarely mentioned and almost never examined in discussions about Israeli security, but their potential impact is so enormous that they virtually beg for much greater scrutiny. The Israelis do not publicly acknowledge their existence and thus never talk about them, but their opponents do not need to be reminded of them. When an Israeli apologist like Beres airily declares that the force "would never be used except in defensive reprisals for massive first strikes," the Arabs almost certainly do not believe them. When Moshe Dayan stated, "Israel must be seen as a mad dog, too dangerous to bother" (quoted in Beres), they undoubtedly pay attention. This warning provides protective cover for Israeli expansionist actions since no one wants to awaken and activate the mad dog. These Israeli policy emphases form the context for American policy directed at guaranteeing the security of Israel and maintaining the special relationship. It is a perspective to that relationship that is not often examined publicly. Maybe it should be.

ISRAELI SECURITY POLICIES

Nuclear weapons and physical expansion have been the synergistic bookends of the Israeli security question since the right-wing Likud Party came to power in 1977 and have been virtually synonymous pillars of policy since Bibi Netanyahu became prime minister over a decade ago. The tight alignment that existed between Netanyahu and the Trump administration effectively tied the United States to this position for as long as that political connection existed.

It is not the only solution that has been part of the American and Israeli debates on Israeli security. In both countries, there is a position associated with more liberal political elements in both countries that calls for a negotiated settlement with Israel's opponents. The historical manifestation of this position has been the "two-state" solution creating a fully sovereign Palestinian state on all or nearly all the West Bank (see Chapter 4). This position was dominant in the American debate prior to Trump, although it has never enjoyed as much support in Israel as in the United States. Advocacy of a negotiated settlement of the current regional "cold war" varies in its compatibility with the two pillars of current policy. The Israeli possession of nuclear weapons can reinforce a negotiated peace, for instance, by providing the ultimate deterrent against a planned attack aimed at destroying Israel. A negotiated settlement is less compatible with Israeli expansionism and thus the Greater Israel policy since limits on future expansion and the probable return of some occupied territories would almost certainly be conditions for any negotiated settlement. The policies and their coordination are difficult and complex. An examination of each element is necessary to see synergies, disconnects, and possible outcomes.

ISRAELI NUCLEAR WEAPONS

Fascination with nuclear weapons to secure the Israeli state is as old as the Jewish state itself. It reflects remembrance not only of the Holocaust but also the mass suicide of freedom-seeking Jews at Masada in 73 AD. The conclusion from that period is captured, according to Hersh, in the cryptic pledge: "Never again!" More elaborately, Beres explains, "Israel must understand that it can never be just another state. It must remain sui generis." The implication, he argues, is the unique imperative of *ein brera* (no alternative) that dictates "that Israel, more than any other state, must not count on others ultimately to protect it, but must be prepared to do so alone." That assertion is extraordinary on several levels. It implies that Israel cannot ultimately count on American protection (a bedrock American promise) and that when international values conflict with Israeli perceived vital concerns, international dictates must be ignored. It also helps explain Israel's obsession with nuclear weapons.

The centrality of gaining nuclear weapons goes back to determinations made by David Ben-Gurion in 1948. As a 2015 National Interest study asserts, Israel's first prime minister "made it his mission to ensure that the one homeland for the Jewish people would be protected from an ever-present threat of Arab attack." To activate that promise, the study maintains, Ben-Gurion "hinted in an April 1948 letter . . . that Israel needed to fast-track their research into building a stockpile of nuclear bombs that would safeguard the Jewish state." In his view, nuclear weapons would provide an "insurance policy" for survival.

According to the Stockholm International Peace Research Institute (SIPRI) and 2019 Federation of American Scientists (FAS) estimates, the Israeli arsenal stands at an estimated 80 warheads, making it the world's second smallest force among possessors (North Korea is last) and represents only a tiny fraction of 1 percent of the world's arsenal of over 14,000 weapons. It is estimated that the Israelis have nuclear material to build another 100 or so bombs, which would surpass the arsenal sizes of India and Pakistan. The United States and Russia, by contrast, each have over 6,000 active warheads.

The arsenal's significance is regional. Israel is the only nuclear power in the region, a condition it works doggedly to maintain. Given the demographic geography of the Middle East, if the arsenal is unleashed on Muslim population concentrations, it could essentially decimate them all. Its opponents know this and that there is nothing they can do to avoid that fate should Israel act. This realization, combined with the Samson Option articulation, gives the Israelis enormous leverage. Most importantly, it means that any other Middle

Eastern state opposing Greater Israel initiatives must measure opposition in terms of potentially courting Armageddon.

As an international, and thus American, issue, the Israeli nuclear program poses unique problems regarding the failure of deterrence. In 1948, this was an abstract concern since only the United States had the "bomb," but today Israel joins eight other members of the nuclear "club." That means today the only danger of war in the region would come from an Israeli launch taken for reasons of its survival. Middle East instability means that seems less farfetched than in other world areas. The fruition of the Iranian nuclear program could lead to a country like Saudi Arabia buying the bomb from Pakistan, for instance, with unforeseeable but potentially disastrous results. Should the "balloon go up" in the region and Israel be part of the nuclear battle space, could the United States avoid the conflict? Who knows? American national security is best served by a nuclear-weapons–free Middle East; the Israelis consider their possession the bedrock of their ultimate security. It is not at all clear the positions are reconcilable.

EVOLUTION OF ISRAELI NUCLEAR WEAPONS

Israeli nuclear weapons have flown under the international radar for most of the program's existence. The beginnings of that program can be traced (as is done by Hersh) to December 1954, when Israel first admitted that, in collaboration with France, it had instituted a peaceful nuclear program under the Atoms for Peace program. This effort fit neatly with what became the French force frappe program in the 1960s. In "early 1958," groundbreaking began for the Dimona EL 102 nuclear reactor at the site of the same name south of the Dead Sea that has been the chief location of Israeli nuclear efforts ever since. Hersh reports that this site engaged both in peaceful (power-generating) and weapons research. With help from the French the first successful underground nuclear test was carried out in the mid-1960s.

Hersh reports that "sometime early in 1968," the Dimona facility was ordered into full-scale production designed to produce four or five warheads a year. Israel also entered a cooperative nuclear agreement with the Republic of South Africa (RSA) in the early 1970s. The South Africans had developed the weapons as a hedge against the black "frontline" states surrounding it. The heart of the Israeli-RSA collaboration was an apparent joint weapons test in the 1960s, which neither country admitted. When black majority rule impended in South Africa, the RSA dismantled its program rather than turn it over to the Mandela regime. Israel did not.

The most notable characteristic of this developmental program was the lack of attention it received. The Israelis never announced nor officially admitted that the program existed, and the only evidence of a major military effort that probably included the nuclear program was the fact that, as Hersh reports, Israeli "defense spending rose 500 percent between 1966 and 1972."

The fruit of the program—and its "coming out" as a major component of Israel's survival strategy—occurred in 1973 during the so-called Yom Kippur War. For the first time, Israeli conventional forces were unsuccessful in rapidly and easily sweeping aside the attacks of their neighbors and faced an increasingly desperate and uncertain fate. In those circumstances, Israel unveiled its nuclear capability and its possible employment against its enemies. As Hersh describes it, the period was "Israel's darkest hour. Israel called its first nuclear alert and began arming its nuclear arsenal." It was both an admission of its capability and a warning to potential antagonists. Hersh adds that "it used the alert to blackmail Washington into a major policy change" that resulted in substantial arms provisions to the Israelis.

The world recognized that Israel had become the world's eighth nuclear power, but the Israelis never specifically admitted it. Instead, the Israeli nuclear capability continued to be governed by two prominent principles that it retains as its rationale for nuclear possession. The first, and most innocuous, is "the bomb in the basement" rationale for not admitting they have the weapons (see Karpin). The second, and more ominous is the "Samson Option," which warns its enemies how and in what circumstances Israel might employ its nuclear weapons and justifies, in Israeli eyes, why it must maintain a regional nuclear monopoly.

The Samson Option draws its name from the biblical legend of Samson, a giant who was captured, tortured, and threatened with death in a Philistine temple. Rather than submit to the humiliation of his fate, Samson used his enormous strength to bring down the pillars of the Temple of Dagon upon both himself and his tormentors, killing them all, including himself. The symbolism is that, if the Israelites were to be slaughtered, they would exact the same fate on those who would destroy them: their act would be suicidal. Martin Van Creveld, quoted in Hirst's *The Gun and the Olive Branch*, states the significance of the symbol: "Our armed forces are not the thirtieth strongest in the world, but rather the second or third. We have the capability to take the world down with us. And I assure you that will happen before Israel goes under." The story is often contrasted with the Masada experience.

THE SAMSON OPTION

The Samson Option is the ultimate deterrent threat. Most superpower deterrence formulations (see Snow, *Nuclear Weapons and Superpower Relations*) are based on the threat of such massive retaliation should an opponent attack that the initial attacking state would be effectively destroyed in the response. The initial attack might be "successful" in destroying the victim, but it would also be suicidal since the attacker would also be destroyed in the response. This suicidal effect is what deters the initial attack.

At one level, the Samson Option threat makes perfect sense for a small country like Israel faced with a hostile and potentially much larger threat, and the recognition that surrender or annihilation are possible fates if Israel is concertedly—and successfully—attacked by its neighbors. Nuclear weapons are the great equalizer in this equation. Israeli weapons could, if targeted against the population centers of surrounding countries, effectively destroy them as functioning societies. It is a matter of demographics: most Muslim countries, given the arid climate, have their populations concentrated in a few urban areas, which are the ideal "target-rich environments" for the Israeli arsenal (Iran is at least a partial exception by virtue of size, population, and physical diversity).

The viability of the Samson threat, however, is predicated on Israeli exclusive regional possession of nuclear weapons. No power—except Russia, at whom the initial Israeli weapons were aimed—could retaliate against Israel if it struck with its arsenal, making its threats credible. If other Middle East states (Iran is the obvious candidate) were also to "go nuclear," the clear applicability of the Samson Option as a deterrent threat would be weakened. This change in dynamic is pivotal to understanding the shrillness of Israeli objections to Iran's obtaining the weapons. The Iran threat is the heart of stated Israeli concern. As Netanyahu put it in a *Time* interview regarding Iranian intentions: "one is to have nuclear weapons, which they intend to use to annihilate Israel. And second, their attempt to bring their army or pieces of their army into Syria, right in Israel's backyard."

Except for North Korea, the Israeli arsenal is thus unique in that it is not part of a nuclear dyad, where two nuclear powers directly deter one another with retaliatory threats as do, for instance, the United States and Russia or India and Pakistan. Mutual deterrence is generally believed to reinforce deterrence. Whether the resulting inhibition to use weapons because of a specific, certain retaliatory response is weakened in the DPRK or Israeli cases is an interesting and largely unexplored theoretical question. The North Koreans are arguably inhibited by the United States, but who restrains Israel? The Israelis maintain, in Beres's words, that "Israel's nuclear force would never be used except in retaliation for massive first strikes. It is almost inconceivable that Israel would ever decide to preempt any enemy aggression with a nuclear defensive strike." This is a significant potential hedge because it adds conventional self-defense to the potential roles of nuclear weapons against an opponent who could not respond in kind with nuclear weapons. Arguably, this dynamic adds to Dayan's needed reputation as a "mad dog."

Thus, the Israeli regional nuclear monopoly has another, and mostly unacknowledged, role for Israel. Since it implicitly threatened to use nuclear weapons in 1973 by activating its arsenal, Israeli regional military dominance—one is tempted to suggest hegemony—has been essentially unquestionable. No Islamic state threatens Israeli actions on a wide variety of issues because Israel is so strong militarily. Nuclear weapons, in other words, deflect some of the existential threat that has formed the basis for Israeli policy and has given the country the capability to engage in geopolitical actions that it might not undertake in more constrained military circumstances. This utility calculation makes the Israeli arsenal unique in the nuclear world.

TERRITORIAL EXPANSION

The second theme of Israeli policy has been territorial expansion. The rationale for acquiring additional territory is normally (and not entirely inappropriately) couched in terms of defense and security and is thus rationalized in existential security terms. It has increasingly been used for additional purposes, such as providing territory for Israeli settlements that it is not clear the Israelis do not intend to incorporate into the Israeli state. Such acts are interpretable as imperialistic.

There are two geographic foci of the territorial question, the West Bank and parts of the Golan Heights. Both have been issues since 1967 since the Israelis occupied both as part of the outcome of the Six Day War and has retained a control over them that they seem decreasingly willing to relinquish or negotiate about the longer their occupation continues. For each area, the major concern among outsiders has become whether occupation has transformed the West Bank and Golan into de facto, and even permanent acts of, annexation to Israel, a position strongly opposed by virtually the entire international community but with considerable support within the political right in Israel itself (prominently including the settler community in the occupied zones) and was with the Trump administration in the United States (Jewish opinion in the United States is fundamentally divided on the issue).

Physically and in terms of international attention, the problem of the West Bank has dominated concern over expansion, but the issue of Golan has re-emerged since the prospects of the end of the Syrian civil war have appeared and the fate of the Syrian state has become important. The West Bank has a population of over three million Palestinian Muslims and about a quarter million Jews, many of them immigrants attracted to Israel by the availability of occupied lands they might inhabit. This factor is important in the overall equation because West Bank expansion is fundamental to Israeli attraction of non-Israeli Jews to the Israeli state: within the pre-1967 boundaries, there is very little land that can be used for additional population. This means the goal of Greater Israel requires annexation and colonization of the occupied territories. By contrast, the part of Golan occupied by Israel is about only the physical size of the District of Columbia and has about only 20,000 Jewish immigrants. It does, however, occupy the highest land on the heights, and the Syrian capital of Damascus, forty miles away, is visible from the top of Mt. Hermon, the highest point in the occupied area at 9,232 feet. Israel has also developed a thriving vacation retreat in the area for Israelis to escape from the heat of Israeli summers. This activity is not widely publicized, but on August 25, 2019, Booking.com listed 95 resort locations in the occupied Golan zone.

The tension regarding both occupied zones is fundamentally similar and is captured in Israeli tension over the questions of maximum security/survival and the desire for Israeli expansion. It is both a geopolitical and an internal political debate within Israel. The geopolitical orientation is largely that of the hardliners, particularly within Israel, who emphasize the security peril of Israeli geography as defined before 1967. They emphasize what Beres terms the "catastrophic threats to Israel" ringed by enemies, vulnerable to invasion that could cut the country in two and for which Israeli conventional forces could prove inadequate, as they nearly did in 1973. Their emphasis is currently on the peril posed by Iran. Ironically, it can be argued that the Israelis need a vibrant Iranian threat to continue the security and territorial position. Tehran thus provides a reason for nuclear weapons and the need to expand.

Their responses are unyielding and rigid, with two emphases. One is the maintenance of more secure territorial buffers making a successful invasion less likely to succeed. This thrust is manifested in the occupation of the West Bank and Golan, both of which extend the land buffer between Israel and its enemies. It also means opposition to a negotiated settlement is a dangerous illusion (part of the "death pact" argument). Occupation, of course, also facilitates and justifies both occupation and colonization, although the Israelis never publicly draw this perfectly obvious consequence and rationale. Thus, territorial security also provides additional space on which to settle immigrants moving to Israel and a prime goal of the Greater Israel thrust of

Netanyahu's policy. Not coincidentally, most of these settlers feel grateful to the prime minister and his allies for creating the opportunity to come to Israel and thus become supporters of the conservative policies of Netanyahu, helping him stay in power. Security-based policies make good electoral politics in this case.

There is an alternate approach to the territorial defense/security question that is held by the international community and more liberal Jewish advocates in both Israel and the United States. That position is that Israel should negotiate with its opponents (especially the Palestinians) to create a political solution wherein Israel agrees to the two-state solution in return to an end of antagonism and violence between Israel and the Palestinian state—a position known for years in Israel as "land for peace." It has essentially been off the table since the hawkish Likud Party came to power in 1977 and is particularly opposed by Netanyahu and his allied hawks, who believe that "political settlements would be nice, but for the moment at least, they cannot be taken seriously. They simply will not work" (Beres).

This position reflects the long-standing Israeli existential obsession. Of the two solutions to the territorial question, the militarily derived solution feeds upon and assuages the existential threat perception by increasing the border protecting Israel, but it does so at the cost of greater enmity from the Palestinians and their champions, currently the Iranians and their surrogates who engage in the campaign of asymmetrical war/terror against Israel that, in turn, reinforces the existential threat/antinegotiation argument of those in power in Israel. It is an entirely circular argument. At the same time, calls for negotiation leading to a two-state solution or of something similar ("land for peace") face the equally circular counterargument that should an agreement be negotiated on which the Arabs reneged, the existential threat would return and Israel's situation could become dire, up to and including a reexamination of the purely defensive, retaliation of nuclear weapons and the Samson Option. Champions of negotiation say negotiation is the only way to break the impasse; opponents say the chance is too great. The current territorial situation allows Israeli strategic depth against attack and thus recourse to a strategy Beres calls "anticipatory self-defense." The circularity of the arguments is heavily weighted toward the status quo. These alternatives deeply divide the Israeli political left and right. The election results of September 2019 did not provide clarity about which approach most Israelis favor.

The status, and more specifically the legality, of the settlements is highly controversial internationally, a concern that becomes especially acute when Israel formally annexes or threatens to annex parts of the occupied territories to the Israeli state. Almost all the international community opposes and regularly condemns Israeli practice, especially when it extends its control over more territory and increases migrant settlement of disputed territories, both practices that have been accelerated since 2017. Opposition is expressed with particular fervor in international fora like the UN and specifically in a series of UN Security Council Resolutions since 1979, all of which demand that Israel reverse the settlement practice and return property to its original owners on the general basis that Israeli actions violate international and specific international conventions. Israel denies these charges and ignores entreaties contained in them.

The substance of the debate is enshrouded in arcane legal argumentation that is not important for present purposes. More to the point, both sides have elaborate legal arguments that are largely moot in their effect on the situation since there is no legal instrument that can authoritatively determine the merits nor issue enforceable judgments or punish transgressors. The Israelis maintain that their continued occupation of what they call the "disputed territories" is legal, and the international community, acting through the UN Security Council, says it is illegal. The issue achieves notoriety only when Israel acts to annex or otherwise change the status of the "occupied territories."

The national security implications for the United States are what principally concern us here. First, they create continued consternation among the Arab states whose territories are occupied (notably Syria and Jordan) and others concerned that their Palestinian brethren are the clear victims of the current situation. What is most notable is how mild and generally ineffectual their expressions of concern have been. Among the Muslim states, only non-Arab Iran has been militant since 1979 in its opposition to the Israelis. Whether Arab relative silence results from fear of Israeli military power or reflects a lack of commitment to rectifying the situation (or both) is debatable. Second, the stalemate clearly comes at the expense of Palestinian statehood, the subject of Chapter 4. Third, the ongoing situation creates difficulties for the United States, which has been both a stalwart champion of Israel and generally an advocate of a more equitable condition for the Palestinians, two positions that are not entirely compatible in practice.

U.S. INFLUENCE, INTERESTS, AND POLICY OPTIONS

The United States has been the third major influence on the Israeli-Palestinian conflict. The commitment of the United States to Israeli security and to Israeli prosperity has been a bedrock tenet of American Middle East policy. The position of the United States has, however, varied on regional issues like the West Bank, depending on Israeli actions and political changes in American politics. The conflict over who will rule the disputed territories will remain a central problem for Israel and all other parties until it is resolved.

The American position begins with what it believes is an ironclad commitment to Israeli security and survival: the bedrock concern around which essentially all Israeli foreign affairs is grounded. Over time, the United States has, according to Lustick, "delivered more than $134 billion in direct economic and military aid to Israel," creating a "cocoon of immunity that successive U.S. administrations have spun around Israeli governments." For 2019, the United States pledged $3.8 billion in government assistance to the Israelis, more than the amount allocated to any other foreign country. Israel, according to the 2019–2020 *CIA World Factbook*, had a population of 8.42 million, including settlers on the West Bank and the Golan Heights, ninety-eighth largest in the world.

This physical commitment is complex, controversial, and politically sensitive. The American attachment to the idea of a Jewish state is controversial in parts of the Islamic Middle East and was a conceptual problem in promoting American access to affordable, reliably available petroleum during part of the Cold War, but Arab avarice and the close ties between the United States and Iran smoothed over that problem. The Arabs wanted American dollars, and Iran made the Persian Gulf effectively an American lake until 1979 when the Iranian Revolution severed that relationship. Before that happened, the problem was manageable. Some Arabs may have disliked American sponsorship and security guarantees about Israel, but they liked petrodollars even more.

The real objection was to the kind of Israel that evolved over time. Israel started its existence decidedly as David in the David and Goliath biblical analogy, but it gradually transformed itself into Goliath and, after 1967, as an assertive, militarily powerful member of the region (see Muravchik for an analysis). Israel's acquisition of nuclear weapons has effectively made it the military hegemon in the region and an arguably arrogant and acquisitive bully. Israelis, and especially their most militant advocates, reject and resent this depiction because it creates the impression of a militaristic, even imperialist, Israel that is unyielding and uncaring about the effects of its policies on others, notably the Palestinians. Palestinian statelessness and misery (how much misery they are forced to endure is an intensely controversial, political question) is simply a fact of regional politics in present circumstances. These relationships are important parts of American policy toward Israel, and they are important parts of how the United States views Israeli expansionism, both on security and Greater Israeli grounds.

American sentiment is ambivalent on the two motives and implications of Israeli territorial policy. The United States understands and supports efforts that lead to a more physically secure Israel, and it fully recognizes the very difficult situation that Israeli geography creates for securing that territory. The Israeli strategic defense position is unquestionably safer with Israel in possession of virtually all the territory it occupies, and American historic efforts have aimed at making those positions more secure through negotiated settlements wherein territory is returned to its pre-1967 owners who enter into treaties guaranteeing a cessation of their efforts against Israel. The 1982 peace agreement with Egypt and the peace treaty with Jordan are cited as precedent. The problem is the Israelis do not trust the other opponents, notably the Palestinians, but also the Syrians and Lebanese to make and honor similar arrangements and refuse to take the chance.

The second Israeli purpose is more controversial: territorial expansion to create the basis for implementing the policy of expanding Greater Israel. That aspect of policy is controversial because it requires excluding people like the Palestinians from returning to their homes as free citizens of the country of their choice. Syrians evicted from the Golan Heights (and viewing the Israeli conversion of their homelands into luxurious vacation meccas for Israelis) feel the same way. Israel, of course, denies the tragedy this creates, but it forms the basis for the Palestinian question that is the feature of the next chapter. The result is a dilemma for American policy.

There is an old homily in foreign policy analysis that interests are basically enduring and do not change very much across time. Rather, what changes are threats to those interests, and it is to ameliorate those conditions and ensure one's enduring interests that underlay policy analysis and actions. American interests in the Middle East tangle of conflicting aspirations and realities changed in the 2010s, but most of those changes were derivatives of basic interests that persist. The hierarchy of U.S. regional interests has been Israeli safety and survival, access to Middle East resources, and the minimization of the presence and influence of the Soviet Union/Russia, that has not changed. Threats to them have.

These principles cumulatively seek to promote peace and stability in the area, which is the overarching American objective. The security of Israel has been served by generous material support for Israel and what the United States (but not all Israelis) view as an ironclad commitment to Israeli survival and safety. Access to resources has meant the security of the Persian Gulf and relations with oil-producing countries. Minimizing Russian influence facilitates achieving both these goals as well as maintaining some control over Russian expansionist mischief.

American actions in these areas has been under some level of stress and scrutiny. The Israeli go-it-alone, nuclear-derived security policy reflects the conclusion of the Israeli right that the American security pledge is not sacrosanct and cannot be entirely relied upon. Partially, this reflects an Israeli belief that the Americans did not come quickly or adequately to Israel's side in the 1973 war and that the only way it can avoid that problem in the future is through unilateral—which is to say nuclear—preparation. Beres represents this thread of analysis: "for a country that is more conspicuously imperiled than any other," he writes, "the nuclear equalizer is necessary to ensure its basic physical survival." The United States is conspicuously mute on Israeli nuclear arms. The Samson Option flows from that kind of analysis and helps explain the growth of the Israeli arsenal and Israeli unilateralist obstinance in the face of global pressure, and resistance to any compromise on security questions. More importantly, it makes negotiating with the enemy (e.g., the Palestinians) on "so-called peace agreements" unacceptable and helps explain the shrill opposition to "a nearly nuclear Iran" (Beres) that Iran denies an intent to develop. Territorial expansion is the other pillar of Israeli security strategy, a policy that changed in the 2010s, as discussed in Chapter 4.

IMPEDIMENTS TO U.S. POLICY

The Israeli obsession with its security and survival is understandable, but it also conflicts with other American security interests and policies. One core part of the Israeli security equation is increased territory to relieve the burden of trying to defend the pre-1967 frontier. This policy dovetails with and reinforces the expansionist instinct that is also a core part of current policy in two ways. One is security: the occupation of the West Bank and Gaza provide real strategic depth for a geographically challenged Israeli territorial base. No one other than the Palestinians seriously questions that priority. Second, the "Greater Israel" goal of making Israel larger to increase Jewish immigration and for physical development is quite a different story. Israel cannot expand its population much within the 1967 boundaries, but does that justify appropriating and displacing others who have occupied territory they believe is theirs? The most controversial example may be the use of part of the Golan for Israeli settlement and as a vacation and recreation mecca that Indyk describes as a "robust tourist industry (all presumably with generous profits for the occupiers)." Security and commercialization and immigration are not entirely compatible goals, and they virtually preclude any possibility of a negotiated settlement where, in Beres's dismissive terms, the result is "possibly still-planned surrenders of land for empty promises—so-called peace agreements." These dismissals do not, it should be mentioned, include any reference to the fact that the "land" is conquered territory, the occupation of which is virtually universally condemned outside Israel. The Trump administration had no difficulty with this expansion, and the president expressed appreciation when one Golan settlement was christened "Trump Heights."

The confluence of overwhelming emphasis on nuclear-based security threats and intransigence on territorial adjustments essentially precludes prospects of negotiating with Israel's neighbors and even entertaining the possibility of a negotiated agreement (a "so-called peace agreement," in Beres's terms). The Israeli right, of which Netanyahu is the chief symbol, does not openly admit this conjunction, although the more liberal opposition within Israel does, but Netanyahu comes from the tradition of a highly militarized state and the advocacy of Greater Israel.

The militarization/expansion agenda did not trouble the Trump administration, which was philosophically and temperamentally closely aligned with the Netanyahu leadership and approach to the point of taking important actions that helped Netanyahu implement his agenda and thus deflected primarily internal opposition that preferred negotiations to continued confrontation. This shift in emphasis was noted by observers in both Israel and the United States, but it was largely ignored in the American foreign policy debate. Various explanations for American silent acquiescence (mostly political in nature based on the power of the so-called Israeli lobby—see Mearsheimer and Waltz's controversial 2007 critique) have not examined in detail the possibly deleterious international effects of this policy direction.

The de facto alignment of American and Israeli policy on the Palestinian question stands at odds both with historic American preferences in the Middle East and overall global policy preferences. If Middle Eastern peace and relative tranquility were the preferred American goals for the region, it is not at all clear how the set of policies, and especially those set out in the stillborn 2020 Trump "peace plan," served that purpose. For most of the period since 1967, American policy preferences have centered on the so-called "two state solution," where most of the West Bank becomes the sovereign Palestinian state and Israel returns, with some territorial adjustments, to the contours of pre-1967 sovereign control, with international (primarily American) guarantees of Israeli security. There has always been division—largely along liberal-conservative lines—within the American policy community and within Israel about whether Israeli existentially driven hardline militarism or the willingness to negotiate (the so-called land for peace approach) wherein Israel negotiates territorial adjustment for reduced tensions, but that debate was overtaken by the militarist/expansionist emphasis of Israeli policy supported by the Trump administration. This problem is raised in the Choosing Policy (CP) section at the end of this chapter and in the body of Chapter 4.

The current problem is one of proportionality. The problem of the existential threat is so deeply ingrained and obviously critical to the Israelis that it overwhelms essentially all other concerns and creates a monomaniacal focus that emotionally negates all other concerns. "Never again" has such obvious vitality and emotional appeal to Israel that it creates a sine qua non parameter on all other concerns that those interacting with Israel simply cannot match. Moreover, it sets the parameter on all conversations and a context that says all contrary arguments are irrelevant: if Israel cannot personally guarantee its own existence, nothing else truly matters. Moreover, that vitality creates a tunnel vision toward all other, and especially potentially compromising, considerations. The territorial question is central.

THE U.S. QUANDARY

The United States is, and always has been, absolutely committed to Israeli survival, but its commitment is simply not the same as the Israeli concern. The United States has other vital interests and concerns, of which protecting Israel is one; Israel has no other totally vital concern. One can argue that the United States has faced an existential threat from Soviet/Russian nuclear weapons, but intellectually, that threat has always been bounded by the recognition of the suicidal consequences of a global exercise of what amounts to a general application of the Samson Option.

This difference in proportionality creates a conflict between Israel and the United States over how to deal with the territorial problem. For the United States, the primary interest is in resolving differences in such a manner that both sides find acceptable and will bring a hopefully stable peace: a win-win outcome. Militant Israelis reject the possibility that such an outcome is possible. Instead, the only approach that can work is one in which Israeli military power makes it impossible or too costly for Israel's enemies to attempt to destroy Israel. To them, a peace agreement through negotiation is not a possibility and cannot responsibly be pursued. The options are a win-lose, zero-sum outcome or a lose-lose result, something like the Samson Option.

This assessment by the Israeli right is the crux of the divide between Israel and the international community, including elements within the United States, on the resolution of the Israeli-Palestinian territorial dispute. The heart of the Israeli argument that a peace agreement too greatly puts Israeli survival at risk is that an agreement weakens the security base for Israel, principally by forcing Israel to relinquish land that, in addition to the nuclear deterrent, forms the basis for Israeli survival. Implicit in this assessment is a belief that the Palestinians and their Islamic co-religionists will not, in the end, honor any agreement they reach and will use a weakened Israeli defense position to attack and try to destroy Israel, leaving it with the unpalatable alternatives of facing extinction (this argument implicitly adds the assessment, based on 1973, that the United States might renege on its guaranteed protection) or defending itself with nuclear weapons, including invocation of the Samson Option. From this assessment, the maintenance of a perpetual garrison state is the only true Israeli option. Only the status quo, possibly augmented by possible Israeli expansion in the name of security, is acceptable.

CHOOSING POLICY: PEACE OR RESISTANCE—
WHICH SERVES WHAT BEST?

Israeli actions since the 1967 war have fundamentally solidified Israeli security. Unlike the early history of the Jewish state culminating in the near disaster of the 1973 war, Israelis have achieved greater security than ever before. For the first quarter century of their existence, Israelis lived in constant fear of a massive attack by their Muslim neighbors that could have decimated them and destroyed the Jewish state. That situation has changed enormously. Israel is now the most powerful state in the region, and fears of its defeat and destruction are now abstract—but not unforgotten—memories. For the foreseeable future, Israeli security is indisputable.

Nuclear weapons and physical expansionism have been chief motors of this fundamental change. Nuclear weapons and the clear willingness to use them under the direst of circumstances is the underlying threat aimed at any potential enemy contemplating hostile actions toward the Israeli state (the Samson Option). Many who wished Israel ill still do, but they now know that acting on their hatred effectively amounts to committing suicide. Adding permanence to their control of territories seized in 1967 helps make Israeli territory more defensible. Other regional states may resent the expansion of Greater Israel, but the shadow of Israeli nuclear weapons stifles their opposition. The Israeli position is not based in cooperation and goodwill, but in fear.

Does this situation serve the interests of the United States? Historical American policy sought to be at least nominally evenhanded, strongly supporting Israel's security but maintaining cordial relations with the surrounding Muslim states. Access to oil and minimizing Soviet influence were the two basic interests served by this posture. U.S. dependence on Middle Eastern oil has declined, and there no longer is a Soviet Union, even if Russia tries to emulate some of its behavior. With these challenges to arguable American vital interests in decline, the United States has tilted more toward support for Israel. Is this wise or short-sighted?

Should American policy toward Israel and especially its more controversial aspects be reexamined? Under Trump, the United States had been supporting the hard-line confrontational Netanyahu approach to Israeli security, but did it yield the greatest security for Israel or serve American interests best?

There are two broad schools of thought about how Israel should deal with the region to maximize its security. Both are present in Israeli and American discussions on the subject. One alternative is militarized and hard line and has as its major tenet that the only way for Israel to remain safe is through such predominant force that no enemy can calculate a successful attack against Israel and is thus dissuaded from even contemplating an attempt. Nuclear weapons and territorial expansion are key elements in this strategy. It is articulated by authors like Beres, was the basic position of the previous government, and had been implicitly endorsed by the Trump administration. The other approach calls for negotiated peace agreements between Israel and its neighbors to create an enduring, noncoercive peace. It is the position of Israeli moderates and liberals and has the traditional position of the United States and most of its allies. Strategy can contain both elements: negotiations reinforced by military strength, for instance.

The Israeli political debate casts these positions as irreconcilable opposites. Given the Jewish twentieth-century experience, there is some predisposition to the hard-line position because it maintains maximum control over its fate in Israeli hands rather than being dependent on what could be fickle outside support. There is no correct answer to the debate.

The United States has a stake in the outcome and has adherents of both positions. The American preference for regional peace and stability suggests a predilection for a negotiated settlement that might create a durable peace such as that in Western Europe since 1945. At the same time, the United States is committed to the security of Israel and the Israelis. Officially, the United States avoids this problem by not discussing Israeli nuclear weapons at all—publicly neither confirming nor denying their existence, thereby avoiding the need to comment on their existence or American attitudes. American officials at least back to Nixon have known of their arsenal, but they remain opaque about them. Is this case of blinders the best policy for the United States? Or should the United States acknowledge them and take some stance on them?

Which approach makes more sense to you? Things have changed since the two positions were articulated in current form in 1973. They were strongly influenced by the Yom Kippur War, the first conflict Israel came close to losing. That war strengthened the appeal of the hardliners, a position reinforced by an Israeli belief the Americans did not resupply them as rapidly as they would have liked. More importantly, it was the first time Israel flexed its nuclear muscle by activating its then small arsenal. The Arab states have not challenged Israel since. Israel is physically safer than it has ever been, a situation for which the hard line is given credit. It may, however, also mean

Israel is secure enough to negotiate peace. Is there room for a compromise that ensures Israeli security within the framework of a negotiated peace? What do you think?

There is one major conflict that has been the major obstacle to improved relations between Israel and its neighbors and most of the international community, including elements in the United States. That problem, of course, is Palestine, and more specifically the question of an independent sovereign country on the West Bank for the stateless Palestinians. The political stability of the Mediterranean Middle East cannot be established without some permanent resolution to the Palestinian question, to which we turn in Chapter 4.

BIBLIOGRAPHY

Alavi, Seyed Ali. *Iran and Palestine: Past, Present, Future.* New York: Routledge, 2019.

Aronson, Shlomo, and Oded Brosk. *The Politics and Strategy of Nuclear Weapons in the Modern Middle East: Opacity, Theory, and Reality, 1960–1991.* Albany, NY: SUNY Press, 1992.

Baker, Alan. *The Settlements Issue: Distorting the Geneva Convention and the Oslo Accords.* Jerusalem: Jerusalem Center For Public Affairs, 2011.

Benn, Auf. "The End of the Old Israel: How Netanyahu Has Transformed the Nation." *Foreign Affairs* 95, no. 4 (July/August 2016), 16–27.

Bennett, Brian. "The Strong Survive." *Time* 194, no. 3 (July 22, 2019), 30–40.

Beres, Louis Rene. *Surviving Amid Chaos: Israel's Nuclear Strategy.* Lanham, MD: Rowman & Littlefield, 2016.

Bregmann, Ahron. *Cursed Victory: A History of Israel and the Occupied Territories, 1967 to the Present.* New York: Pegasus, 2015.

Cohen, Avner. *Israel and the Bomb.* New York: Columbia University Press, 1998.

———. *The Worst-Kept Secret: Israel's Bargain with the Bomb.* New York: Columbia University Press, 2010.

Cohen, Eliot A. "America's Long Goodbye: The Real Crisis of the Trump Era." *Foreign Affairs* 98, 1 (January/February 2019), 138–146.

Dowty, Alan. *Israel/Palestine.* Fourth Ed. London: Polity Press, 2017.

Feldman, Shai. *Israeli Nuclear Deterrence: A Strategy for the 1980s.* New York: Columbia University Press, 1983.

Freedman, Lawrence, and Jeffrey Michaels. *The Evolution of Nuclear Strategy.* New, Updated and Completely Revised. Fourth Ed. New York: Palgrave Macmillan, 2019.

Gerges, Famaz A. *Making the Arab World: Nasser, Qtub, and the Clash That Shaped the Middle East.* Princeton, NJ: Princeton University Press, 2018.

Gordis, Daniel. *Israel: A Concise History.* New York: Ecco, 2016.

Gorenberg, Gershom. *The Accidental Empire: Israel and the Birth of the Settlements, 1967–1977.* New York: Times Books, 2007.

Hersh, Seymour M. *The Samson Option: Israel's Nuclear Arsenal and American Foreign Policy.* With a New Afterword. New York: Vintage, 1992.

Hirst, David. *The Gun and the Olive Branch: The Roots of Violence in the Middle East.* San Diego, CA: Harcourt Brace Jananovich, 1977.

Karpin, Michael. *The Bomb in the Basement: How Israel Went Nuclear and What That Means for the World.* New York: Simon & Shuster Reprints, 2006.

Katz, Yaakov, and Yoaz Hendel. *Israel versus Iran: The Shadow War.* Washington, DC: Potomac, 2012.

Krisborn, Hans, and Robert Norris. "Israeli Nuclear Weapons 2014." *Bulletin of the Atomic Scientists* 7, 6 (2014), 97–115.

Larsen, Jeffrey A. and Kerry M. Karchner. *On Limited Nuclear War in the 21st Century.* Palo Alto, CA: Stanford Security Studies, 2014.

Malka, Haim. *Crossroads: The Future of the U.S.-Israeli Strategic Partnership.* Washington, DC: CSIS Press, 2011.

Mattson, Roger. *Stealing the Atom Bomb: How Denial and Deception Armed Israel.* Second Ed. Woodbury, NJ: Roger J. Mattson, 2016.

Mearsheimer, John J., and Stephen M. Walt. *The Israel Lobby and U.S. Foreign Policy.* New York: Farrar, Straus and Giroux, 2007.

Muravchik, Joshua. *Making David into Goliath: How the World Turned Against Israel.* New York: Encounter, 2015.

Murray, Donnette. *US Foreign Policy and Iran: American-Iranian Relations Since the Islamic Revolution.* New York: Routledge, 2009.

The National Interest. "Welcome to Israeli Nuclear Weapons 101." September 20, 2015.

Oren, Michael. *Six Days of War: June 1967 and the Making of the Modern Middle East.* New York: Presidio, 2003.

Piper, Michael Collins. *The Golem: Israel's Nuclear Hell Bomb and the Road to Armageddon.* Washington, DC: American Free Press, 2007.

Pollack, Kenneth M. *Armies of Sand: The Past, Present, and Future of Arab Military Effectiveness.* Oxford, UK: Oxford University Press, 2018.

Rabin, Lawrence, and Adam Stulberg. *The End of Strategic Stability? Nuclear Weapons and the Challenge of Regional Rivalries.* Washington, DC: Georgetown University Press, 2018.

Rosenbaum, Ron. *How the End Begins: The Road to a Nuclear World War III.* New York: Simon & Schuster, 2011.

Segev, Tom. *1967: Israel, the War, and the Year That Transformed the Middle East.* New York: Henry Holt and Company, 2007.

Shavit, Ari. *Does This Mean War? Top Israeli Strategists Debate the Iranian Bomb.* Tel Aviv: Haaretz, 2012.

———. *My Promised Land: The Triumph and Tragedy of Israel.* New York: Spiegel and Grau, 2015.

Simon, Steven. *Iran and Israel: The Iran Primer.* Washington, DC: United States Institute of Peace Press, 2019.

Smith, Charles (ed.). *Palestine and the Arab-Israel Conflict: A History with Documents.* Ninth Ed. New York: St. Martin's Press, 2016.

Snow, Donald M. *Cases in International Relations: Principles and Applications.* Eighth Ed. Lanham, MD: Rowman & Littlefield, 2020.

———. *The Necessary Peace: Nuclear Weapons and Superpower Relations.* Lexington, MA: Lexington Books, 1987.

———. *Nuclear Strategy in a Dynamic World.* Tuscaloosa: University of Alabama Press, 1980.

Sobhani, Sohrab. *The Pragmatic Entente: Israeli-Iranian Relations, 1948-1988.* Westport, CT: Praeger, 1989.

Sokolsky, Henry D. (ed.), et. al. *Nuclear Weapons Material Gone Missing: What Does History Teach?* Washington, DC: Department of the Army (Strategic Studies Institute), 2015.

Stockholm International Peace Research Institute (SIPRI). "Nuclear Weapons, 2017." July 2017.

United States Central Intelligence Agency. *2019-2020 World Factbook.* New York: Skyhorse Publishing, 2019.

Uris, Leon. *Exodus: A Novel.* New York: Doubleday and Company, 1958. (The motion picture version of *Exodus* was released in 1960.)

Van Creveld, Martin L. *The Culture of War.* New York: Presidio, 2008.

———. *The Land of Blood and Honey: The Rise of Modern Israel.* New York: Thomas Dunne, 2010.

Zertal, Idith, and Avika Eldar. *Lords of the Land: The War Over Israeli Settlements in the Occupied Territories, 1967-2007.* New York: Hatchette Book Group (Bold Type Books), 2009.

Zraick, Karen. "A Look at the West Bank Area Netanyahu Viewed to Annex." *New York Times* (online), September 10, 2019.

4

The Tragedy and Dilemma of Stateless Peoples
Palestine

The most famous—or notorious, depending on one's vantage point—conflict in the region has been the ongoing confrontation for physical and political control of areas adjacent to pre-1967 Israel that have been occupied and in some cases physically annexed by Israel for reasons discussed in the last chapter. The heart of the issue is whether substantial parts of these territories rightfully "belong" to the Palestinians who fled Israel in 1948 as part of the nakbah reaction to Israeli sovereignty and control over territories they believe are theirs. The issue has spread to several areas with Muslim majorities that were seized by the Israelis as part of that conflict like Gaza, the Sinai Peninsula, and Golan Heights. The Egyptian territories were returned to Egyptian control in the peace treaty between Israel and Egypt in 1982. The Golan Heights remains under Israeli occupation in an increasingly permanent-appearing relationship.

The heart of the continuing conflict has been over the West Bank of the Jordan River. It is important for several reasons. These include its seizure and de facto annexation from Jordan, of which it was a part until 1967, and was an act that deprived the Jordanians of some of their most valuable, productive land. Second, when the Palestinians fled the new Israeli state in 1948, many went to adjacent states like Lebanon and Syria, and a large percentage migrated to the West Bank, where they took refuge in austere refugee camps run by the UN Relief and Works Agency for Palestinian Refugees (UNRWAPR). International underfunding ripened rebellious desires to organize an insurrection to return these lands to control of Palestine to form the basis for a sovereign state centered on the West Bank. Third, the contested territory is valuable. The West Bank had the most developable land in the region and was thus a prize for the Israelis. Prior to the occupation, there was very little developable land suitable for the expansion of Greater Israel by providing undeveloped lands to immigrants. The West Bank thus appealed to the basic Israeli policies of security and expansion.

In addition, the land itself has great symbolic importance to Muslims, Jews, and Christians. The physical focus is Jerusalem and its environs. It contains basic religious symbols for Jews (e.g., the Wailing Wall) and Muslims (e.g., the Dome of the Rock) as well as Christians. The city has a multiethnic and multiconfessional population, largely living in effective ghettos in different parts of the city, and both Israelis and Palestinians maintain it as their capital. The city has further been divided by the border between pre-1967 Israel and whoever rules the West Bank. Since 1967, the city has been effectively unified under Israeli rule, a status the Palestinians and most members of the international community reject. When President Trump became the first leader of a major state to recognize all of Jerusalem as the legal capital of Israel, it delighted the Netanyahu government and was universally condemned by the rest of the international community. The disposition of Jerusalem is at the heart of the conflict.

These factors have coalesced to make the disposition of Palestine the longest-standing and most highly publicized aspect of the Middle East conflict. The heart of the competition between Israel and the Palestinian people is over rightful sovereign control of the lands that became Israel when that state was formed in 1948 and their quest for a sovereign state. Many fled the new Israeli state and have been living as part of a stateless nation ever since. This central issue has for some time been the core of the so-called Arab-Israeli conflict. It provided the framework within which the Israelis and their Islamic neighboring states fought wars in 1948, 1956, 1967, and 1973. Israel was triumphant in all those conflicts and that focus has faded from centrality. The Arab states no longer physically or verbally threaten Israel, mostly out of fear of possible, including nuclear, consequences of doing so. Other forms of conflict, much of which still concern the territorial disagreement between Israel and most of the rest of the world community is about a Palestinian home. That conflict has significantly spread to other regional actors such as Syria and Iran. For as long as this conflict continues, it colors, arguably taints, the politics of the entire region, and it is the lynchpin both of regional geopolitics and the key to change. It is the center of the operational environment of interconnected problems in which the regional actors and the United States interact.

One way to distinguish Middle Eastern problems and situations is their apparent endlessness. The Israeli-Palestinian problem is the prototype. The basic structure of the conflict was established in 1967, and periodically the conflict flares back up, as in the declaration of East Jerusalem as the capital of Israel and the Israeli proposal to annex greater parts of the territory to the

Jewish state, a proposed action that regularly meets with international verbal condemnation but little action.

The Palestine problem is a major point of disagreement within Israel as well. The most recent episode in this "drama" surrounded the Israeli Knesset (parliament) elections of September 17, 2019, that have been extended to follow-on elections in 2020. The main protagonists have been Prime Minister Benjamin Netanyahu and his right-wing Likud Party and retired General Benny Gantz and his slightly more centrist Blue and White Party. Netanyahu campaigned vigorously on a pattern of territorial accession of more of the occupied territories on security grounds, while Gantz and his supporters favored a more moderate direction that might include negotiations with the Palestinians. The 2019 election could have been a watershed election; in typical Israeli political fashion, it was not. Reflecting deep divisions in the Israeli electorate, neither Likud nor Blue and White came close to attaining the majority in the Knesset necessary to form a government in this parliamentary democracy. Building a successful coalition that could represent a majority was confounded by internecine squabbles among minor parties and corruption charges hanging over Netanyahu's head. The issue remained unresolved well into 2020. What was advertised as a potential watershed political event turned out to be Israeli-Palestinian business as usual.

BASIC PARAMETERS AND OPTIONS

The basic dynamic of the Israeli-Palestinian impasse remains at the center of the conflict, although it has changed significantly as the balance of forces and arguments surrounding it have evolved. Israel remains in physical control of the West Bank and strategic portions of the Golan Heights overlooking both Israel and Syria. The Palestinian majority in the West Bank still has lesser rights and prosperity than Israeli settlers who have established what are clearly permanent presences in the area. In a July 2019 *Time* interview, Netanyahu said some of these areas "have already become basically part of Israel." In the process, the likelihood of a negotiated settlement between the antagonists has receded greatly, despite the appearance of a movement toward a settlement in terms of a "peace proposal" presented by the Trump administration in February 2020 that was little more than a reiteration of a plan consistently advocated by Israeli prime minister Benjamin Netanyahu and consistently dismissed out of hand by the Palestinian leadership. It has been likened to an Israeli form of apartheid by some observers.

Any assessment of the Palestinian situation begins with the basic interests and positions of the two major contestants, Israel and Palestine. They both have basic and deeply held convictions regarding the territorial heart of the dispute, the West Bank (a physical piece of territory roughly the size of Delaware), and parts of Golan. The basic problem in international terms is a matter of real estate. Inhabitable territory in the disputed area is not abundant, especially for cohabitation by Palestinian Arabs and additional Jewish immigrants to Israel. Moreover, the shape of boundaries and geography potentially leave Israel vulnerable to aggression (as noted in Chapter 3) and possible conquest. For the Palestinians, the West Bank provides the only regional parcel of land in which they can achieve national self-determination. Some Israelis counter derisively that there already is a Palestinian state called Jordan. For Israelis, defending the long, narrow strip of land that constitutes pre-1967 Israel creates extremely difficult logistics, and if its enemies should launch a successful invasion (which they came close to doing in 1973), they might conquer Israel and even threaten or attempt to annihilate the Israeli Jewish population. The vivid memory of the Holocaust makes this prospect seem all too realistically possible, and its shadow creates among the Israelis a deep existential fear that inspires resolve: "Never again" is the watchword.

American interests are different. For the United States, the primary interest is in resolving differences in such a manner that both sides can accept and will bring a stable peace: a win-win outcome. Militant Israelis like Beres reject the possibility that such an outcome is possible. Instead, the only approach that can work is one in which Israeli military power makes it impossible or too costly for Israel's enemies to attempt to destroy Israel. To them, a peace agreement through negotiation is not a possibility and cannot responsibly be pursued. The options are a win-lose, zero-sum outcome or a lose-lose result, something like the Samson Option.

APPROACHES TO THE PROBLEM

Perspectives on the need to resolve the Palestinian issue vary. The Israeli government and its supporters find the need less compelling because they have the upper hand. The Palestinians have greater motivations to gain (or regain) their sovereign status and find a negotiated settlement the only path to that end. Many Israelis do not want to take a chance that might, at worst, imperil their survival; the Palestinians have less to lose.

There are two basic approaches, the so-called one-state and two-state solutions, each with two substrategies. The Israeli government and hardliners prefer a one-state solution, and Israeli policy has acted to create that outcome. The Palestinians obviously prefer a two-state outcome since a second state would be Palestine. This approach is also favored by most of the world outside Israel.

The Israelis have moved relentlessly toward the one-state solution since 1967. The vehicle has been the physical occupation and development—including populating—of the territories, a process that has accelerated under Netanyahu. Most of the disputed territories have not been legally annexed due to negative international reactions. The Israelis have made some token proposals for limited Palestinian autonomy on parts of the West Bank that the Palestinians reject out of hand. This de facto one-state solution continues to be the heart of Israeli strategy. The other variation of the one-state solution would be the physical annexation of occupied territories as part of sovereign Israel. The annexation of Jerusalem, which was endorsed by the Trump administration, may be a precedent, although the option includes granting full citizenship to the inhabitants (including the Palestinians).

There are also two variations of the two-state solution. The first and by far most widely advocated, has been the creation of a sovereign Palestinian state on all or most of the West Bank and Gaza Strip. The Israeli and Palestinian states would be reasonably pure sovereign entities, with provisions for migration from one state to the other and creation of a corridor connecting Gaza to the West Bank. This solution would end Palestinian statelessness and international charges of Israeli illegal occupation. The principal barrier is where to draw the boundary between Palestine and pre-1967 Israel as well as the division of Jerusalem. Neither are small problems.

Israeli hardliners oppose this solution on familiar security grounds. They argue a Palestinian state on the West Bank would like to be a terrorist nation hiding behind sovereignty as it continued launching attacks against Israel. This case, of course, fails to admit the reason for terrorism has largely been to pressure Israel into negotiating the Palestinian claim. Were that motivation removed, so might the reason for terror. This position is held by liberal Israelis who favor negotiation as the key to "land for peace." The other reason is that an independent Palestine would no longer be a destination point for Israeli immigrants. Israel's occupation also makes Israeli control of all Jerusalem simpler. The land for peace rallying cry has been moribund since the early 2000s, although a pair of competing articles in *Foreign Affairs* in summer 2020 have raised the question of whether regional conditions may have changed enough to revisit it. Minister Yitzakh Rabin said that "Israel cannot—and does not want to—permanently control a large population that seeks independence." Backers of Netanyahu disagree, as Doran argues: Israel will not "give back at the negotiating table what it has taken on the battlefield."

Some form of the two-state solution has been the official American preference for most of the post-1967 period before Trump. Successive American administrations have argued in favor of both major aspects on the two-state argument. They have joined almost all the international community opposing Israeli continued occupation, colonization, and annexation of progressive parts as violations of international law and obligations under the UN Charter and as denials of basic human rights of the Palestinian people to statehood. They are joined in this position by liberal Israelis and American Jews.

ADDITIONAL CONCERN: THE DEMOGRAPHIC "TIME BOMB"

There is also a more geopolitical argument that adherence of the current status quo is short-sighted and will ultimately result in a worse dilemma for Israel than it already faces. The basis of this argument is demographic and reflects population trends among both the Israeli Jewish population and the Muslim, Palestinian populations. A few Israeli demographers like Della Pergola have pointed to the demographic "time bomb," the central dynamic of which is that the Palestinian population is growing more rapidly than are the Israelis, that those populations in the affected geographic areas (pre-1967 Israel, the West Bank, Gaza, and Golan) are today roughly equal in total and that projections of current realities suggest that Palestinians will be in the physical majority in essentially all those areas except pre-1967 Israel in the next few years.

These strands (which I have discussed in the various editions of *Cases in International Relations*) affect basic values held by Israelis about the nature of their state and alternate factors. Although population statistics are not precise, the Israeli population in the four combined affected population areas currently contains a narrow Jewish majority, but it is narrowing due to higher Palestinian birth rates, and it is only a matter of time until the population majority for the entire region is non-Israeli/Jewish. Israel's birth rate approximated that of the Arabs in 2018, but the only way for Israel to sustain its claim to majority status is through increased immigration. Current inflow comes disproportionately from Russia (about one-third) and Ukraine (about one-fifth). The major problem is that there is inadequate habitable land in pre-1967 Israel on which to settle immigrants, making retention of the West Bank much more important than it would otherwise be as a place where immigrants can live. Meanwhile, UNRWAPR maintains on its website that there are "five million" Palestinian refugees in Gaza and the West Bank and more in Lebanon and Syria, many of whom would like to return to Palestine as they define it.

The result is a demographic decision for Israel. Which is preferable, a Jewish or a democratic Israel? If one accepts the notion that the demographics will continue to move in the direction they have (not a certainty but a high likelihood), the outcome potentially threatens the traditional value base of Israel: its status as both Jewish and democratic. Simply put, if Israeli Jews become a minority in the combined territories, any resulting single country cannot effectively be both. The details are difficult to pin down due to unreliability of census data and thus counting of groups that would become part of any settlement. Aggregating statistics from various sources, the population balance in the four major areas under discussion appears to be about 6.7 million Israelis to 6.25 million Arabs in 2019, but those figures include about a half million Arabs in East Jerusalem, which is claimed by both sides as its capital. The Netanyahu government and its supporters rarely even mention this problem and dismiss it as inconsequential when they do.

This creates the conjunction between the basic question of political control and the nature of the future Israel. The Greater Israel policy requires Israeli control of much of the West Bank (except Gaza), Golan, and pre-1967 Israel. The problem, very simply, is that demographics (and the possibility of Palestinian migration from UNRWA care) will shortly mean the Arabs will be the majority in the overall area. If one assumes confessional political preferences will rule in such a situation (which they almost certainly would), Jews would be a minority and could only maintain control by manipulating political participation so that Jewish "votes" counted more than Arab votes, a weighted majority that former U.S. president Jimmy Carter suggested in 2006 would create an "apartheid" state of unequal citizen status like that in South Africa until black rule came to that country, a suggestion Netanyahu has dismissed as "nonsense." Greater Israel, in other words, would remain Jewish but not democratic unless it negotiates an apartheid-like arrangement such as that endorsed by the Trump administration in 2020 wherein the Palestinians would have limited political rights.

There is a way to solve this problem, although it is anathema to the Israeli right. If Israel wants to be both democratic and Jewish, it must adjust the boundaries of Israel such that the result is a reliably long-term Jewish majority. The major possibility for that is a return of Israel to something like the pre-1967 borders, where it has a three-to-one majority that will likely endure for a long time (many of the 20 percent of that population who are Palestinian would probably migrate to the Palestinian state, thus reinforcing the permanency of that control) and removing the demographic pressure on Israel. That is, of course, the crux of the two-state solution that is anathema to the current Israeli leadership.

Debate over the attractiveness of the two-state solution reflects the Israeli debate over Israel's approach to the world, and especially its region. Those Israelis who emphasize the existential question and thus the need to expand to increase the viability of Israel's ability to defend itself in a hostile, predatory world argue that negotiation leading to the "so-called peace agreements" (Beres's phrase) is too risky to entertain because outcomes in which Israel traded "land for peace" could (or would) reduce Israel's ability unilaterally to defend itself and could lead, in the worst case, to a choice between extinction or exercising the nuclear/Samson Option.

The other side of this is that Israeli unwillingness to negotiate at least the possibility of carving a Palestinian state from the West Bank perpetuates a situation of injustice and suffering among Palestinians and their supporters that guarantees the very condition the Israelis act to avoid. Current Israeli policy, in other words, not only isolates the country from the rest of the world and thereby perpetuates a self-fulfilling existential us-or-them scenario. In this situation, what are the aggrieved Palestinians to do? Their options are stark: continue to accept an unacceptable condition or resist. Lacking the means to employ effective force of their own, what else can they do but accept the help of others like agents of Iran? The result is a circle: Israeli actions further frustrate the Palestinians who respond with asymmetrical, terrorist actions (mostly carried out by surrogates), which the Israelis use to justify perpetuation of the security policies that caused the problem.

That leaves Israel with continuation of the highly militarized garrison state status and the occupied territories and thus the militarized Greater Israel posture and policy. This has been the approach of the Netanyahu administration, and it was supported by the Trump administration in its 2020 plan. This support not only facilitated the continuation of Israeli expansionism, but it placed the United States more formally in opposition to those who back Palestine. As Lustick argued, "nothing makes it easier for the Islamic State or Al Qaeda to recruit terrorists than U.S. support for a state that blockades the Gaza Strip, shoots and gases Palestinian protesters, and takes Arab land in the West Bank and East Jerusalem to construct settlements." One can agree or disagree with this assessment, but it does raise the possibility that American action had the effective result of supporting anti-Palestinian outcomes to the Israeli-Palestinian confrontation, a position at some odds with historic American positions and an endorsement (implicitly or explicitly) of a pro-Israeli hard-line solution in the region.

The Trump January 2020 "peace plan" and reactions to it were remarkable. The proposal itself was condemned both as unoriginal (a reprint of well-publicized and universally rejected Israeli hard-line positions) that Peter Beaumont, writing in the *Guardian* the day it was released, said, "reads like a series of Israeli talking points that places its emphasis on Israeli security rather than Palestinian self-determination." It did this by creating a series of Palestinian enclaves on the West Bank that would be separated by Israeli settlements where Palestinian transit would be regulated by Israeli security forces and Palestinian "sovereignty" would be limited to maintaining internal order within enclaves (see Chapter 5) that resemble South African Bantustans and thus inspire accusations of an apartheid design and which Liel argued grants the Palestinians territory "without granting them real freedom or basic political rights." Liel argued the attraction of this arrangement may reflect the close relations between Israel and white South Africa from 1974 until the end of white rule in 1994. The heat of the arrangement is a devil's bargain where, according to Shikaki, "Israel receives a large compensation."

The other remarkable aspect of the proposal was its reception. It is not unfair to say the proposal was dead before Trump and Netanyahu (who was present at the White House ceremony—the Palestinians were not invited) left the room in which it was proclaimed. Trump hyperbolically described the proposal as "the deal of the century." Shikaki reported that 94 percent of Palestinians polled after the rollout rejected it. Ominously, the same poll reported only 39 percent continued to support the two-state solution, the lowest percentage since that goal was articulated in the Oslo accords of 1993. Trump and Netanyahu beamed at the presentation and proposal. Nobody else did.

BIBI'S DREAM

In the heat of his reelection campaign of September 2019, Netanyahu articulated the heart of the Trump plan to promote his election. On September 10, 2019, he announced that if reelected, he would annex roughly one-third of the West Bank to Israel. The area in question is along the eastern border of the West Bank from the Sea of Galilee 185 miles south to the shoreline of along the Dead Sea. The effect would be to surround a Palestinian state on the West Bank with Israeli territory, a variation of Netanyahu's plan for limited autonomy for the Palestinians in a West Bank state wherein Israeli Defense Forces personnel were stationed in roughly the same territory to provide security and leaving Palestine a semi-sovereign entity at best. Netanyahu further stated that he would not implement this plan without the assent of the Trump administration, which he expected with the Trump peace plan coordinated by son-in-law Jared Kushner. Netanyahu maintained the heart of this proposal was "more and more investments, in the private sector, to the Palestinian areas for joint Israeli-Palestinian efforts." These would occur in an

Israeli-controlled state. In effect, it proposed to buy off the Palestinians in return for their docility. It was unlikely to be accepted by the Palestinians.

EFFECTS ON OTHER PARTIES

The Israelis and the Palestinians have the most important, but not the only, regional interest in the situation. The other states most clearly impacted are Syria and Iran. The situations of these countries, how and why they could become more enmeshed in the conflict, and how their involvement becomes part of the regional spiderweb are all discussed in subsequent chapters: Syria in Chapter 6 and Iran in Chapter 7. They are introduced here as obvious parts of the central equation.

Syrian interest is the most obvious. The situation on the Golan Heights is essentially analogous to that on the West Bank in the sense that Israel has occupied part of the Heights since 1967, has fortified it against artillery attacks on the Israeli valleys to its west, have colonized it (20,000 Israeli "settlers" compared to 27,000 Syrians), and have even converted parts of their occupation zone (especially near the Sea of Galilee) into a resort and vacation area for Israelis. From a Syrian vantage point, all these actions are obnoxious and, in the eyes of most of the international community, illegal. Like the Palestinians, the Syrians have historically been physically incapable of rectifying the situation in their favor by force, and this limit has been especially true since the Syrian civil war broke out in 2011. Meanwhile, Israelis standing on the top of Mt. Hermon, the highest point in the heights at 9,232 feet, can stare down the mountainside and eyeball Damascus, forty miles away.

The situation will almost certainly change when the civil war finally ends. The Syrian government has been preoccupied with that conflict and has thus devoted little effort to seeking restitution for or control of those parts of Golan that Israel has effectively appropriated and exploited. The way the civil war has been conducted has deflected international attention from Israeli actions on Golan so that international disapproval of those actions has been muted, thereby facilitating Israel's effective annexation of the occupied areas. Syria has been in no position to prosecute complaints about the situation. Israel has, of course, been fully aware of this Syrian disability. The Trump administration supported Israeli actions.

This situation could change once the civil war ends and something resembling peace returns to Syria. That will be a formidable and expensive process, but it will be one where Syria's pariah status will probably wane as the international community tries to find ways to help rebuild it. One way that the government could seek to restore public support would be to ignite national indignation over Golan and particularly by asserting the ironic proposition that continued Israeli occupation of territory overlooking Damascus imperils Syrian security.

The other Syrian factor is the physical fate of the Syrian state after war ends. As discussed in Chapter 6, there is a chance that Syria will break apart after the war ends. Syria has always been a multinational, multiconfessional state of peoples only tenuously united as Syrians, and the conduct and bitterness of the violence has torn apart the fabric of commonality that preexisted the civil war. The major questions are into how many parts will it break, who will be dominant in which parts, who will support new entities, and how the process of adjustment will affect the international politics of the region. The fate of the Golan Heights is a major part of those calculations.

Iran is one of the states that will play a part in that process of adjustment. Largely through its association with and sponsorship of Hamas and Hezbollah (both Shiites like the Iranians) organizations mostly headquartered in Lebanon, the Iranians have been involved both with opposing the anti-Assad resistance in Syria and in equipping and aiding anti-Israeli forces resisting Israeli actions in Gaza and the West Bank. It is not clear how Iran will react to a breakup of Syria, particularly if it includes a Kurdish state that Iran opposes.

U.S. POLICY OPTIONS AND CONSEQUENCES

It is difficult to project policy solutions that will lead to resolving this knotty, twisted conflict that serves as the single most destabilizing problem set in the region and the greatest threat to American interests and regional stability since the 2014 ISIS attempt to establish a caliphate in the Levant. In these circumstances, all the United States can do is to return to its basic interests and try to influence events to achieve those interests, knowing they are subject to the swirling winds of change that blow across the desert sands. It is not an easy task, and it is often frustrating.

American interests have not fundamentally changed since the establishment of the state of Israel. The three pillars in 1948 remain: the integrity of Israel, secure and reliable access to natural resources, and the minimization of Soviet (now Russian) influence. Each of these interests is best served by conditions of peace and stability, but they have not been universal parts of the Middle Eastern architecture. The confrontational trajectory of contemporary regional politics and the antagonisms between the United States and some other states (primarily Iran) reinforce the cacophony.

If the basic American value preference is peace and stability in the Middle East, why is the Palestinian-Israeli conflict such an important barrier to achieving that condition? The key problem, of course, is the disposition of Israel's security dilemma in a manner that reassures the Israelis and reduces antagonisms among the parties. The territorial question is key. Both sides claim the same land. Before World War II, the real estate was Palestine, and its shepherds were the Palestinian Arabs. Israeli settlers shared the land, but they were the minority. Since 1948 and especially 1967, the Palestinians have lost their domain, and the Israelis have expanded theirs. Actions contemplated and announced by the Netanyahu regime seek to make the current divisions permanent under Jewish rule.

Both sides have articulated a claim to the land as theirs, and both sides have a point. The region would be safer and more peaceful (clearly the historic American preference) if both sides had their own secure sovereign territory. They do not, and until they both find and mutually accept an outcome with which they can live, the situation will remain conflictual and violent. The cycle of violence is deep in the Palestinian fabric, each side continues to act in ways that perpetuate and even exacerbate that situation, and their venom spreads beyond its physical bounds.

BARRIERS TO ACCORD

There are two defining, contradictory characteristics of the conflict that stand as barriers to positive change. The first is the concern—arguably obsession—with physical security. That factor particularly consumes the Israelis, whose historical experience makes many of them justifiably paranoid about their situations. It is less well publicized for the Palestinians, but the simple fact is that Palestinians in the occupied zones and Gaza live in a condition of uncertainty, fear, and deprivation, and their claim is also understandable and defensible. Both sides want safety for themselves; unfortunately, both act in ways that increase their sense of insecurity and reinforce their felt need for security measures at the expense of the other, the classic structure of an arms race. Palestinians and their allies pummel Israel with rocket attacks and suicide bombings; the Israelis respond with military attacks and further isolate and leave helpless and defensive Palestinians whose claimed lands go from occupied to annexed parts of Israel. Both sides want to make things better for themselves, but they do so by making life more miserable for the other. Both want to make life better for themselves but treat the situation like a zero- or negative-sum game.

The other problem is available land: there is simply not enough inhabitable land in the mutually claimed area for both sides to meet their felt needs. The inhabitable portion of pre-1967 Israel was largely occupied with the population of around five million, and the Netanyahu dream of a Greater Israel requires additional living space—the basic function of settlements on the West Bank and Golan. Without these lands, further Israeli expansion is problematic. The West Bank is small and can hardly support both a larger Israeli immigrant and a Palestinian population augmented by an influx of refugees from the UNRWAPR. Land is scarce.

It is hard to envisage an acceptable negotiated solution that meets all needs for both groups. Israeli physical security requires expanded borders to provide military depth, and annexation of the occupied territories serves both, making it more difficult for its enemies to attack it and providing additional space to absorb immigrants. Palestinian needs include sovereign control of space to end their status as a stateless people as well as guarantees of their security. The two sides have not been capable of reconciling these differences themselves. Can (or should) the United States be more helpful in this process?

Part of the answer to the question is the effect of the impact of American actions on other interests in other parts of the Middle East and the world. There is probably no regional solution that will be universally embraced. Continued support for the Israeli hard line on Palestinian self-determination will not be embraced by any of the Muslim states, although experience since 1973 suggests that none of these states will do much physically to alter the Palestinian plight because of Israel's nuclear-based military hegemony. Other regional states have the bad options of physically ignoring the problem or engaging in low-intensity complaints about Israel. For the foreseeable future, nobody in the region can violently challenge the Israelis; the Iranians are the only ones who even try, and they are condemned for their efforts. The international community complains about the occupation/annexation efforts, but their objections have not had negative enough consequences for Israel to heed them. Only Iran seems interested in championing the Palestine cause, and their motives are almost certainly not philanthropic.

AMERICAN CHOICES

The United States has supported a two-state solution, but that advocacy was basically shelved by Trump. Many observers have declared that Israeli actions have rendered this option dead because of the reality of increasing Israeli settler presence and actions leading toward annexation. It remains a prominent proposal for change, and it is advocated by most of the rest of the world. Future possibilities include embracing the progression of Israel's drive toward expansion (the heart of the 2020 Trump proposal) or maintaining the territorial status quo (the Israeli preference). None of these embrace Palestinian aspirations.

Short- and long-term interests and policies for all parties collide in current circumstances. Two competing realities dominate the ongoing situation and must be resolved in any long-term resolution. The first is that Israeli military power clearly dominates the current situation. No individual state or coalition in the region can threaten or compel Israel to change its current policies, at least not for the foreseeable future. Iran's efforts in supporting asymmetrical, including terrorist acts, will continue to annoy the Israelis, but they will not force real change. Nuclear-backed Israeli military power will remain the overriding factor in regional reactions to Israeli actions. The Israelis know and exploit this; regardless of what they say to the contrary, ending their nuclear monopoly is the core of their opposition to and concern with Iran. Were Iran to gain nuclear weapons, Israeli intransigence would become more problematical. The only country that can even possibly put geopolitical pressure on Israel is the United States. Everyone shudders at the prospect of a nuclear arms race in the region.

The other reality is demographic. The internal existential debate in Israel is about more than the military destruction of the Israel state and extinction of its population. The immigration policies of the Netanyahu government have successfully delayed that problem for the foreseeable future, but there has been a price in terms of Israel's standing in the world community and in the suffering of people like the Palestinians. Both problems are matters that will eventually have to be resolved, and it is not clear the current Israeli leadership will address them.

The demographic dilemma is not so literally existential, but it surrounds the question of what kind of Israel the future may hold. There are two Israeli perceived imperatives that are reinforcing in principle but contradictory in application. The first directly addresses the kind of political and ethnic combination most Israelis want: to live in a Jewish, democratic state. That is what they had before 1967, but it left Israel with a security dilemma that has prevailed since. As noted, demographics mean that unless adjustments of borders and inhabitants occur, Israel will likely be faced with the need to be one or the other. Which is more important, especially given the security implications of the choice? It is not clear, and it is a question that Israeli leaders like Netanyahu have avoided forcing the citizenry to make. The other imperative is the attraction of as much of the Jewish diaspora to Israel as possible. Obviously, the two imperatives are related by the shortage of available land for more Israelis and Palestinians. Without current immigration—which creates the need for expansion, Israel would face the choices between being democratic or Jewish in the future. The Israeli government is only deferring the inevitable choice. It is as simple as that.

CHOOSING POLICY: ASSISTING OR IMPEDING THE PEACE PROCESS

What, if anything, should the United States do about the creation of a Palestinian state? The first question this raises is whether that outcome is desirable and should be promoted. Before the Netanyahu incumbency and its expansionist, hard-line approach to the problem, opinion in Israel was split into a lively debate, while the international community (including the United States) backed the Oslo accords commitment to a sovereign Palestinian state. That has changed. The Trump-Netanyahu "peace" proposal falls far short of creating such a state, and if it remains the dominant voice in the conversation, never will move toward that goal (which appears to be its intent).

There is also the question of what kind of outcome is desirable. The Israeli right has answered that concern negatively, and reinforced by the Trump administration, it did prevail. Even though factors like demographics suggest current Israeli policy may be short-sighted and will be ultimately counterproductive, it currently dominates. If it does, there will be no sovereign state of Palestine: the Palestinians will remain a stateless nation.

The United States is the only country in any real position to move Israeli policy, and that capability is limited and depends on what assessment of the Israeli predicament one advocates. The United States wants a safe, prosperous Israel, but does current Israeli policy really promote both those goals? Territorial acquisition may make Israel more secure in the short run, but it also makes the likelihood of peaceful negotiations about the region and international acceptance less likely. That policy also defers the demographic time bomb and faces the future dilemma of an Israel that is democratic or one that is Jewish.

It is not an easy choice for the Israelis or the Americans. There is strong Israeli division on the question. Israel's primary foreign constituency and support base has been American Jewry, which is also divided. As Mearsheimer and Walt pointed out over a decade ago, the Jewish vote is divided strategically in different states in the United States, and American politicians tend to defer to what they perceive as policies that might alienate that constituency. Israelis uniformly want to be safe, but they are still divided on whether their security should be based on territorial expansionism or negotiation.

There is also the question of American leverage on Israel. The American government has provided enormous financial aid sums, primarily to the

Israeli military: Israel does receive more American military support than does any other country in the world. The current rationale is as a counterweight to Iranian support for Hamas and Hezbollah, but is there more? An invasion sweeping across Israel is no longer a major possibility, and Israel's conventional and nuclear capabilities assure none of its neighbors can contemplate conventional war against it. Although it is rarely publicly articulated, conventional military assistance also means that Israel does not have to put the Samson Option high on its contingency list, a condition the United States certainly wants to nurture.

What options does the United States have? The current situation creates peace of sorts in the eastern Mediterranean, but it is fragile and imperfect. Its fragility is that it creates inequity for some parties (the Palestinians) and perpetuates the shadow of the demographic time bomb. The basis of stability is a military balance that favors and is only truly advocated by one state, Israel. All others grudgingly accept the status quo, but none are truly happy with it. Israeli policy has been premised on hedging against this possibility. Should the military situation destabilize, what would happen to peace and stability? Israeli policy has been premised on hedging against this possibility; its hard-line aggressiveness may have made it worse. Would some different configuration of regional power not potentially be more stable? Changing the situation would require negotiation of some arrangement that would alter the power map of the area, probably to Israeli security disadvantage. Whether peace entailing territorial adjustment is worth the risk remains the major debate within Israel—and within policy elites in the United States. Does the military status quo serve American interests?

If the United States wants to support the militarized solution, it should continue much of the Trump era support for Israel: pumping more military aid into Israeli coffers, supporting the continued occupation and annexation of the West Bank and Golan, and formalization of Jerusalem as the permanent capital of Israel, for instance. If it prefers some form of the two-state solution, it should return to a policy of bringing pressure on Israel to negotiate toward an outcome that can satisfy both parties: providing sovereignty for a Palestinian state free of Israeli infringement on that sovereignty, and obtaining an enforceable physical condition that does not imperil Israeli security. The goal of such initiatives must be a situation where Israel feels safe and the Palestinians (and citizens of occupied Golan) feel free. Going back to that position creates some risks for Israel, but Israeli nuclear weapons condition those risks.

The imperfection of the status quo is its current inequity for all actors, and especially the Palestinians. The Palestinians have, after all, lived in some condition of servitude for seventy years and have not had a sovereign, unoccupied home for a half century. Beyond questions of equity, this situation has roiled the politics of the region, and while one can be sympathetic for the hard-line view in Israel, the status quo has produced unquestionable deprivation for what will soon become the largest population segment in the Israeli/West Bank/Golan/Gaza region. The Israelis have reason both to encourage and to resist change that requires them to take a conceivably existential gamble in the name of a peace that may or may not be the result of negotiations. The Palestinians have less—arguably nothing—to lose from resistance or negotiation. The choices between strategies for the parties, and both approaches and outcomes as they affect the United States are not easy ones. It is arguable, however, that the status quo does not serve either the American interest in regional stability or national self-determination. It is such a difficult problem that no one has been able to come up with a solution. What do you think? Should the United States return to a commitment to Palestinian self-determination and hopefully peace, or should it continue to support Israeli intransigence toward perpetuating Palestinian statelessness? Or is there some acceptable outcome between the extremes?

BIBLIOGRAPHY

Aly, Abdel Monem Said, Shai Feldman, et al. *Arabs and Israelis: Peacekeeping in the Middle East.* London: Palgrave, 2013.

Avashai, Bernard. "Confederation: The One Possible Arab-Palestinian Solution." *New York Review of Books*, February 2, 2018.

Beaumont, Peter. "Trump's Middle East Plan: Key Points at a Glance." *Guardian* (online), January 28, 2020.

Bennett, Brian. "The Strong Survive." *Time* 194, no. 3, July 22, 2019, 30–40.

Beres, Louis Rene. *Surviving Amid Chaos: Israel's Nuclear Strategy.* Lanham, MD: Rowman & Littlefield, 2016.

Blecher, Martin. *Israeli Settlements Distorting the Geneva Convention and the Oslo Accords.* Jerusalem: Jerusalem Center for Public Affairs, 2011.

Bregmann, Ahron. *Cursed Victory: A History of Israel and the Occupied Territories, 1967 to the Present.* New York: Pegasus, 2015.

Brown, Nathan. "The Occupation at Fifty: A Permanent State of Ambiguity." *Current History* 116, 704 (December 2017), 331–36.

Carter, Jimmy. *Palestine: Peace Not Apartheid.* New York: Simon & Schuster, 2006.

Della Pergola, Sergio. "Israel's Existential Predicament: Population, Territory, and Identity." *Current History* 109, no. 731 (December 2010), 383–89.

———, and Rebhun Uzi (eds.). *Jewish Population Identity: Concept and Reality.* New York: Springer, 2018.

Dowty, Alan. *Israel/Palestine.* Fourth Ed. London: Polity Press, 2017.

Falk, Richard. "Apartheid and the Future of Israel/Palestine." *Foreign Affairs Journal* (online), September 21, 2017.

Fawcett, Louise. *International Relations of the Middle East.* Oxford, UK: Oxford University Press, 2019.

Gerson, Alan. *Israel, the West Bank, and International Law.* New York: Routledge, 2012.

Gordis, Daniel. *We Stand Divided: The Rift Between American Jews and Israel.* New York: ECCO, 2019.

Hammond, Jeremy R. *Obstacle to Peace: The U.S. Role in the Israeli-Palestine Conflict.* New York: Worldview, 2016.

Hanafi, Sari, Leila Hilal, and Lex Takkenberg (eds.). *UNRWA and Palestinian Refugees: From Relief and Works to Human Development.* New York: Routledge, 2014.

Harms, Gregory, and Todd M. Ferry. *The Palestine-Israeli Conflict: A Basic Introduction.* Fourth Ed. London: Pluto Press, 2017.

Hirst, David. *The Gun and the Olive Branch: The Roots of Violence in the Middle East.* New York: Nation Books (Bold Type Books), 2003.

Indyk, Martin. "Disaster in the Desert: Why Trump's Middle East Plan Won't Work." *Foreign Affairs* 98, 6 (November/December 2019), 10–20.

Khalili, Rashid. *The Hundred Years' War on Palestine: A History of Settler Colonialism and Resistance, 1917-2017.* New York: Henry Holt, 2020.

Laqueur, Walter, and Dan Schueftan. *The Israeli-Arab Reader: A Documentary Reader.* New York: Penguin, 2014.

Lesch, David. *The Arab-Israeli Conflict: A Reader.* Second Ed. Oxford, UK: Oxford University Press, 2018.

Liel, Alon. "Trump's Peace Plan for Israel Looks a Lot Like Apartheid." *Foreign Policy* (online), February 20, 2020.

Lustick, Ian S. "We Need to Talk about Israel." *Foreign Affairs* 98, 4 (July/August 2019), 190–92.

Mahler, Gregory S. *Politics and Government in Israel: The Maturation of a Modern State.* Third Ed. Lanham, MD: Rowman & Littlefield, 2016.

Mearsheimer, John J., and Stephen M. Walt. *The Israel Lobby and U.S. Foreign Policy.* New York: Farrar, Straus and Giroux, 2007.

Munayyer, Youssef. "There Will Be a One-State Solution: But What Kind of State Will It Be?" *Foreign Affairs* 98, 6 (November/December 2019), 30–36.

Oren, Michael. *Ally: My Journey Across the American-Israeli Divide.* New York: Random House, 2015.

———. *Six Days of War: June 1967 and the Making of the Modern Middle East.* New York: Presidio, 2003.

Osman, Tarek, and Michael S. Doran. "Will Power Shifts in the Middle East Revive 'Land for Peace?'" *Foreign Affairs* 99, 3 (May/June 2020), online.

Pollack, Kenneth M. *Armies of Sand: The Past, Present, and Future of Arab Military Effectiveness.* Oxford, UK: Oxford University Press, 2018.

Ross, Dennis. *Doomed to Succeed: The U.S.-Israeli Relationship from Truman to Obama.* New York: Farrar, Straus and Giroux, 2015.

Said, Edward W. *The Question of Palestine.* Reissue Ed. New York: Vintage, 2015.

Selengut, Charles. *Our Promised Land: Faith and Militant Zionism in Israeli Settlements.* Lanham, MD: Rowman & Littlefield, 2015.

Shikaki, Khalil. "What Comes After the Middle East Peace Process: The Palestinians Propose an Alternative to Trump's Plan." *Foreign Affairs* (online), March 6, 2020.

Smith, Charles (ed.). *Palestine and the Arab-Israeli Conflict: A History with Documents.* Ninth Ed. New York: St. Martin's Press, 2016.

Snow, Donald M. *Cases in International Relations: Principles and Applications.* Eighth Ed. Lanham, MD: Rowman & Littlefield, 2020.

Tyler, Patrick. *Fortress Israel: The Inside Story of the Military Elite Who Run the Country—and Why They Can't Make Peace.* New York: Farrar, Straus and Giroux, 2012.

United States Central Intelligence Agency. *2019-2020 World Factbook.* New York: Skyhorse Publishing, 2019.

Uris, Leon. *Exodus: A Novel.* New York: Doubleday and Company, 1958. (The motion picture *Exodus* was released in 1960.)

Van Creveld, Martin L. *The Culture of War.* New York: Presidio, 2008.

———. *The Land of Blood and Honey: The Rise of Modern Israel.* New York: Thomas Dunne, 2010.

Zraick, Karen. "A Look at the West Bank Area Netanyahu Viewed to Annex." *New York Times* (online), September 10, 2019.

5

The Tragic Fate of Stateless People II
Kurdistan

The other major instance of Middle East statelessness afflicts the Kurds. Their situation resembles that of the Palestinians in that the Kurds represent a coherent, defined group of people who consider themselves a nationality that deserves a sovereign state of their own. The territory they claim is by others unwilling to honor their desire. Israel is the sole, and controversially legal, governing power in Palestine; Kurdistan, by contrast, spans territory that is part of four sovereign states (Iran, Iraq, Syria, and Turkey), parts of which are claimed as rightful parts of the Kurdish state.

The modern quest for a Kurdish state goes back to the dismemberment of the Ottoman Empire after World War I since all the areas claimed by the Kurds were parts of that empire. Kurdish leaders petitioned the conferees at the Versailles Peace Conference of 1919 to create Kurdistan as part of the redrawing of the Ottoman map. Caught in the literally byzantine power politics of the conference (see Anderson), they were denied, and what they considered parts of Kurdistan were assigned to various other states, from which Kurdish nationalists have been trying to free themselves ever since. They have not yet succeeded.

Kurdistan as envisioned by the Kurds is a classic enclave state—a country fully within another country (or in the Kurdish case, countries). This designation is reserved for sovereign states that are landlocked within a state. Vatican City and San Marino in Italy and Lesotho (a former Bantustan) are examples. A subset are "semi-enclave" states that are surrounded by another state but have direct access to the sea. Monaco, Gambia, and Brunei are examples. Kurdistan is a hybrid: it is surrounded by four states, parts of which are claimed by the Kurds; it could become a semi-enclave if it could achieve a Kurdish corridor to the Mediterranean Sea.

Because it is occurring outside the Israeli-Palestinian spotlight, Kurdish nationalism receives less international publicity than does its Palestinian counterpart, but it is quantitively a larger problem. There are 35–36 million Kurds who are potential citizens of Kurdistan, and should their dream be realized, the Kurdish state would be a major actor in the Shiite Crescent that stretches from Iran to Syria and Lebanon. The critical role Kurdish militias played in vanquishing the Islamic state in 2016 demonstrates they would be a force to be reckoned with.

The Kurdish problem is large and complex. There are more Kurds than other stateless peoples, and they form majorities in the largely contiguous parts of four states. The dream of the Kurds is to unite each of the areas into a single state of Kurdistan. The geography is internally propitious because the areas are largely contiguous. The problem is that each of the states from which Kurdistan would be fashioned opposes the creation of the Kurdish state. Each has a different reason for opposing the Kurds, but the underlying dynamic is that a united Kurdistan would be a major regional player and factor in the geopolitics of this volatile part of the world. The geopolitics of the region would change with an independent Kurdistan.

Statelessness and its elimination pose both a political and a moral conundrum in the contemporary world. Since the agreements that ended World War I, the international system has been putatively devoted to the ideals of freedom and self-determination for all peoples. Under Wilsonian principles enshrined at Versailles, one major goal was to allow peoples to decide where, with whom, and under what form and constitution of government they would live. In the case of kindred groups who did not enjoy these conditions, statelessness was a frequent preventative condition. Statelessness, in other words, is inconsistent with professed ideals and thus both a conceptual and practical limit on self-determination.

The previous chapter introduced the Palestinian example of statelessness, but it did not place it in the larger theoretical framework of international politics. The story of Kurdish statelessness thus begins by placing the phenomenon in the broader political perspective.

THE PROBLEM AND IMPORTANCE OF STATELESSNESS

The notion of people being part of a "stateless nation" seems initially anomalous, even confusing. The large reason for this confusion arises because in normal discourse about politics, the root terms—*state* and *nation*—are often used interchangeably. The two terms are, however, distinctly different in meaning and connotation. The term *nation* is anthropological and reflects the affinity and identification that groups of people have for one another. It is expressed in terms of and reflected in characteristics like ethnicity, physical appearance, language, religion, and shared experience as a group. At heart, a person's nationality is some combination of these characteristics and particularly of the conviction that one belongs to a national group: the belief that one is a Kurd, a Palestinian, an Israeli, or an American is based in the belief of people that they are part of that nation.

The term *state*, by contrast, is a political and legal term that refers to physical territories and the rightful ability to govern the particular territory. The root characteristic of states in international politics is the possession and recognition of sovereignty over territory and its inhabitants, including the recognition by other states that the possessor has a valid claim to sovereignty. There are currently more than 200 recognized states in the international system; nationality, by contrast, is much more diverse and extensive. There are, for instance, countries (a useful synonym for states) in Africa that have literally hundreds of groups of people who believe they belong to distinct national groups.

The fact that physical territory and human loyalties do not match up completely in many countries is the source of conflict that creates considerable instability and violence in the world, and nowhere are these problems more evident than in the Middle East. The most common form of discontinuity between the two concepts occurs when at least two nationally defined lives within a particular state and find themselves at odds when they cannot overcome their more basic political affiliations and influences (which Chua prefers to think of as tribal) and transfer their loyalties from their more parochial base to attachment to the state. This situation is the definition of multinationalism and is the most common form of imperfection in the world's map and thus the source of most of the internal instability in the world.

This situation is common to almost all of the developing world, and especially those countries that were subject to European colonial rule and where their founding fathers were either unaware or unmindful of the ethnic conflict they were creating in drawing national boundaries. Writing in 1993, for instance, Welsh surveyed the world's countries and concluded that 160 of the then 180 recognized sovereign states were multinational in one way or another. It becomes a destabilizing source when one or more of the groups in these multinational states decides they want to change the physical or political balance by eliminating or suppressing one another of the other groups in the state. Either motive can result in internal violence to overthrow the existing state or to secede from it.

Multinationalism is virtually universal in the Middle East. With the exception of the remnants of historic empires like Iran/Persia and Egypt, almost all

Middle Eastern states have boundaries that were artifacts of the aftermath of the two world wars, and most were drawn imperfectly to accommodate the influence of one or another of the victors of those conflicts rather than as a reflection of national realities on the ground. The most extreme examples are Syria and Iraq, countries that almost certainly should not exist but whose existence and configuration are primarily a testimony to British (Iraq) and French (Syria) desire to maintain influence in the region in 1919. They are the regional countries considered most likely to break apart.

The other form is irredentism, a term with an interesting genesis that describes what is, in many ways, an even more tragic and intractable situation. It derives from the Italian word that means "unredeemed," and it was first used to describe aspirations various groups had about lands that became part of Italy during the unification process in 1870. It has become a more generic term to describe what the Free Dictionary calls a movement or sentiment the purpose of which is "the recovery of territory culturally or historically related to one's nation but now subject to a foreign government." The broad purpose of multinational efforts is to alter an existing state to make it more congenial to other nationalities that reside in a particular sovereign territory. Irredentists challenge the rightful possession and exercise of sovereignty in territories they consider theirs.

The Kurds are a classic irredentist group. Their purpose is to create a state in which all people of Kurdish nationality can reside and be in the majority. Their problem is that the areas where the Kurds are in the majority and that would form the sovereign state of Kurdistan are in parts of four existing states—Syria, Iraq, Turkey, and Iran. Each has an area with a Kurdish majority, and those areas are roughly contiguous so that drawing a single set of geographic boundaries for a sovereign Kurdistan is not an insurmountable physical task. The problem is that none of the states wants the Kurds to secede and annex their independent territory to a Kurdish state. The existing states all fear—with some justification—the problems that a Kurdish state in their midst would cause for them. As a result, they all vigorously oppose Kurdish irredentist claims and actively seek to defeat Kurdish separatists. Given the number of states involved and the variety of reasons on which their opposition to Kurdistan is based, the problem of Kurdish self-determination is physically and conceptually a good bit more complex than the multinational situation surrounding Palestine.

The fundamental purpose of both kinds of these groups is to attack the problem of stateless nations. Groups making irredentist claims are basically arguing one of two pernicious conditions prevents them from achieving what they view as their assertion as their rightful endowment. One of these is territorial occupation that precludes their ability to assert their sovereign authority and form the state that marries their nationality and statehood. The other is that territory they feel is rightfully theirs is within the unjust sovereign jurisdiction of one or more states. Their intent and purpose are to unite these areas into a single state. The problem is easy to state; it is extremely difficult to resolve.

Statelessness can become the basis for violence and instability when a stateless group asserts its determined intention to alter political jurisdictions of which they are part and in which they feel trapped. The problem is basically the scarcity of territory to accommodate the various nations that assert a claim and desire their own statehood, the heart of a scarcity situation. It is a classic zero-sum situation where only one side can win (have all the resources—sovereign territory—they desire). If the possessor of contested territory will not willingly forfeit part of its territory to the stateless claimants, they must either compromise and somehow divide the territory to create a tolerable, satisfactory outcome for both in which neither of their claims (which by definition they view as legitimate) or no agreement is possible. If the latter is the case, the result is likely to be frustration on the part of the deprived group (usually the stateless people). It is the nature of zero-sum games that one side wins and the other side loses. When the "game" is national existence and political freedom, losing carries a heavy burden that may make the recourse to violence attractive to the frustrated party and counterviolence attractive to the dominant group.

Territorial disputes arising from statelessness are not common in contemporary international relations, but where they do exist, they are particularly difficult and furtive. There is likely not to be an accepted and stable agreement on national boundaries because boundaries were poorly drawn in ways that created conditions of statelessness. This dynamic describes much of the developed world, and especially Africa and the Middle East. In both areas, but especially in the Middle East, divisions, disagreements, and violence have, among some groups in some locales, sporadically occurred since Old Testament days.

American direct involvement with the Kurds is relatively recent, dating back to the aftermath of American leadership in evicting Iraq from Kuwait (Operation Desert Storm). In the aftermath of that event, Iraqi leader Saddam Hussein attacked both Iraqi Shiites and Kurds for their failure to support his invasion. This included using poison gas against Kurdish civilians, which caused many to flee to the Turkish mountains across the border where large numbers of Kurds lived. The Turks insisted they leave, and the solution was Operation Provide Comfort, where the United States guaranteed and enforced Kurdish protection when they returned from Turkey to their homes in Iraq. Americans and Kurds have interacted mostly positively ever since.

Chapter 5

IRREDENTISM: THE CASE OF KURDISTAN

The "Kurdish problem" is simple to state but excruciatingly difficult to solve. The basic problem is that the Kurds, who meet all the criteria of nationality, desire to create a state in the specific parts of the four countries where they are in a majority from territory currently a part of those states. The Kurdish zones of these states are essentially contiguous with one another, making the drawing of boundaries for a Kurdish state reasonably straightforward. Because the Kurds are a majority in each of these areas, there would not be a major problem of multinationalism. Kurdish populations in two of those states (Iraq and Syria) have exercised de facto political control and thus have experience in governance. There is, and has been, a particularly active Kurdish movement in Turkey to withdraw Kurdish-majority regions from Turkish control, which the Turks act to suppress more violently than any of the other Kurdish regions. The Kurds have the least active difficulties with the Persians, but that could change.

The problem may seem relatively straightforward, but it is not. The central problem is that all the states part of whose territory would become Kurdish are, for various reasons, opposed to Kurdish independence. All are rivals with differences among them—Sunni Turkey versus Shiite Iran, Arab Iraq versus non-Arab Turkey, and mixed ethnic countries like Syria and Iraq—there is little commonality about why they oppose the Kurds. But they are all do.

The problem is irredentism. The Kurds want to carve their own state from parts of their neighbors. For Kurdistan's neighbors, one aspect of the problem is close to classically multinational. All four neighbors are, to one degree or another, polyglots of ethno-religiously based nationalism, of which being Kurdish is one prominent example. This is the serious problem that is particularly likely to occur in the most marginal and artificial states: Iraq and Syria, but the Kurds represent roughly 22 percent of the population of Turkey, and their loss would have serious consequences for the Turks that make them the most furtive opponents of Kurdistan. An independent Kurdistan in the middle of these competing, conflicted countries would have serious consequences for the geopolitics of the region as well. The United States has conflicting interests because it has conflicting interests in all the parties to the process.

BACKGROUND OF THE CONFLICT

The Kurdish people number 35–36 million concentrated in an arc of territory that conjoins the independent states of Turkey, Iraq, Syria, and Iran. Syria and Iraq are inventions of twentieth-century great power politics, but Iran/Persia and Turkey have been staple powers of the region that includes Kurdistan for centuries or longer and remain the largest states in the area. Kurdish history includes periods when the Turks or the Persians have ruled them. In a part of the world where empires have been frequent and have changed over time, the Kurds have never had their "turn" as imperial forces.

The Kurds are unlike their neighbors, although for different reasons. The Kurds are moderate Sunni Muslims, differentiating them from the more radical, conservative kingdoms of the Persian Gulf. They are of Indo-European ethnicity, which makes them racially similar to the Persians, and their languages are similar. The Persians, of course, are non-Arab Shiites. The Iraqis include both Sunnis and Shi'a, but they are also Arab. The Syrians are a more mixed group of religious sects and ethnicity, but the Kurdish area of Syria is important geopolitically to Turkey, and the small Syrian oil industry is located in Syrian Kurdistan. Kurds are the largest minority group in Turkey and claim a large part of eastern Turkey as part of Kurdistan. The Turks and the Kurds have been locked in a civil war for years. The incursion into northern Syria to establish a "neutral zone" between Turkey and the Syrian territory the Kurds consider part of Rojava in October 2019 exemplifies the very bad blood between the two peoples.

The geopolitics of the region are ambivalent. The Kurds essentially stand alone. The fact they have differences with each of the other states from which Kurdistan would be carved means they have no natural regional ally. Kurdish self-defense militia forces (the pesh merga) are useful in situations where other regional states are imperiled, as in the case of Islamic State forces in the parts of Syria and Iraq annexed to the caliphate on Kurdish lands, which Kurdish militias protected, but such arrangements are expedient and dissolve once the crisis passes. All of these states have differences with one another that preclude them from finding adequate common cause to try to wipe out the Kurdish movement. It is not clear how successful any of them would be against the Kurds, unless Kurdish forces were deprived of adequate arms (which have historically been provided by the United States) to defend themselves. This possibility arose briefly in the October 2019 crisis with Turkey.

The Kurdish areas (the territories claimed as part of Kurdish irredentism) are roughly contiguous territories in the middle of those four states. Should their movement succeed, the state of Kurdistan would nestle among and border each of those states. Based on demographics and other factors, Kurdistan could be a viable state and a major factor in its region if the geographic problem of being landlocked can be solved. The problem is that none of the states from which it would be carved want this to occur.

STRUCTURE OF THE PROBLEM: COMPETING INTERESTS, CONSEQUENCES, AND BARRIERS TO STATEHOOD

Kurdish self-determination is opposed for different reasons and with varying intensity by all four of the countries from which Kurdistan would be formed. The opposition is not uniform in content or intensity. The greater the impact would be, the stronger the resistance to the Kurdish idea is, and each individual bilateral relationship is different and complex.

Syria. The country has the least overt opposition to the Kurdish cause. Eastern Syria, which encompasses Syrian Kurdistan (Rojava), is the least populous part of Syria. This country has fewer Kurds than any of the other three states. There are about two million Kurds in Rojava, basically an arid, bleak, lightly populated piece of territory that has generally been neglected or ignored by Syrian authorities. Simply put, the Assad regime has and continues to invest its resources in the Mediterranean parts of the country, which will form the core of Syria once the civil war ends. The Assad regime decided in effect to ignore the problems of the east. This neglect is one reason the Islamic State began its quest to form the Caliphate in this region and why they were so apparently successful.

The opposition came from the Kurds, since the Islamic State (IS) was expanding into sections of Syrian and Iraqi Kurdistan. The Kurds became the shock troops of resistance, but they were acting to protect the Kurdish population (who were brutally suppressed by ISIS as heretics). As Kurdish militias defeated and drove IS out of their territory, they established governance in Rojava and expanded their hold on the Kurdish Autonomous Region of Iraq. A de facto internationally constituted state of Kurdistan was emerging from the ashes of the caliphate. Iraqis and Syrians were just glad to see someone attenuate the IS threat.

The results are evolving and will be affected by future events. Syria and Iraq are the most artificial and thus centripetal states in the region, and the Kurdish situation will affect and be affected by forces that may tear either or both apart. If, for instance, Syria dissolves, what will the fate of Rojava be? Will it become a pillar of Kurdistan? The Syrian government is influenced by Russia, which also has interests in Turkey. At the same time, the small Syrian oil industry is located essentially totally in Rojava. The oil revenues from that industry are not great, but much of it has historically gone to Turkey. It could also become part of a thriving Kurdish oil-producing capability if combined with oil reserves in Iraqi Kurdistan. President Trump said on October 29, 2019, that the exports from Syrian sources produced $45 million a month. The Syrians are also prime candidates for providing the Kurds with a transit route to relieve the trauma of their enclave status.

Iran. The Kurdish-Iranian relationship is different. Around eight million Kurds live in Iran, but because Iran's population is over 80 million, it is a smaller proportion than in other states. Most Kurds live in the western part of Iran adjoining Iraq. The Kurds are ethnically and linguistically akin to the Persians and both are rivals of the dominant Arabs of neighboring Iraq. Kurdish reluctance to support the Baghdad regime in the Iran-Iraq War of the 1980s was the major reason Saddam Hussein attacked Kurdistan in 1991.

For now, Iranian-Kurdish relations are not a major factor in Kurdish separatism. They could become more problematic if Kurdish irredentism becomes more successful and aggressive. The Kurds and Iranian "militias" cooperated in the expulsion and destruction of IS, even though the Iranians are Shia and the Kurds are Sunni. Neither regime (despite some protestations from American and Israeli sources) is militantly aggressive. Should the Kurds succeed in establishing Kurdistan, there is the possibility of either cooperation or conflict with Iranian efforts to spread their influence westward into places like Syria or Lebanon.

Iraq. The tumultuous relationship between the Kurds and the government in Baghdad has been the most public and well-publicized aspect of the Kurdish quest. The Kurds have been effectively self-governing in Rojava since early in the campaign against IS; the Kurdish Autonomous Region of northern Iraq (where most Kurds reside) has enjoyed virtual self-rule since the United States overthrew the government of Saddam Hussein in 2003.

In terms of Iraqi instability, the Kurdish assertion of virtual sovereignty in northern Iraq is a central feature of the struggle between Iraqi Arabs and the Kurds. The population of Iraq is about 20 percent Kurdish and mostly lives in the northern part of the country. The rest are Arab. Of the Arab total, about twice as many Iraqis are Shiites in the southern part of the country; the rest are Sunnis who reside in the middle, an area known as the Sunni triangle. The Sunnis predominated government and the military until the United States overthrew the Sunni-dominated government of Saddam Hussein and dismantled the Iraqi armed forces in 2003. Since then, the Kurds have consolidated effective control of Iraqi Kurdistan, a dynamic that continues.

The critical geopolitical importance of Iraq is petroleum. Iraq statistics are often suspect, but in 2015, Iraq was considered to have the fifth largest reserves in the world, located in the Shiite south and the Kurdish north. There is essentially no oil in the Sunni triangle. This has a profound effect on Iraqi politics since control of the Iraqi political system is the only way the minority Sunnis can control oil wealth. Centripetal dynamics that weaken both Sunnis and Shia serve Kurdish interests; the weaker the central government, the more institutionalized Kurdish autonomy becomes. Pesh merga fighters, for instance, act as a de facto border guard between Kurdish Iraq and the other regions.

The IS threat illustrated the anomalies involved. Although it was seldom recognized in 2014 when IS began its sweep across the region, most of that conquest occurred in sparsely populated areas in Syria and then across the border into northern Iraq. Syrian armed forces were occupied by the main theater of the civil war, and the Iraqi army did not perform well in the face of the highly motivated, often savage Sunni fundamentalists (many of whose leaders were former members of Saddam's Sunni-dominated armed forces). The only highly capable, disciplined, and motivated forces confronting IS were Kurdish self-defense forces. Because much of the territory being occupied by the Caliphate was on what the Kurds considered part of Kurdistan, they fought resolutely against the less disciplined IS "fighters" and prevailed.

The result was twofold in Kurdish-Iraqi terms. The first was heightened conflict between the Kurds, those Iraqis who supported IS, and those who resisted ineffectually the inexorable sweep of IS. The prospect created great concern, even panic regionally and in the West, which feared a rogue, evangelical IS caliphate would become a launching pad for terrorism. The second effect flowed from pesh merga's prowess in leading the resistance to IS. The Kurds gained publicity for their cause and established themselves as a significant power within the region. This impact was to some extent double-edged because it also created greater paranoia among their neighboring rivals about the Kurds. This was particularly true of the Turks.

Turkey. The Turks are more opposed to the success of Kurdish irredentism than any other state with a stake in Kurdistan. The reason is straightforward: if the Kurds succeed in establishing Kurdistan, Turkey would be more affected than any other state. The Turks and the Kurds are natural rivals, even enemies, within Turkey. When the Kurds failed to gain sovereign status after World War I, the largest number of Kurds became part of Turkey, a status many of them have rejected, often violently, ever since.

The basis of the Turkish concern with the Kurds is demographic and geographic. There are more Kurds in Turkey than in any of the other states in which they reside. Exact numbers are unreliable: the Kurdish Project in 2016 estimated it at around 18 million, about half of the Kurdish population and around 22 percent of the population of Turkey of 81 million. There is some disagreement on how many of the Kurds are separatist. The Turkish government argues most of the hard core (of about 8 million) is concentrated in the eastern Anatolia region: the Kurds argue the separatist sentiment is far more widespread. The Kurds claim that upward of a quarter of Turkish territory as part of Kurdistan. The core is Anatolia, one of the country's most developed regions, which contains the sources of much of the region's water and hydroelectric power generated by dams on those rivers.

Without the territory claimed as part of Kurdistan, Turkey is a considerably reduced power, a fact of which the regime in Ankara is acutely aware. Much of Turkish power and geopolitical prestige is tied to its status as the southern flank of NATO, a role that is potentially diminished in a reduced Turkish state. Other states may resent or dislike the Kurds, but their presence in Turkey is integral to the status and prosperity of that country, and it helps explains both their concerted efforts against the Kurds and their courtship of alternate "friends" in the region. Suppressing Kurdish separatism is more important to Turkey than to any of the other states in the region. It is an emotional issue to which the Turkish Erdoğan government has invested great energy and emotion. When the Turkish president visited Washington in November 2019, he brought with him film footage of what he alleged was evidence that Kurdish separatists are terrorists and should be treated accordingly by the international community. It was crudely propagandistic, and when the film was shown at the White House on November 13, 2019, to the president and a contingent of Republican lawmakers, its amateurism and credulity was widely assailed, making the effort appear farcical and counterproductive.

AMERICAN CONFLICTING INTERESTS

The United States has episodic interest in the Kurdish cause, but it is neither consistent nor intense enough to cause the United States to devise a policy either to champion or oppose Kurdish statehood. The Kurds lack a patron in the area on whom they can count to advocate their cause and to provide support they need to prosecute their quest for statehood. Their neighbors will not do so because Kurdish success comes at their physical expense. The Kurds yearn for the Americans to provide at least some version of the support it accords Israel. It has not been systematically forthcoming.

The Kurds also face an enormous and to date insurmountable geographic/economic problem. An independent Kurdistan carved from the four states is landlocked by those countries: it is a physical enclave with no secure accessible route to the rest of the world. To get into or out of Kurdistan, one has to pass through one of the countries from which Kurdistan would be formed, and it is hard to imagine that any of them would grant that permission on acceptable terms. Gibson describes this as the "basic problem that the Kurds have always faced." Being landlocked leaves "it unable to participate in the international economy without being reliant on external—and hostile powers such as Turkey, Iran, Iraq, and Syria." Exporting oil is a prime example. The only change that might break this dilemma is the dissolution of Iraq or Syria and the emergence of new territorial boundaries that could create a corridor for the Kurds.

Kurdish-American relations have been uneven. They have tended to peak when situations raise American consciousness of the Kurdish plight to an unignorable level. Two events in post–World War II Middle Eastern politics illustrate both the kinds of situations and the extent and depth of American concern. Both represent situations where events of which the United States was a part drew them into union with the Kurds, although for quite different reasons. In both cases, the motivations of the two "partners" were different and more transient than they initially appeared.

The first came in the aftermath of the first Gulf War (Operation Desert Storm). The impetus was the 1990 invasion of Kuwait. Sunni-controlled Arab Iraq had gone to war with Shiite Iran from 1980–1988 to limit Iranian (thus non-Arab) expansionism stimulated by the 1979 Iranian Civil War. The prosecution of that conflict was expensive for the Iraqis, and they believed they should be compensated for the debts they had incurred by the principal beneficiaries, notably oil-rich Kuwait and Saudi Arabia. When both these countries refused Iraq's demands, Saddam Hussein responded with a massive invasion and occupation of Kuwait that placed his forces on the border with Saudi Arabia a short dash from the Saudi oil fields. His apparent motivation was to gain control of the oil to recoup Iraq's sacrifices as well as to establish himself as a regional leader.

The aftermath raised the Kurds into the American consciousness. American president George H. W. Bush, who had ordered Desert Storm, was under considerable pressure to send coalition forces into Iraq and overthrow the Hussein regime in 1991. When he demurred, Saddam Hussein felt free to take revenge against his internal opponents. Neither the Kurds of the north nor the Shiites of the south had supported the Kuwaiti invasion and had even initiated a post–Desert Storm rebellion against Saddam's continued rule.

Hussein unleashed the Iraqi armed forces in retributive violence against both groups, but especially the Kurds. His government attacked Kurdish urban areas with poison gas. Many Kurds, fearing a continuation or even expansion of this campaign, fled across the nearby border into Turkey, where they gathered in squalor on Turkish mountainsides. The Turks were appalled since they fled to Turkish Kurdistan and posed a significant financial burden to Turkey. Their plight was discovered and publicized on worldwide television largely by a fledgling new Cable News Network (CNN), which televised their misery for the world to see. The United States suddenly became aware of the Kurds. The Turks were unhappy and insisted that the Kurds return to Iraq. Most of them refused, fearing that Saddam's chemical weapons awaited them on the Iraqi side of the frontier. The question was how to make the Kurds feel safe enough to get them to leave Turkey, and the United States was drawn into finding a solution. Growing sympathy for the Kurds' plight, Turkey's status as a NATO ally, and a realization that the United States had indirectly promoted the crisis by not acting to support the rebels before the chemical attacks provided the incentive.

The result was Operation Provide Comfort (later renamed Northern Watch). Its problem was how to convince the Kurds to return to Iraq, which they were reluctant to do given the fate Saddam likely had in store for them. The problem was pressing because the Turkish government insisted that they leave. Thus, the dilemma was how to convince the Kurds they could feel safe returning home. The United States provided the solution, and it joined the fates of the Kurds and the Americans.

That solution was to create a no-fly zone over northern Iraq (basically Iraqi Kurdistan) where Iraqi air and land forces would be excluded from operating, thereby eliminating their physical ability to attack the Kurds. The arrangement would be enforced by American air forces supported by NATO allies, principally the British and the French. It was a clear violation of Iraqi sovereignty, but it persuaded the Kurds to leave Turkey. A recently defeated Iraq was in no physical position to contest the restrictions physically. The military effort was extended to the Shiites to ensure Saddam did not unleash his retributive fury against them (Operation Southern Watch).

There were two important side effects of this action. The first was that it created the precedent of the United States acting to protect the Kurds, the kind of patronage they had sought and been denied previously. A bond was established between the Kurds and the Americans. Many Kurds believed the Americans were now their "allies," which most Americans did not acknowledge. The perception of a Kurdish-American connection was, however, established, possibly misleadingly, in the minds of the Kurds.

The second effect was to create an open-ended military commitment for the United States. Operation Northern/Southern Watch was an active arrangement only for as long as the United States physically enforced it. Had the Americans abrogated the commitment, they could have done so by removing the air shield they surveilled and allowing Saddam to send forces into the protected regions. The result could well have been a bloodbath. Such a prospect would have been viewed internationally as perfidious, and it meant the U.S. commitment to the Kurds was potentially perpetual.

Ultimately, what ended the no-fly policy and ushered in the second phase of U.S.-Kurdish relations was the American invasion and conquest of Iraq in 2003. A major effect was to change American policy toward the Kurds. The invasion overthrew the Iraqi government. The Hussein government was dismantled and replaced by an American-run occupation regime. It also ended the effective period of Sunni dominance of Iraq and Saddam's tyranny. Among the beneficiaries was the Kurds, who created a de facto independent regime in the Kurdish region that was transformed into what Filkins called "the semiautonomous Kurdish region of Iraq" in 2014, and thus lay the basis for the continuing movement toward a Kurdish state.

American-Kurdish cooperation was natural in some ways. The Kurds are among the most Westernized people in the region. As Filkins adds, Kurdistan "is pro-western, largely democratic, largely secular and economically prosperous." Moreover, they are fierce and effective allies in Filkins estimate: "Since 2003, not a single U.S. soldier has lost his life in Kurdish territory." During the American occupation of Kurdish Iraq between 2003 and 2007 (when Iraqi sovereignty was officially reinstated), the United States presided over an effectively independent Iraqi Kurdistan.

New trouble, however, was not far below the surface. In 2007, Al Qaeda in Iraq arose as an offshoot of the bin Laden organization. Composed mostly of dissident Sunnis, it went underground after the so-called Sunni Awakening of that year and reappeared as ISIS in 2013 as the Caliphate. As the Caliphate developed and emerged publicly in 2014, the Americans and the Kurds were once again thrown together. It joined them in the common cause of overthrowing and hopefully destroying a menacing force that frightened much of the world. For the Kurds, defeating IS was primarily a territorial matter: most of IS's early conquests were in Syrian and Iraqi Kurdistan; liberating their brethren from the barbaric atrocities of IS occupiers was a natural response. The American interest was to suppress and hopefully destroy a menacing new manifestation of the war on terror.

The problem was how to stop a military campaign that seemed inexorable and unstoppable to many outsiders. The pace of IS expansion was, of course, largely due to geography—conquering lightly populated and defended territory in Syria and Iraq. Syrian forces were preoccupied with their civil war, and when the attackers entered Iraq, it was mostly in the Sunni triangle, where some Sunnis welcomed them as liberators and which mostly Shiite Iraqi armed forces did not defend with any enthusiasm. Americans decried the spread of IS as a terrorist threat to the United States, but there was no support for reinserting American combat forces into the area.

Only the Kurds cared because much of the territory IS attacked and occupied was part of Syrian or Iraqi Kurdistan, making it a foreign invasion to Kurdish nationalists. In addition, the Kurds practice a moderate form of Sunnism that is far short of what the Caliphate demanded in terms of what they view as adequate piety and deviations from which they treated harshly, including summary execution of apostates. Resistance and defeat of IS was in the vital interests of the Kurds.

The Kurds were the heroes of the war against IS. Effectively, Kurdish pesh merga militias served as the foot soldiers in stopping and expelling and defeating ISIS particularly after the Shiite Iraqi armed forces showed little stomach for dying to liberate the Sunni triangle.

The Kurds were aided, trained, and supplied by the Americans. It was an informal alliance, but it worked. It was also remarkably durable. When the Turks invaded and occupied northern Syrian parts of Rojava adjacent to Turkey, relations seemed strained, and some commentators complained about a betrayal of the "alliance" (in parentheses because no formal alliance obligation exists) and wondered if it would cause a breach in the common effort.

POLICY OPTIONS AND CONSEQUENCES

The Kurdish situation reflects the two contradictory problems the United States faces dealing with ISIS and Kurdish independence. The United States and the Kurds both want to extinguish the ISIS movement, if for different reasons. For the Kurds, ISIS is an existential threat. For the Americans, ISIS is essentially a terrorist problem: the Caliphate provided a potential launching pad for international terrorist activity aimed at the United States and elsewhere. The two goals are asymmetrical. For the Kurds, ISIS is a territorial problem, a matter of vital self-defense of the Kurdish "homeland." The international terrorism aspect that activates the Americans is decidedly secondary to the Kurds. For the United States, the priorities are reversed. The United States is ambivalent about Kurdish self-determination, but it is very interested in international terrorism.

This combination makes the Kurdish-American relationship fragile. As Filkins noted in 2014, "the (Obama) administration wants the Kurds to do two potentially incompatible things. The first is to serve as a crucial ally in the campaign to destroy ISIS. The second is to resist seceding from the Turkish state." The first matter is both political and strategic. From a U.S. perspective, having the Kurds concentrate on destroying ISIS reduces its major concern without great American personal involvement (which was a concern of President Trump): it avoids entanglement in Kurdish statehood.

Kurdish secession from Turkey and elsewhere is trickier for the United States. It is clearly the paramount concern of the Kurds, and their problem is the lack of a strong supporter to help. There are, indeed, some attractions to association with Kurdish statehood. The Americans have been deprived of access to Iraqi oil (of which Kurdish oil is a part) for decades, and have shown periodic interest in an Iraqi Kurdish oil deal, an interest blocked by Baghdad and effectively blocked by Kurdistan's landlocked position that makes it impossible to ship that oil independently to Western markets. The problem is that none of Kurdistan's contiguous neighbors accepts the creation of a Kurdish state. Turkey (and potentially Iran) resists the idea with force. The Kurds are different in ethnic, religious, and historical terms, and a Kurdish state would not have natural allies in the region.

There is an additional factor, however, that is rarely included in discussions of Kurdistan, but it is at the heart of the problem and the resistance. That factor is geopolitical: an independent Kurdistan would upset a very delicate power balance in the region to the potential detriment of virtually all other regional states. Simply put, all those states would lose territory and population to Kurdistan. The only way to avoid this problem is to keep Kurdistan from coming into being; the method is to ensure that Kurdistan remains an enclave incapable of getting its goods to market, and thus economically nonviable.

This is the heart of the geopolitical threat: the effect of Kurdish statehood is to weaken the power of each of the states from which it is carved and to transfer some or all of that power to the Kurds. As potential losers, it should be no surprise that Turkey, Iran, Iraq, and Syria all oppose the creation of a sovereign Kurdish state in their midst. Two of these, Iran and Turkey, are the largest and most influential, each with populations in excess of 80 million. Not coincidentally, they would lose the most people and land to a fully independent Kurdistan. Iraq and Syria would also be affected adversely.

There is little analysis of this phenomenon in the public record. Most of what little speculation exists is about Iraqi Kurdistan, where the prospects of a breakaway are especially high given the fragile, divided condition of both the Shiite and Sunni Arab population of that country and the de facto development of independent governance by the Kurds. The major opponents of that development are said to be the Iranians, who allegedly would find a neighboring Iraqi Sunni state on its border to be an unwanted neighbor. Turkish opposition is the most adamant, and a concerted Kurdish attempted secession of the Northern (Turkish) Kurds from Turkey would likely be very bloody.

The basic configurations of the states from which Kurdistan would be carved is shown in population and geographic terms in Table 5.1. It also includes summary Kurdish figures (in parentheses as a point of comparison). The parentheses are because the Kurdish totals are currently part of the others.

Table 5.1. Total Area and Population for Kurdistan-Affected States

State	Current Area (square miles)	Current Population (in millions)
Iran	636,372	83
Turkey	302,536	81
Iraq	169,235	40
Syria	66,500	19.5
Kurdistan	151,000	35–36

Sources: *2017 CIA World Handbook*. Washington, DC: Skyhorse, 2017.
The Kurdish Project (online), 2016.

The geographic and human changes that would occur can be roughly depicted in terms of pre- and post-Kurdistan population and physical territory. The results are dramatic. The Kurdish Project summarizes the distribution and locations of the areas that would be part of Kurdistan. It is displayed in Table 5.2.

Table 5.2. Kurdish Population and Land Area by Location

Location	Designation	Claimed Land Area (in millions)	Estimated Population (square miles)
Iran	Eastern Kurdistan	48,000	8
Turkey	Northern Kurdistan	73,000	18
Iraq	Southern Kurdistan	25,000	5
Syria	Western Kurdistan	5,000	2
Total		151,000	35–36*

*Includes 2 million classified as "all other" by the Kurdish Project, which is the source of the figures.

These Kurdish figures are important because they form the basic demographics an independent Kurdistan would have on the totals for the other states. This subtraction is depicted in population and land areas for the region with a Kurdish sovereign state in its midst. Table 5.3 shows that the redistribution of power (to the extent that is what the population and geographic figures depict) is dramatic.

Table 5.3. Regional Population and Land Area Including Kurdistan

Country	Population (in millions)	Land Area (square miles)
Iran	75	588,000
Turkey	63	232,000
Kurdistan	35–36	160,000
Iraq	35	145,000
Syria	17.5	66,500

Notes: Figures are rounded given imprecisions in measurements and claims. The rough comparisons, however, hold.

One can make both too much and too little of these demographic changes in the region. They do not, for instance, address the fundamental Kurdish problem of lack of physical access to the outside world arising from their landlocked condition. A solution to the enclave situation is a virtual sine qua non for a Kurdish state. The Kurds must develop arrangements to provide them with a secure, reliable way to get from Kurdistan to the outside world. If they cannot, the result could be a wretched failure that would arguably leave the Kurds worse off than they are now. None of the states surrounding the Kurdish state is predisposed to provide the cordon sanitaire that Kurdistan needs to be a full and competitive member of the international system since each would have territory taken from them to form that state. The question becomes under what circumstances can that barrier be surmounted.

CHOOSING POLICY: A KURDISH STATE?

How one views the future of Kurdish statelessness depends on how one answers two questions: Should there be a sovereign Kurdish state? and What must be done to make such a state a reality? The answers to both questions are crucial to whether the Kurdish people will live in a country of their own or remain minority citizens in states they do not control. The answers are difficult, difficult and interrelated.

The desirability of an independent Kurdistan is contentious. The Kurds meet the criteria of nationhood, and a Kurdistan uniting the populations of the parts of the four states from which it would be carved could almost certainly form a viable state that might well be a pillar of regional stabilization. The self-determination of the Kurdish people would certainly be an expression of principles within the United Nations Charter on the rights of people. Unfortunately, of course, none of this can occur (at least not easily) without the support or at least tacit cooperation of the states from which Kurdistan would be forged, and it is not clear if the objective is obtainable. Moreover, as Table 5.3 suggested, an independent Kurdistan alters, in some unpredictable ways, the power balance of the region. Moreover, it could set the precedent for irredentists elsewhere. An independent Kurdistan needs the agreement of others who so far have opposed it.

The agenda for moving toward Kurdistan requires at least two giant steps. The first is gaining the support (or dampening the objectives) of those who oppose it. Activating a process to accomplish that would be a difficult task that would require the intervention of some outside power(s). The United States might seem an unlikely candidate; its record on Palestinian statehood is not encouraging. The second, and logistically both the more difficult and essential, is removing the new country's enclave status by establishing a corridor to the sea for the Kurds. Syria is a key in both cases: Rojava would clearly be a fundamental element of the new Kurdish state, and a post–civil war Syria is key to this possibility (see Chapter 6).

Where does the United States fit into this process? Predictably, the answer is ambivalently. The United States has some affinity for the Kurds, who want to view the Americans as their advocates. The United States loves pesh merga; Americans are unaware of or indifferent to Kurdish statehood. Also, the United States has ties to Iraq and Turkey, and adversarial relations with Syria and Iran. Advocacy of the Kurds stirs the pot: Is it worth it? The key element is NATO ally and historical friend Turkey. The Turks are the most adamant opponents of Kurdistan: they have the most to lose, and they will oppose any change that might result in increased Kurdish secessionist sentiment in Turkey. U.S.-Turkish relations are already strained: Is the advocacy of Kurdistan worth straining them further?

These are all difficult questions and barriers. If they were not, Kurdistan would probably already exist. As the situation now stands, the prospects seem forlorn. Do you have any ideas how to answer the situation facing American options? Should there be Kurdistan? If so, what should the United States do to make it a reality?

BIBLIOGRAPHY

Allsop, Harriet. *The Kurds of Syria: Political Parties and Identity in the Middle East.* London: I B Tauris, 2015.

Ambrosio, Thomas. *Irredentism: Ethnic Conflict and International Politics.* Westport, CT: Praeger, 2001.

Anderson, Scott. *Lawrence in Arabia: War, Deceit, Imperial Folly, and the Making of the Modern Middle East.* New York: Anchor Books, 2013.

Aziz, Mahir. *The Kurds of Iraq: Nationalism and Identity in Kurdish Iraq.* London: I B Tauris, 2014.

Bengio, Ofra. *The Kurds of Iraq: Building a State within a State.* Boulder, CO: Lynne Rienner, 2012.

Central Intelligence Agency. *The CIA World Factbook 2017.* Washington, DC: Skyhorse Publishing, 2016.

Chaliland, Gerald, and Michael Pallis. *A People without a Country: The Kurds and Kurdistan.* Northampton, MA: Interlink Publishing Group, 1993.

Chazam, Naomi (ed.). *Irredentism and International Politics.* Boulder, CO: Lynne Rienner, 1991.

Chua, Amy. *Political Tribes: Group Instincts and the Fate of Nations.* New York: Penguin Press, 2018.

Dowty, Alan. *Israel/Palestine: Hot Spots in Global Politics.* Fourth Ed. London: Polity Press, 2017.

Eccarius-Kelly, Vera, and Michael Gunter (eds.). *Kurdish Autonomy and U.S. Foreign Policy: Continuity and Change.* Bern, Switzerland: Peter Lang, 2019.

Eppel, Michael. *People without a State: The Kurds from the Rise of Islam to the Dawn of Nationalism.* Austin: University of Texas Press, 2016.

Filkins, Dexter. "The Fight of Their Lives: The White House Wants the Kurds to Help Save Iraq from ISIS. The Kurds May Be More Interested in Breaking Away." *The New Yorker.* September 22, 2014 (online).

Gibson, Bryan R. "The Secret Origins of the U.S.-Kurdish Relationship Explain Today's Disaster." *Foreign Policy* (online), October 14, 2018.

———. *Sold Out? US Foreign Policy, Iraq, the Kurds, and the Cold War.* London: Palgrave Macmillan, 2015.

Gunter, Michael. *The Kurds: A Divided Nation in Search of an Identity.* Princeton, NJ: Markus Weiner, 2018.

———. *The Kurds: A Modern History.* Princeton, NJ: Markus Weiner Publishers, 2015.

Izady, Mehrdad. *The Kurds: A Concise History and Factbook.* London: Taylor and Francis, 2015.

King, Diane E. *Kurdistan and the Global Stage: Land and Community in Iraq.* New Brunswick, NJ: Rutgers University Press, 2013.

Krishnadev, Calamur. "Where Is Kurdistan?" *The Kurdish Project*, 2019.

———. "Why Doesn't the U.S. Support Kurdish Independence?" *The Atlantic* (online), October 20, 2017.

Lawrence, Quil, et al. *Invisible Nation: How the Kurds' Quest for Statehood Is Shaping Iraq and the Middle East.* New York: Walker Books, 2008.

Mansfield, Stephen. *The Miracle of the Kurds: A Remarkable Story of Hope Reborn in Northern Iraq.* New York: Worthy Books, 2014.

Marcus, Aliza. *Blood and Belief: The PKK and the Kurdish Fight for Independence.* New York: NYU Press, 2009.

McDowell, David. *A Modern History of the Kurds.* Revised ed. London: I. B. Tauris, 2004.

Meiselas, Susan. *Kurdistan: In the Shadow of History.* Chicago: University of Chicago Press, 2008.

Phillips. David L. *The Kurdish Spring: A New Map of the Middle East.* New York: Routledge, 2017.

Randal, Johnathan. *After Such Knowledge, What Forgiveness? My Encounters with Kurdistan.* New York: Routledge, 2019.

Roblin, Sebastien. "The Kurds Served as America's Ground Troops in the War Against ISIS: And Washington's Betrayal of Them Is Quite Cruel." *The National Interest* (online), October 13, 2019.

Rudd, Gordon W., and U.S. Army Center for Military History. *Humanitarian Intervention: Military History.* Military Bookshop, 2012.

Schmidinger, Thomas. *Rojava: Revolution, War, and the Future of Syria's Kurds.* London: Pluto Press, 2018.

Smith, Charles D. *Palestine and the Arab-Israeli Conflict: A History with Documents.* Ninth Ed. New York: St. Martin's Press, 2016.

Snow, Donald M. *The Case Against Military Intervention: Why We Do It and Why It Fails.* Lanham, MD: Rowman & Littlefield, 2016.

———. *Cases in International Relations: Principles and Applications.* Eighth Ed. Lanham, MD: Rowman & Littlefield, 2020.

———. *National Security.* Seventh Ed. New York: Routledge, 2020.

———, and Dennis M. Drew. *From Lexington to Desert Storm: War and Politics in the American Experience.* Armonk, NY: M. E. Sharpe, 1994.

Valentine, Simon Ross. *Pesh Merga (Those Who Face Death): The Kurdish Army, Its History. Development and the Fight Against ISIS.* Seattle, WA: Kindle Direct Publishing, 2018.

Verini, James. *They Will Have to Die Now: Mosul and the Fall of the Caliphate.* New York: W.W. Norton, 2019.

Welsh, David. "Domestic Politics and Ethnic Politics," in Michael E. Brown, ed. *Ethnic Conflict and International Security.* Princeton, NJ: Princeton University Press, 1993.

White, Paul. *The PKK: +Coming Down from the Mountains.* London: Zed Books, 2015.

6

The Syrian Pivot after the Civil War

In a region where enigmas and incongruities are the political norm, Syria may be the most enigmatic country of them all. In many respects, it (like Iraq) should probably not be a state at all in its current configuration. It was more the product of European maneuvering and posturing at the end of World War I that created a series of influence zones for major European powers (notably Britain and France) carving up the Mediterranean remains of the collapsed Ottoman Empire than anything else. The Sykes-Picot agreement provided the blessing for this arrangement that ended with the states of Syria, Iraq, and Lebanon, each of which has been unstable ever since. The bloody civil war that has raged since 2011 as the most visible and tragic outcome of the Arab Spring is the latest attempt to rationalize the status of the territory known as Syria.

Syria has been a controversial player in the region since the aftermath of World War II created fully sovereign states in the countries "liberated" from the Turks in 1919. In 1920, an area called "Greater Syria" (composed of territory including parts of contemporary Israel, Lebanon, and Syria) was proposed as a democratic constitutional monarchy, but its creation was effectively blocked by the European powers and never came into being (see Thompson). As Waterbury puts it in his review of the Thompson volume, "European powers strangled Syrian independence in its crib." Whether the success of the independence movement would have produced a different Syria is impossible to know; by the time World War II broke out, it was replaced by what Waterbury depicts as "an intolerant form of Islam and autocratic Arab nationalism that came to prevail in the Middle East." Syria was part of that problem.

Syria became a sovereign state in 1946, as the British and the French retreated from their self-appointed interwar responsibilities. The French had done virtually nothing to prepare the new Syrians, composed of multiple ethnicities and religious groups, for political independence before it was granted, and the result was considerable political instability, marked by a series of coups and countercoups.

Syria has suffered through uncertainties throughout its existence. It is a classic artificial, multinational, multiethnic country that contains a volatile mix of ethnic and politico-religious groups that does not result in a rational, defensible Syrian nationality, and it joins Iraq (for most of the same reasons) as a state that probably should not exist. Syria is the kind of place it is because that is what European diplomats created at the end of World War I. Syrians have struggled to create a Syrian national identity and kindred spirit that the civil war reveals have largely failed. One of the major questions after the civil bloodletting has concluded is whether Syria will remain a single entity or split into several successors. The same question is asked about Iraq.

Speculation abounds about the Syrian future. The outcome is obviously important for the Syrian people and for the geopolitics of the western Mediterranean area of the Middle East. The first problem will be how to recover from the physical and human carnage of the war. A large portion of the population has been displaced or killed in the fighting, and many reside in internal or external exile. Most fervently hope to return to their homes after the war is over. Rebuilding the country will be an enormous task the cost of which is estimated in the trillions of dollars, and it is not clear who will foot the bill. It is a more complex problem than simply writing checks and importing rebuilding capacity. The geopolitics of that aspect of the Syrian future will go a long way toward determining what Syria or its successor states will physically and politically look like. Only one thing is certain: postwar Syria will be different than prewar Syria. The question is how, and what that means for the region at large.

Syria is a critical part of the Mediterranean Middle East. It joins several other countries with an interest and a geopolitical stake in the regional political and geopolitical balance. From an American point of view, the impact on Israel may be the most important. The successor Syria, once freed of its internecine focus, is almost certainly going to turn some of its attention to the aggressive Israeli development of the Golan region and will want to reverse that trend, to which the Trump administration had voiced its active approval. The successor Syrians are likely to be aided in anti-Israeli efforts by the Iranians. Lebanon, which shares a border with northern Israel, probably cannot remain entirely aloof from the struggle. Turkey sits on the northern boundary of Syria, and it has regularly impinged on areas of Syria, especially parts the

Kurds call Rojava and claim as part of greater Kurdistan. The Russians have a physical stake in the Alawite region of northern Syria, both because of their naval base in Tartus and Assad and his supporters are from that region. To the east, northern Syria falls into possible avenues where the Kurds want to break their land-locked status as a prerequisite to establishing Kurdistan.

The result is a bubbling witches' cauldron of regional possibilities with uncertain impacts on the United States and its regional interests in the region. The Trump administration effectively tied American interests tightly to those of Israel. Based largely on its aversion to the prospects of involvement in more regional "endless wars," it remained largely aloof from personal involvement in the civil war, a policy inherited from an Obama administration also reluctant to engage in policies that might drag into yet another Middle East maelstrom. The result is a yeasty mix involvement that may become unavoidable.

SYRIA: THE EYE OF THE STORM

Syria, one of the artifacts of the Versailles Conference of 1919, has been an unstable wild card in the region ever since. Thanks to Sykes-Picot, it was administered by France during the interwar period. Some of its more sympathetic chroniclers maintain that this assignation, which the Syrians did not seek, destroyed any chances of success of a "liberal-Islamic alliance" in what became Syria, and the country has been basically an unstable entity ever since. Syria achieved independence in 1946 and suffered a series of coups among competing ethno-religious groups within the country. In 1958, Syria became a member of the short-lived United Arab Republic with Egypt. Elites in both countries believed they should dominate the union, and it dissolved in 1961, replaced by the Syrian Arab Republic that is still the official name of the country. In 1970, Hafiz al-Assad led the minority Alawite ethnic region to control (although only about 13 percent of the population are Alawite Shiites). Syrians from this region dominated both the military and the civil service in the country. When Hafiz al-Assad died in 2000, he was succeeded by his son Bashar al-Assad, the current president of the country. He still holds that office.

Syria has always represented a radical element in the region. It has been staunchly anti-Israeli and was prominent in the various wars by the Arab states against the Israelis. It and Lebanon share the northern border of Israel and have thus posed a major part of the Israeli security problem. The most visible aspect of that challenge has always been the Golan Heights region of Syria, from which the Syrians historically bombarded settlements in Israel, and it was a primary reason for the Israeli occupation and annexation of the Heights in 1967. Lebanon has been a staging area for anti-Israeli attacks from Hezbollah and other groups, some of which are affiliated with and sponsored by Iran. The Israeli frontier with these two countries has thus been a major point of regional contention, and after the civil war ends in Syria, whoever emerges in control is likely to reignite the dispute over Golan.

The civil war has been the most tragic outcomes of the Arab Spring. That movement started in Tunisia in 2010 as a pro-democratic outpouring primarily led and supported by young people demanding an end to corruption and repression in Muslim states of the region. The initial success of the Tunisian movement emboldened pro-democratic elements in other countries, and it spread like an apparently inexorable force for the rest of 2010 and into early 2011, when it arrived in Syria. Demonstrations broke out across Syria protesting the autocratic rule of Alawite Shiite president Bashar al-Assad, focusing both on the repressive nature of his regime and his failure to enact reforms he had promised when he succeeded his father. Protests were particularly vocal among members of the Sunni majority, which had been in tactical alliance with the Alawite government whereby the regime provided benefits for Sunni businessmen in return for support of the regime.

The precipitating spark for the bloody conflict occurred when teenagers were arrested for spray-painting anti-government slogans on buildings in major cities. Police reacted harshly to the vandalism, arresting fifteen of the protesters. One of the prisoners died suspiciously while incarcerated, and the event ignited protests and anti-government demonstrations among members of the Sunni majority. The situation quickly deteriorated, and hastily assembled Sunni militias took to the streets, where violent clashes broke out with government forces. The "perfect maelstrom" (a term I coined in a 2019 book, *Cases in U.S. National Security*) was set in motion. Its waters continue to spin.

THE CIVIL WAR

The Syrian civil war that has raged since 2011 is arguably the darkest outcome of the Arab Spring. The various elements of the resistance have failed to coalesce in any meaningful way to oppose the Assad government in Damascus and have shown little likelihood of improvement, leading McGurk glumly to conclude, "Assad is not going anywhere. . . . There is no chance that the United States or anyone else will unseat him." The fighting has produced nearly a half million casualties, and roughly half the population of twenty million—almost but about 5 percent of whom say they want to return home and resume their prewar lives—are in either internal or external exile.

Both groups place a significant burden on outsiders: most are in either Lebanon or Jordan, neither of which is well equipped to add their welfare to those of the Palestinian refugees already there. They pose a social and economic burden within the EU countries to which many have fled, as well. No one knows for sure what the final bill will be, but the postwar cost of physical rebuilding will be enormous, universally predicted in the trillions of dollars. Nobody knows who will pick up the tab.

Geopolitics have complicated an already complex situation. The war saw the emergence of ISIS and its campaign beginning in 2014 to create a fundamentalist, Salafist caliphate in eastern Syria and Iraq as a springboard to a broader new Arab empire. Virtually nobody saw this rebirth of Al Qaeda in Iraq (AQI) coming since that organization had been publicly moribund since the Iraqi "awakening" of 2007. ISIS quickly claimed largely unpopulated and marginally productive areas of eastern Syria and into Iraq, at their zenith moving to what many feared was striking distance of Baghdad. In 2014, they seemed an inexorable force and expression of international terrorism that caused occasionally hysterical responses in the West. Fortunately for the rest of the world, the land they conquered (and the populations they terrorized) were largely part of what the inhabitants considered Kurdish land, and the Kurds led the movement that stopped and reversed their campaign of conquest. ISIS has retreated from the global center stage, but it remains a factor lurking in the background that could become a player in postwar Syrian politics.

The geopolitics of intra-Muslim rivalry also come into play. Assuming Assad's government will survive the war's end—which almost all observers predict—the question is how Syria will attempt to recover. There are over ten million internal and external exiles who want to come home, but for many, that means a return to war-caused rubble. Someone will have to pay the bill for rebuilding structures and infrastructure as well as recreating Syria's economic structure. The Syrians themselves cannot undertake the task alone. As McGurk dourly notes, "Since 2011, Syria has had the steepest GDP collapse of any country since Germany and Japan at the end of World War II."

Where does the estimated two trillion dollars needed for the task come from? Under the most favorable conditions, raising that amount of capital would be daunting, and the problem is made even more formidable by the worldwide recession caused by the coronavirus pandemic and expenditures within countries to mitigate its effects.

Geopolitics enter and confound the picture. Despite the 2020 collapse of the oil market, the potential regional source of funding comes from the deep pockets of the conservative Sunni monarchies, but will they come forward? There are barriers. For one thing, most of the money is controlled by very conservative Wahhabis in places like Saudi Arabia. Many of these potential donors were privately ideologically and liturgically sympathetic to ISIS and its "principles," and ISIS has no likely place in rebuilding (or rebuilt) Syria. Will the Wahhabis, many of whom supported ISIS financially, open their checkbooks for a solution that excludes their political progeny? At the same time, the current government is Shiite, and given the state of Islamic power politics, fundamentalist Sunnis cannot be expected to bankroll their enemies. Assad and his potential bankers are in a Mexican standoff on this issue.

Other sources are no more promising. Fellow-Shi'a Iranians would like to help, but strangling American-imposed sanctions inhibit their ability to do so, and their mere effort would be widely condemned (see Chapter 8). The Russians would like to assist Assad, but their economy is tied to petroleum, and most of the wealth it creates is effectively dedicated to keeping Vladimir Putin in power.

Overshadowing the efforts or desires of potential benefactors is the coronavirus (COVID-19) crisis that has dominated the international scene since early 2020. In addition to the worldwide human health crisis the pandemic has caused, it has had enormous domestic and international effects globally. Countries have had to invest enormous sums dealing with the crisis that continues and which will have to be somehow paid for when the crisis abates. The international economic system has also been effectively shut down, and no one knows how long it will take to rebound. Assad is a medical doctor and has acknowledged that the spread of the virus to his country could have catastrophic effects.

Until the pandemic recedes and ceases to be a paralyzing drain on global economic activity, it is thus not clear where the funds can or will come from to fund Syrian recovery. Countries around Syria have reported outbreaks, and it is probably just a matter of time until they appear in Syria. Refugee camps in the country, in which at least half a million reside, are particular areas of concern for the spread of infectious diseases generally, and the Syrian medical community has both been disrupted by the war and is largely involved in treating victims of the war. It is unclear what levels of international assistance will be available to countries like Syria given the uncertainties of the situation. From the perspective of mid-2020, Syria appears to be an odd country out in the hierarchy of dealing with COVID, just adding to the country's general misery index.

THE POST–CIVIL WAR PROSPECTS

The war will end sometime, and the question is what happens next. There are several possible outcomes in the short and longer run, and they become more uncertain the further in the future one projects. Each has different ramifications for countries with interests in Syria and the Middle East generally. In turn, these possibilities impinge on the overall stability and politics of the region, and thus on American interests.

Because the states directly involved in the Syrian conflict are not—other than Israel—major players in global geopolitics, attention to and concern about what is happening in that gravely injured state have retreated from prime international concern partly because the conduct of the war has been so one sided on the ground. Although the Sunni majority that forms the target base of government suppression contains about 70 percent of the Syrian population, they have been incapable of mounting an effective resistance to continued Assad rule, despite the fact that numerous resistance groups have emerged to oppose effective sovereign rule by the Assad regime.

There are effectively three reasons resistance has been ineffective. The first and most obvious when fighting broke out has been the absence of unity or even cooperation among the various Sunni groups opposing Assad. The initial reaction of the United States, for instance, was to provide (Nixon Doctrine–style) aid to the rebels, but the problem was identifying who could be trusted with that aid. When ISIS emerged in 2014, the fear that aid would be captured by them and used both in its campaign of conquest and against the United States, the Americans never provided any real direct military assistance to those opposing Assad.

Second, the emergence of the ISIS threat diverted attention from some of the most vicious, atrocious actions by the government toward its opponents in the early days of the rebellion, including the virtual leveling of parts of Aleppo, the country's largest predominantly Sunni city and even more appallingly, the use of poisonous gas against civilians in urban areas that displayed opposition to the Assad regime. These actions created international appall and heightened calls for regime change, including charges of genocide against Assad and his government that resulted in Assad's indictment for war crimes by the International Criminal Court (ICC) in the Hague. That indictment still stands and will have to be dealt with somehow when the war ends—a nettlesome holdover the ultimate disposition of which is uncertain. The Syrians were provided effective cover for these operations from Russia.

What ultimately diverted public attention away from regime atrocities was the emergence of ISIS as a major player in the region. The Islamic State is the lineal descendant of Al Qaeda in American occupation of Iraq in the early 2000s. It was a Sunni-based organization that operated primarily in the Sunni triangle of Iraq wedged between the Shiite south and the Kurdish north. The area had been the home grounds of most of the Sunni leadership (including Saddam Hussein). In 2007, the Americans convinced enough Sunni tribal leaders to revolt against AQI as part of the Anbar Awakening, after which the Al Qaeda affiliate went apparently dormant and apparently moribund.

The organization minus Zarqawi (who was killed in an American bombing raid in 2006) reappeared as one of the Sunni opposition groups to Assad during the chaotic and unsuccessful attempt to form a united front against him. The United States, seeking Syrian rebel allies to arm, discovered the identity of the movement as AQI reincarnated, and the fear that American assistance might somehow come under AQI control helped inhibit the provision of any aid to the rebels. When AQI began its conquest of eastern Syria and parts of Iraq in 2014, concern for the Syrian war moved to the back burner of regional national security concerns, replaced by the Caliphate threat.

The emergence of ISIS was useful geographically to the Assad government as well. The eastern regions of Syria have not been important to the regime since they are lightly populated, barren, and the source of little economic activity other than the production of oil. The regime has concentrated its efforts on western Syria, which is where most of the population resides and most Syrian commerce and wealth is located. In addition, Mediterranean Syria is where the Alawite region is located and where the Russian naval base at Tartus (the most obvious source of Russian interest in the country) is located. As Western attention moved from the heart of the warfront in the west to territory mostly claimed by the Kurds (about whom the regime had shown marginal concern) in Iraq and western Iraq, the change of attention facilitated Syrian efforts against the various revolutionary factions without much appall after the Assad regime ceased its campaign of chemical attacks. Particularly since 2017, there has been relatively little detailed coverage of the situation on the ground beyond periodic updates of casualty figures. Even with the ISIS threat in apparent (if possibly temporary) abeyance, the international spotlight has apparently moved on as Assad and his allies subdue the remaining opposition.

The demographics of support in the civil war are of continuing relevance; they affect the balance on the ground and provide a harbinger on likely influences on postwar Syria. The Alawite base and other Shiites on which the government military are based constitute a distinct minority of about 15 percent of the population of 21 million, most of the rest being either Sunni Arab (50 percent), Kurds (10 percent), and others, according to figures in the *2020 World Almanac and Book of Facts*. Their control of the military provides the Alawites with a preponderance of force, but that is not enough to explain their dominance in the fighting. The disarray of the opposition and lack of outside support for it from outside helps explain this, but in addition, the government has benefited crucially from military assistance from Russia and from "volunteers" from fellow Shiite state Iran. It is inconceivable that these benefactors are not accumulating "chits" that they will seek to call in when the civil war ends.

INTERNATIONAL RAMIFICATIONS

Several states have an interest in the outcome of the Syrian civil war. Throughout the conflict, most of the tragedy has been physically confined to Syria itself, although it has occasionally reached across the Turkish border, where the Turks are anxious to ensure that its effects do not embolden the Kurds' aspirations to statehood, a cause that has been enhanced by its leading military role in calming the ISIS threat. Other states with a vested interest in the war and its outcome prominently include Syria's neighboring states, Lebanon and Israel, although for different reasons, and other states have greater or lesser interests depending on what kind of Syria emerges from the ashes. Beyond humanitarian concerns (not a high priority during the Trump administration), direct American concerns are largely derivative: the United States has relatively few direct interests in the country, but some outcomes affect countries where it does, notably Israel. There are also larger regional impacts of the outcome largely discussed in the next chapter.

IMPACTS OF OUTCOMES ON REGIONAL ACTORS

The Syrian civil war is rarely examined as an international political, including national security, event, although some of its more important ramifications are in what impact various outcomes have on other actors. The sheer magnitude and scale of human suffering has rightly been the "lead story" regarding the conflict, although the deadly drumbeat has faded as it has dragged on. Once the ISIS threat it seemed to spawn retreated as an immediate problem, so too did concerted concern for the bloodletting, except by humanitarian groups interested in ending the slaughter and figuring out how to rebuild the war-torn country and make it inhabitable for its returning citizens.

There are three major possible outcomes to the conflict. The first, which most observers in 2020 viewed as most likely in the short term, is that the Assad regime will prevail, effectively crushing the organized resistance and reinforcing Assad/Alawite domain in the country. The balance of force, including that provided by outsiders like Iran, Russia, and Hezbollah, clearly supports belief in this outcome, but it is likely that it will be an interim rather than a long-term, stable solution. It is unlikely that any source will come forward with the funding to underwrite the rebuilding of a Syrian state that resembles the pre-2011 country. Funds for such a massive, multi-trillion-dollar endeavor were, as noted earlier, problematical before the world redirected its resources to the COVID pandemic. In the short to medium term, they are essentially nonexistent. The Assad regime will have an exceedingly difficult time escaping the consequences.

The second possible outcome, probably following on the travails of reconstituted, Assad/Alawite rule, will be the evolution (or return) to some form of coalition between the regime and the Sunni majority. Prior to 2011, this was the informal manner by which Syrian politics had been conducted since the 1970 ascent of the Assad regime (father and son): the Alawite-dominated military and government bureaucracy ruled, supported by the majority Sunni businessmen, who formed the economic backbone of the country. Rule was less than democratic, but the regime effectively bought off the business community concentrated in western Syria (especially Aleppo and Damascus) with preferential treatment. This relationship had frayed by 2011, as Sunnis chafed at what they considered excessive authoritarianism by Bashar al-Assad.

The third possibility, and what some observers view as the likely long-term outcome, is the partition of Syria into several sovereign entities. As has been mentioned repeatedly, Syria joined Iraq as an artificial creation of the post–World War I European maneuvering and manipulation, which was reflected in the Sykes-Picot agreement. The country has areas where one group or another is in the majority, making it possible to draw at least a rough map subdividing the current map into three or more jurisdictions. The northern coastline is predominately Alawite and could form a small state; the large center is overwhelmingly Sunni and could be reconfigured as the largest part of the reconfiguration, possibly retaining the Syrian name. The eastern area is heavily Kurdish, and the area they call Rojava has been under their effective control since they expelled the Islamic State from it. There is a Druze minority in the south that might break away as well.

Which of these outcomes eventually prevails affects Syria and those other countries with an interest in it in different ways. The status quo (Assad stays in power) appeals to those who currently benefit from the situation, notably the Alawites internally, their Russian "allies," and the Iranians, fellow Shiites who use parts of the country to launch operations into Israel. An independent Sunni state in central Syria would have a far better position to reach out to the conservative Gulf states than under any other alternative, for instance. Partition would present the Kurds with their best opportunity to declare a Kurdish state, although doing so would create other regional problems, notably with Turkey.

OTHER AFFECTED/INTERESTED STATES

Possible outcomes affect other regional states differentially, and they thus have contrasting preferences for how to restore peace and reconstitute the Syrian polity. No one exults or condones the slaughter that is occurring, and all would presumably prefer the cessation of the violence on terms from which they benefit. They differ substantially on the kind, including composition, of the successor state to the current Syria.

Israel. Among the states with the greatest but least discussed interest is Israel. Of all the regional states, Israel has arguably benefited most from the ongoing chaos because it effectively removes a competitor and opponent on Israel's border in the Golan Heights. Israel has maintained its occupation since 1967 and has annexed that part of the Heights it occupies, but that territory remains contentious. Hezbollah, acting as an ally and surrogate for Iran, continues a campaign to dislodge the Israelis from the occupied zone they have converted into a tourist and vacation attraction (see Chapter 4). Perched on the top of the Heights, the Israelis literally command the high ground and maintain control. This status is unlikely to change until the civil war concludes. The Israelis are moving to become so entrenched that they cannot be removed, completing the assimilation of the territory to Israel, their preferred outcome. The Israeli position on Golan is physically very secure, and that security is made more secure with an ongoing civil war that effectively precludes any concerted Syrian campaign to return Golan to Syrian sovereign control. The possibility that Iran will retain interest in a successor regime or over the regime in a spinoff state adjacent to Syrian Golan is the largest problem the civil war created for the Israelis. Several analysts have suggested that Israeli security is, however, enhanced by an ongoing war. Unlike other neighbors, Israel does not have to deal with the refugee problem the war creates for neighboring states like Lebanon or even European states to which those refugees have fled. The Trump-blessed annexation of Syrian Golan adds to Israeli leverage over the area.

Turkey. The Turks also have a stake in how the war ends. As a mostly Sunni country, the Turks have no sectarian affinity for the Alawite regime in Damascus. The major source of Turkish interest is in the northern Syrian borderland and its Kurdish activists, a concern they expressed forcefully in late 2019 by invading part of the Kurdish area of Syria. The area of their interest is otherwise reasonably inconsequential. The area is lightly populated, and its only real economic importance is that it is the site of the relatively small Syrian oil industry (estimated at producing 14,000 barrels a day in 2015), from which the Turks gain some profit and energy.

The Turks' underlying interest in Syria focuses almost exclusively on the Syrian Kurds. The Kurds are the largest minority group in Turkey (about 18 percent of the total population, most of the rest being ethnic Turks, according to the *CIA World Factbook*). They number nearly 18 million, are the largest Kurdish diaspora in any of the countries in which they live, and they would thus form the largest single population element in a Kurdish state. The Kurds participate in Turkish governance but are also mostly supporters of an independent Kurdistan. The Erdoğan administration in Turkey considers them to be terrorists. The Kurdish area of Turkey is concentrated in the east, especially Anatolia, a valuable tourist area and source of both Turkish water and hydroelectric power. With the Kurdish lands and population removed from their sovereign domain, Turkey is a significantly diminished power.

Given the Kurdish situation in Turkey, the eventual outcome of the civil war on the status of the Kurdish area in northeastern Syria represents the clearest Turkish interest in the war. The Kurds have gained valuable, and apparently successful, experience in governing the areas they reclaimed from ISIS in Rojava and Iraq, and this experience and precedent could easily—and likely—be the springboard for expanding the Kurdish state into other areas. Turk-Kurd animosity combines with nationalism evident among Turkish Kurds to suggest that movement could easily spread across the lengthy border into Turkey. Turkey would (and has) resisted such an incursion with force.

Kurdish-claimed areas of Turkey are thus extremely important to both the Turkish government and the Kurdish nationalist movement. Turkey desperately needs a Syrian government that reasserts both its interest in and intention to control Rojava. The Assad regime has never shown much interest in its least productive region, and if Assad maintains control, it is difficult to see why that would change. The outcome of the Syrian war could thus be the fuse for a major conflict endangering the historic southern flank of NATO.

Lebanon. The Lebanese are caught in the uncomfortable position that seems to be the perpetual fate of this small country. Wedged between Israel and Syria, it has 3,950 square miles of sovereign territory (about one-third the size of Maryland and 170th in area in the world). About six million people live in the country. Ninety-five percent of the population considers itself Arab, 54 percent of whom are Muslim (divided almost evenly between Sunnis and Shi'a), 40.5 percent are Christian, and most of the rest are Druze.

It is politically democratic, with leadership roles (e.g., president, prime minister) allocated to specific religious groups based on demographics established in the 1926 constitution and gradually modified as the original Christian majority has been eclipsed by Muslims. It has historically seen itself as neutral on religious grounds and to preserve the regional political role it has occupied as the financial and investment hub of the Middle East. This historic position and preference have been tested by internal conflict and a war with Israel in 2006.

The Syrian War has affected both Lebanon's stability and prosperity, leaving it on what Shinkman describes as a "high wire tightrope" with "the potential to become an influential partner for Western countries seeking some resolution" to the conflict. Although its role (befitting its size and power) is not central either to the war or its military outcome, Lebanon is both affected by the conflict and could have an important role in the postwar environment.

The refugee problem facing the country is daunting. The numbers change at the margins, but there are approximately a half million Palestinian refugees in the country, some of whom have been there since the foundation of Israel and many of whom live in refugee camps that are underfunded and have been the historic source of discontent and antigovernment activism. In addition, over a million Syrian refugees (1,000,513 in 2016) have fled to Lebanon during the civil war, meaning the total refugee population is about one-quarter the size of the Lebanese citizenry in the physically small land. That burden will not be meaningfully relieved until the civil war ends, including peace terms by which at least the Syrian refugees feel safe to go home.

Partisan issues that affect Lebanon but are not part of the Syrian predicament arise from the war. Some of the most prominent surround the Shiite crescent. Lebanon stands at the western end of that geostrategic area, washing on the eastern shores of the Mediterranean. It also shares a border with Syria and stands as a buffer between Israel and Syria. Lebanon is thus surrounded by Israel and a Shiite-ruled Syrian state and houses Shiite Hezbollah insurgents who use its territory as a base for attacking Israel. This factor in turn causes Israel to move periodically into Lebanon with armed force to attack Hezbollah and has meant Israel and Lebanon are at military odds that sometimes erupts as fighting between them (as in the 2006 war). Given this set of circumstances, it is probably not surprising that the Lebanese government has joined Iran in support of the Assad regime in the civil war. Should the war end with the overthrow of Assad or partition of Syria, the relationship between Lebanon and Syria would be one of the matters that would have to be adjusted. That adjustment could include the possibility of a Kurdish corridor from Syrian Kurdistan/Rojava to the Mediterranean.

More than any other country in the Crescent, Lebanon is a victim and, upon occasion, a pawn of the more powerful states surrounding it. When the country was founded, the hope was that it could be a kind of intercommunal refuge, a place that demonstrated the people in the region could coexist in peace. That has not always been the case, and the result is considerable anxiety and instability in the country. Lebanese feel a sense of victimization, a sentiment vividly demonstrated on August 4, 2020, when a powerful cache of poorly secured ammonium nitrate explosive detonated in a warehouse by the Beirut port, sending a mushroom-shaped cloud of destruction into the sky and killing literally hundreds of Lebanese. Critics like Bazzi blame the accident on the indecisiveness of a fragile political system, in which all sectarian groups have an effective veto over policy decisions.

Russia. Syria is Russia's point of entrée into the Middle East, a part of Vladimir Putin's campaign to return Russia to a position akin to the one it had as the Soviet Union during the Cold War. That effort had limited appeal when Russia was the USSR because of the basic philosophical incompatibility between consciously atheistic communism and highly theistic Islam. Syria, which heralded itself as the leader of so-called "Arab socialism" along with Egypt, was one of the few places where the Russians could gain a foothold, which it reinforced by providing arms for Syrian military efforts against Israel and in return for which the Soviets negotiated their naval base in the Alawite area of Mediterranean Syria—the only Cold War source of permanent Soviet military presence in the region.

The Syrian-Russian relationship fell into disrepair with the implosion of the Soviet Union in 1991 and did not revive during the political turmoil of the 2000s in Russia. The spark that reignited Russian interest in its Muslim fellow traveler was the ascension of Vladimir Putin to power in 2012. One of his major goals was to return Russia to the international status it enjoyed as the Soviet Union. The vehicle has been Russian involvement in the evolving Syrian civil war in support of Assad. The Russians remain the most prominent nonregional actor in that war on that basis, and are, in the view of many outside observers like Erlich, "the only clear winners" in the situation. That status will, however, be tested once the fighting ends because Russia will almost certainly be either unable or unwilling to bear much of the cost of recovery reconstruction, and all other potential sources (e.g., the West, the Gulf States) oppose the Russian presence.

Putin's regime has, however, become the most prominent nonregional source of support for a Syria that has largely been isolated from most of the non–Middle Eastern international system. The extreme violence and brutality of the regime's campaign to suppress or eliminate the opposition has played a major part in this reaction. Highly publicized and condemned elements of the campaign include the virtual leveling of sizable urban centers—mostly Sunni areas in places like Aleppo—and has been a major point of condemnation, but the most egregious alleged acts have involved the use of poison gas against urban elements in some of these cities (these actions have been at the heart of ICC accusations of war crimes against Assad).

The Russians have both participated in some Syrian government actions and defended the Assad regime in international fora. The Russians have provided arms to the government, and Russian air assets have engaged in support of the bombing of rebel-held enclaves and civilian areas. When condemnations of the government have been introduced in places like the UN Security Council, the Russians have protected their allies by vetoing the resolutions.

Russia is clearly betting heavily on Assad's defeat of the insurgency and retention of political power to secure its two major interests in the country. The first of these, of course, is to reinforce a physical, military presence in the country and the region. The large naval base at Tartus has been a symbol of Russian military reach since the Cold War as well as the only Russian military presence in the area. That presence has widened and deepened with continuing Russian aid to Assad and the connection between the Assad and Putin regimes. Second, Syria is about the only place in the region (other than those former Soviet republics that border the Middle East) where the Russians have a political presence, which is clearly part of Putin's goal of reestablishing Russia's global status. Russia thus has a sizable stake in the Assad regime and is counting on its continuing tenure in the country to maintain a Middle East presence. It has been attempting to improve relations with Turkey, a traditional rival, and it has been economically and militarily generous, at least by Russian standards, in supporting the Assad regime.

But what happens when the shooting stops and the rebuilding begins? Making Syria whole again is going to be a multi-trillion-dollar enterprise that possible donors who need that money for pandemic recovery will be reluctant to commit to Syria, and Russia can be of limited assistance. Can Assad survive if he cannot find funding for the enterprise? If funding must come from the Gulf monarchies, would a commitment of those resources require jettisoning the Russians? Assad is left with a devil's choice. If he cannot stay in power without turning away from the Russians, where is the source of funding he needs to maintain his military, without which he is in a very vulnerable situation? If he keeps the Russians, will the war restart? The Russians have no interest (beyond remaining relevant) to fund an endless continuation of the civil war, so what do they do? Do they abandon Syria to facilitate other rebuilding funds becoming available to the Assad government? Russia's foothold is much more secure while the civil war continues than it will be after it is over.

Iran. Iran is the wild card in Syria. As the only state in the region whose Muslim population is virtually entirely Shiite and whose population is almost entirely non-Arab (the ethnicity of most of its citizens is Persian), it has a long history as the world's second oldest civilization. In regional terms, it is the second largest state (behind Saudi Arabia), with an area of over 636,237 square miles (2.5 times the size of Texas and about the size of Alaska). Its population is over 82 million, exceeded regionally only by Pakistan and Egypt, neither of which is a major player in the part of the Middle East politics discussed here. Sitting at the top of the Persian (or Arabian) Gulf, it also is among world leaders in global oil reserves. By any measure, Iran is a country that cannot be ignored in Middle Eastern politics, including those surrounding Syria.

Iran has a special place in the regional politics of endless war for two reasons. First, it is "different" than other Middle Eastern countries. It has the largest non-Arab population in the region, along with the Turks, and when this distinction is combined with its adherence to the Shiite interpretation of Islam, it is markedly distinct from those states that are nominally Arab and who practice the dominant Sunni sect of Islam. Iraq forms a transition between the two characteristics: it is roughly two-thirds Shiite (and the holiest symbols of Shiism at Najaf and Karbala that are that sect's version of Sunni Mecca in Saudi Arabia).

Iran also has a special place in regional and international geopolitics. Iran's military was partially developed under the tutelage of the United States during its quarter-century of the Shah's rule, and should it exercise the nuclear option (see Chapter 3), it would be the dominant military force in the region. This potential makes the Iranians the principal regional problem for both the Israelis (whose policy toward the occupied territories puts it at odds with Jerusalem) and the Saudis, who entertain dreams of regional hegemony and are locked in a rivalry with the Iranians (see Chapter 7). In these circumstances the cooperation between the Israelis and Saudis makes much more sense than does their historical relationship, which is highly conflictual.

Iran is a leading world example of what I referred to in the 2015 edition of *Cases in International Relations* as a "pivotal state." Such states are not as powerful as the strongest members of the international system (e.g., the Soviets and Americans during the Cold War), but they are the most prominent states within their geographic regions and generally expect to be accorded major power status. The problem often arises when these states interact with a larger power that has become interested in their "turf." In this situation, the regional power is likely to be offended by this intrusion, and the result can be a rocky relationship between them. The post-1945 relationship between the United States and Iran is a primary example and helps frame the international politics of the region and American policy in it.

The postwar history of Iran, especially with the United States, is distinct. Iran as Persia is one of the world's oldest civilizations, and a return to Persian greatness is never far beneath the surface in dealings between Iran and its rivals like Saudi Arabia, which only became an independent state in 1933. In the period since World War II, much of Iran's regional prominence has centered on its schizophrenic relationship with the United States.

Iran and the United States first interacted during World War II as part of the Allied effort to deny German access to Middle Eastern oil, a role reprised after the war when the Soviets also tried to incur on Gulf oil by gaining influence in Iran. The Americans and others resisted, and in the process, the United States developed a taste for Middle Eastern petroleum, and this led it to an interest in Iran. After the Shah was overthrown in 1950, the United States (see Kinzer) led the forces that overthrew his successor, Muhammad Mossadegh (the only fully democratically elected history in Iranian history) and reinstalled Reza Pahlavi to the Peacock throne in 1953. The two countries were the closest of friends until 1979: the Shah guaranteed the unimpeded flow of oil westward, and the Americans developed and Westernized Iran. Ultimately, conservative Shiites were outraged by Westernization and overthrew the Shah in 1979, in the process evicting the Americans. The superpower and the pivotal state have been antagonists ever since.

CHOOSING POLICY: IMPACTS ON THE UNITED STATES

The United States has not been a major player in the evolving geopolitics of the Syrian civil war. The American government has never been a major supporter of the Assads, and the antipathy is mutual. During the Cold War, American regimes condemned the close relations between the Syrians and the Soviets, the primary sore thumb of which was the Tartus naval base, which gave the Soviets a military foot in the Middle Eastern door. When fighting broke out in 2011, the United States was initially drawn to support the Syrian opposition, but it faced two problems that were augmented by evolving conditions and related regional concerns. Neither the Obama nor the Trump administration were predisposed to involve American power in any major way, and both succeeded in avoiding a major intervention politically or militarily. The situation has, however, evolved as the war has dragged on.

The initial U.S. response was twofold and at least partly contradictory. The first element was a mixture of horror and appall at the brutal repression Assad inflicted on Syrians who protested the harsh retributions and suppressions the government meted out to those protesting the actions taken against the original protests of early 2011. The Obama administration expressed appall and sought natural allies in the emerging resistance whom they could aid. The disarray and incoherence of the anti-Assad response made finding a reliable side to back impossible. The second response was a very public resolve not to involve American forces in the fighting. On the heels of recently concluded adventures in Iraq and the ongoing conflict in Afghanistan (see Chapter 9), this decision was clearly dictated by the "endless war" fear.

The effects have paralyzed and limited America's role in Syria ever since. They have defined American policy as peripheral: the United States is appalled by the situation and especially the Assad government's reaction to it, but it is personally unwilling to take a lead role in ending the fighting or punishing the war criminals. There was an uptick in that involvement when ISIS was expanding physically. Some American politicians argued that the Caliphate's success could lead to increased terrorism against U.S. soil (a prospect that has not publicly been demonstrated). This interest was most openly directed at arming and supporting the Kurds in their eviction of ISIS from Kurdish-claimed lands.

The United States remains a limited participant in the conflict. If projections are accurate, the United States will not react strongly if Assad retains power, leaving the struggle over postwar Syria to be conducted by Syrian elements, outsiders like Turkey, Russia, and even Iran, and influenced by those with vested interests in one neighbor like Lebanon or Israel rather than the United States. It is a self-limited American role.

Do you think this is the correct path for the United States? While essentially no one advocates a major intrusion by the Americans in the area, there are clearly impacts that the outcome will enshrine. Will Russia emerge as the prime extra-regional actor? Or Turkey? Will a weakened or dissected Syria create a weaker opponent that will encourage Israeli annexation of additional areas, with negative reactions in the Islamic world? Will Syria simply dissolve into several states, and what will that mean?

Some of these possibilities are explored in the next chapter. There is no consensus on what any of them portends, and you are not expected to know the answers. The question that can be addressed is whether the comparatively passive role of the United States in this crisis serves or deserves American interests in the region. Should the United States be more involved than it is in the consequences of how the Syrian war ends? Why or why not?

BIBLIOGRAPHY

Andelman, David A. *A Shattered Peace: Versailles 1919 and the Price We Pay Today*. New York: Wiley 2014.

Anderson, Scott. *Lawrence in Arabia: War, Deceit, Imperial Folly and the Making of the Modern Middle East*. New York: Anchor Books, 2013.

Anson, Andrew. *Lebanon: A Country in Fragments*. London: Hurst, 2018.

Bazzi, Mohamad. "The Corrupt Political Class That Broke Lebanon." *Foreign Affairs* (online), August 23, 2020.

Berdine, Michael D. *Redrawing the Middle East: Sir Mark Sykes, Imperialism and the Sykes-Picot Agreement*. London: I. B. Tauris, 2018.

Central Intelligence Agency. *CIA World Factbook, 2019-2020*. Washington, DC: Skyhorse Publishing, 2019.

Cooper, Tom. *Syrian Conflagration: The Syrian Civil War, 2011–2013.* London: Helion and Company, 2016.

Dagher, Sam. *Assad or We Burn the Country: How One Family's Power Destroyed Syria.* Boston, MA: Little, Brown and Company, 2019.

Erlich, Reese. "In Syria, Russia Is the Only Winner." *Foreign Policy* (online), October 30, 2019.

Eytain, Freddy, and Yossi Kuperwasser. *The Failures of the International Community Since the Sykes-Picot Agreement, 1916–2016.* Jerusalem: Jerusalem Center for Public Affairs, 2016.

Farha, Mark. *Lebanon: The Rise and Fall of a Secular State Under Siege.* Cambridge, UK: Cambridge University Press, 2019.

Fisk, Robert. *The Great War for Civilisation: The Conquest of the Middle East.* London: Fourth Estate, 2014.

Friedman, Thomas L. *From Lebanon to Jerusalem.* New York: Farrar, Straus and Giroux, 2010.

Fromkin, David. *A Peace to End All Wars: The Fall of the Ottoman Empire and the Creation of the Modern Middle East.* 20th Anniversary Ed. New York: Holt Paperbacks, 2010.

Harris, William. *Lebanon: A History, 600-2011.* Oxford, UK: Oxford University Press, 2012.

Kerr, Robert M. (ed.). *Syrian Civil War: The Essential Reference Guide.* New York: ABC-CLIO, 2020.

Khatib, Lina. "Bashar al-Assad's Hollow Victory: Subservient to Profiteers, the Syrian Regime Is Weaker than Ever." *Foreign Affairs* (online), January 17, 2020.

Kinzer, Stephen. *The Brothers: John Foster Dulles, Allen Dulles, and Their Secret World War.* New York: Times Books, 2013.

Lederer, Edith M. "UN Warns of Potential Coronavirus Tragedy in Syria." *Times of Israel* (online), April 30, 2020.

Levitt, Matthew. *Hezbollah: The Global Footprint of Lebanon's Party of God.* Washington, DC: Georgetown University Press, 2015.

McGurk, Brett. "Hard Truths in Syria: America Can't Do More and It Shouldn't Try." *Foreign Affairs* 98, 3 (May/June 2019), 69–84.

Metlugo, John. *Syria: A Recent History.* London: Saqi Books, 2001.

Nour, Ayman Abdel. "How Trump Can End the War in Syria: Putin and Erdogan Are Finally Ready to Negotiate." *Foreign Affairs* (online), April 26, 2020.

Phillips, Christopher. *The Battle for Syria: International Rivalry in the New Middle East.* New Haven, CT: Yale University Press, 2016.

Provence, Michael. *The Last Ottoman Generation and the Making of the Modern Middle East.* Cambridge, UK: Cambridge University Press, 2017.

Rogan, Eugene. *The Fall of the Ottomans: The Great War in the Middle East.* New York: Basic Books, 2015.

Shinkman, Paul D. "Lebanon's Precarious Place in the Syria War." *US News* (online), April 16, 2018.

Simon, Sykes Christopher. *The Man Who Created the Middle East: A Story of Empire, Conflict, and the Sykes-Picot Agreement.* London: William Collins, 2016.

Snow, Donald M. *Cases in U.S. National Security: Concepts and Processes.* Lanham, MD: Rowman & Littlefield, 2019.

———. "Pivotal States: Confronting and Accommodating Iran," Chapter 7 (pp. 125–44) in *Cases in International Relations.* Sixth Ed. New York: Pearson, 2015.

Thompson, Elizabeth F. *How the West Stole Democracy from the Arabs: The Syrian Arab Conference of 1920 and the Destruction of Its Liberal-Islamic Alliance.* New York: Atlantic Monthly Press, 2020.

Traboulski, Fawwaz. *A History of Modern Lebanon.* Second Ed. London: Pluto Press, 2012.

Van Dam, Nikolaus. *Destroying a Nation: The Civil War in Syria.* London: I. B. Tauris, 2016.

Waterbury, John. "Middle East." *Foreign Affairs* 993 (May/June 2020), 210–212.

World Almanac and Book of Facts. New York: Infobase, 2020.

Yassin-Kassab, and Leila el-Shami. *Burning Country: Syrians in Revolution and War.* New Ed. London: Pluto Press, 2018.

7

The Chaotic Shiite Crescent
Iran, Iraq, Syria, Lebanon

The outcome of the Syrian civil war is particularly important for those countries wedged between the Turkish north and the Arab south in the Middle East. What has become known as the Shiite Crescent is composed of those countries between the Mediterranean Sea on the west and Iran as the eastern anchor between Turkey, Israel, and the Arab states. The designation "Shiite" Crescent refers to the existence of countries (Iraq, Syria, and Lebanon) that have significant but not majority Shiite populations; only Iran is virtually exclusively Shiite. It is a crescent because the member states curl around parts of the historical Levant, from Lebanon through Syria and Iraq down into the Arabian Peninsula. Lebanon is at the western tip of the crescent; Bahrain is at its eastern and southern end. Its shape is inverted like a waning moon.

The Crescent area has been the seat of considerable instability and sporadic violence for some time. Because two of its states (Lebanon and Syria) are on Israel's border, there has been violence whenever supporters of the Palestinians headquartered in one of those countries (e.g., Hezbollah) attacks into Israel and the Israelis retaliate. The war between Lebanon and Israel in 2006 is a particularly vivid example, particularly since the Israeli Defense Force has some difficulty dispatching guerrillas employing asymmetrical warfare methods. The two major artificial, dysfunctional states in the region (Iraq and Syria) are prominent parts of Crescent instability. Looming at the eastern end of the Crescent are the Iranians, for whom leadership of the Crescent countries is clearly a major underlying part of their desire to expand their role as a regional pivotal state and because of an affinity between its post-1979 leadership and militant Palestinians. The brief and possibly resurgent influence of the Islamic State as a Crescent disrupter lurks not far in the background.

The Syrian civil war and its outcome is an obviously crucial element in the evolution of the geopolitics of the Crescent. Extra-Crescent Russia, Turkey, and Iran are important variables in that outcome based on their size, location, and interests in the region. The Kurds are among the non-Shiite elements in the region, and their interests in constructing a viable (i.e., nonlandlocked) Kurdistan could be vitally affected by what happens to postwar Syria. In addition, the balance between Sunni and Shiite power in the Crescent is affected by the fate of ISIS, which has remained in the geopolitical background since it was driven from power, but continues to have support and to represent many Sunnis in Iraq and to a lesser degree Syria. For better or worse for the Syrian people, how the war ends and its aftermath affect more people than just the Syrians. Major traumatic events have helped shape the ongoing landscape and will doubtless affect the political shape of the Crescent after a settlement is established in Syria.

AN OVERVIEW OF THE CRESCENT CONCEPT: THE REGION

The designation of a Shiite Crescent is a historically recent construct, and most Americans are either unfamiliar with the concept or its substance. The physical crescent, of course, is one of the major symbols of Islam, and thus the crescent is a common enough idea that it is attached to many phenomena in the Muslim world. As a geopolitical construct impinging on the volatility of the contemporary Middle East and how it may impinge in profound ways on the outcome of the Syrian Civil War, it has become a potentially crucial part of the regional geopolitical maelstrom. One cannot fully understand the political machinations of the region without taking the Crescent into account.

The term was first used by King Abdullah II of Jordan in 2004 in response to accusations of Iranian interference in the affairs of other Shia-dominated or -influenced countries. Wikipedia, borrowing from a 2008 *NBC News* interview, quotes the king's assessment of that influence. "If it was a Shiite-led Iraq that had a special relationship with Iran, and you look at that relationship with Syria and Hezbollah-Lebanon, then we have this new Crescent that appears that would be very destabilizing for the Gulf countries and actually for the whole region." The Crescent, in other words, occupies a significant physical and intellectual place in the contemporary area. Definitions of the Crescent are imprecise. Originally, it referred to countries or areas with a significant Shiite population—where Shia are in a physical majority or influential minority. All are areas where the Iranians have or are seeking to establish premier influence based in Shiite theology. Countries generally considered parts of the Crescent include (alphabetically) Azerbaijan,

Bahrain, Iran, Iraq, Lebanon, Syria, and Yemen. Not all citizens of these countries embrace the designation or its policy implications. Other regional states with significant Shia minorities include Saudi Arabia, Turkey, India, Pakistan, and the United Arab Emirates. As a practical matter, Iran, Iraq, Syria, and Lebanon are the Crescent areas where the geopolitical "action" centers, most of it originating in Iran.

The Iranians are the overwhelming force in the creation and dynamics of a Crescent that symbolizes the great change in Iranian international activity since the Iranian Revolution of 1979 and the emergence of a militantly successor regime to that of the basically secular rule of the Shah of Iran. The region, including its primary actors, is a remarkably diverse area, as Table 7.1 indicates. By essentially any of the measures depicted in the table, Iran is the largest and most powerful of the major Crescent states. Israel is the object of much of the common Iranian-led geopolitical activities, and so its comparative characteristics are displayed, as well, as a point of contrast.

Table 7.1. Characteristics of Major Shiite Crescent States

Size	Iran	Iraq	Lebanon	Syria	Israel
Area	636,372[1]	438,317	4,015	71,498	8,019
	19th[2]	60th	169th	90th	153rd
Population (in millions)	84.9	48.1	5.49	19.35	8.67
GDP/Capita	$20,100	$16,700	$19,600	$3,300	$36,400
	89th	107th	91st	194th	55th
People[3]					
Ethnicity	Persian	Arab 75–80	Arab 94	Arab 50	Jewish 75
	Azeri	Kurds 15–20	Armenian 4	Alawite 13	Arab 21
	Kurd			Other 37	
Religion	Shia 90–95	Shia 64–69	Shia 30.5	Sunni 74	Jewish 75
	Sunni 5–10	Sunni 29–34	Sunni 30.6	Shia 13	Muslim 18
			Xian 33.7	Xian 10	Xian 2
Politics					
Govt.	Theocratic R.	Fed. Parl. Rep.	Parl. Rep.	Pres. Rep.	Parl. Demo.
Govt. Head	Rohani	Abdak-Mahdi	Hasan Diab	Bashar al-Assad	B. Netanyahu
	2013[4]	2018	2019	2000	2009

Source: CIA World Factbook, 2010-2021. New York: Skyhorse Publications, 2020.
[1] In square miles
[2] Rank in world
[3] In percentages
[4] Year assumed power

The first two categories of the table display indicators of the physical size of the major states in terms of territorial and population sizes. The geographic measures are reasonably precise, although there are disputes that affect them, such as disagreements over things like occupied lands. If the land claimed as part of Kurdistan is subtracted from the relevant states (all but Lebanon), the numbers are diminished, but rankings remain largely unchanged (see Chapter 5). Population sizes change marginally based on the accounting of disputed territories (e.g., occupied parts of Golan). Given the refugee problem and flow, the numbers for Syria are the most problematic and will probably change when the war ends. Because of size, Iran is clearly the dominant member, with an area half again that of Iraq, the next largest state, and a population over twice that of the Iraqi state. By most measures, Syria is the third largest state, followed by Israel and Lebanon. These measures basically hold for the economic metric, gross domestic product (GDP) per capita (a measure that approximates comparative well-being). Israel leads the economic comparison, followed by Iran, Lebanon, Iraq, and Syria, the latter's numbers skewed by the effects of the civil war.

Population characteristics are more diverse and complicated in ways that make it difficult to typify what being a part of the Crescent means and that makes relations between them more difficult than they might otherwise be. Three of the states have ethnically Arab majorities (Iraq, Lebanon, and Syria), while the two most geopolitically consequential states, Iran and Israel, do not. Both are racially distinct from the Arabs and historically have considered the Arabs (people who trace their origins to the Arabian Peninsula) foes. It is noteworthy that they are the two regional states around which most controversy and conflict swirl. Among the identified Crescent states, only Iran's profile in the 2020–2021 *CIA World Factbook* contains no mention of Arabs as an ethnic group, and this is a reason Teheran places an emphasis on Shi-ism in its regional appeal. Among states in the table, only Iran and Iraq have Shiite majorities, joining Bahrain in that distinction.

There are economic and political differences as well. Despite crippling American sanctions, Iran has the highest GDP per capita, followed by Lebanon and Iraq. Due to the impact of a decade of civil war, the Syrian economy has largely been destroyed and will require massive rehabilitation, as noted in Chapter 6. Israel is by far the wealthiest state in the region at $36,400 GDP per capita, although that figure ranks only fifty-fifth worldwide. Among the Crescent states, only Lebanon is listed as democratic, and its head of government, Hasan Diab, has been in power only since the end of 2019. Iran's "theocratic republic" (the *CIA World Factbook*'s designation) is headed by Hassan Rohani, who has ruled since 2015, Iraq's "federal parliamentary republic" has been led by Adil Abdal-Mahdi since 2018, and Syria's "presidential republic" has had Bashar al-Assad as president since 2000. Benjamin Netanyahu has been prime minister of Israel's "parliamentary democracy" since 2009.

LANDMARK EVENTS

Less attention has historically been given to the Shiite Crescent as a distinct geopolitical space than to other dynamics of the Middle East. There are probably two basic reasons for this. One is that, as a region, it has been comparatively tranquil during the 2010s. The major protagonists in or abutting on the Crescent region have been Israel and its neighbors, but since the brief 2006 invasion of southern Lebanon by the Israelis, overt Israeli-Arab conflict in the area has been relatively subdued as the attention of the Crescent countries has been turned inward or otherwise away from that source of conflict. The nuclear-armed government of Netanyahu has systematically sought to solidify its hold over the territories it has occupied to the point of making its acquisitions virtually irreversible. The multiple events in Syria have kept that country in the geopolitical spotlight, but as a discreet rather than as a Crescent phenomenon. The other reason is that the instabilities and violence that have plagued the region have not been thought of as problems of the Crescent as such. Iran seems a problem to many regional and other powers and notably the United States, but the context is rarely conceptualized in terms of the geographic Crescent region but as a part of protecting Israel. Much is going on in the Crescent; the dynamics of that area are rarely given much credit or blame for what happens.

These dynamics are, however, important in and of themselves and because of their wider effects. One reason for embracing the idea is because it announced to the world that the Middle East is not exclusively a Sunni Arab area; it includes both a non-Arab and non-Sunni element that must be considered as well. The leading proponent of these characteristics is, of course, Iran, and it is no secret that the post-1980 Iranians have been the sponsors, organizers, and enthusiasts of the Crescent concept. Since Iran aspires to an expanded regional role as the pivotal Middle Eastern power, geopolitics blends in with the general Shiite promotion theme. Those who fear Iranian expansionism and assertion thus treat the Crescent idea with a sense of jaundice that goes well beyond sectarian rivalry.

The individual countries and the overall region have, of course, been buffeted by the several sources of international upheaval that have complicated the relations of the general Middle East. No list is comprehensive, and individual events and trends affect the member states in different ways. There was, for instance, virtually no discussion of anything like a Shiite region before the latter 1970s, when events leading to the overthrow of the Shah activated regional awareness of Shiism as a major component of regional politics. Now the resultingly expanded Iranian presence is a routine part of geopolitical calculi partly because Iran has dominated Crescent politics.

The thread of events and influences that has produced the current interest in the Crescent began with the 1967 war. Israel's stunning victory in the Six-Day War began the process—along with the recognition of its nuclear acquisition the next year—and established Israel as a dominant force, not as a besieged victim. The occupation Israel undertook on the West Bank and Golan changed the physical map of the western Mediterranean, and additional Israeli actions have made the western Crescent a much more integral part of the overall pattern of Middle Eastern conflict than it previously had been. After the Iranian Revolution and the rising militance it infused in Iranian politics, it also accentuated Iranian-supported anti-Israeli elements in Lebanon and thus created a role in the military geopolitics of the area for the Lebanese.

The Iranian Revolution of 1979 ultimately created a new assertiveness among the Iranians that is an important continuing emphasis of Iranian foreign policy. Part of that change, as discussed in the next chapter, has been directed at the Saudis and part in support of revolutionary elements in the region through relationships with movements like Hezbollah in Lebanon and the Alawite Shiite regime in Syria. In the process, Iranian expansionism moved westward from Iran and Iraq into the western end of the Crescent in Syria and Lebanon. As Iranian activism was building, Sunni militants seized the Grand Mosque in Mecca, Saudi Arabia, in November/December of the same year. The Iranian revolution and the Saudi response to the Mosque crisis helped shape the confrontation between the two countries that has been a major regional characteristic of the region, highlighted in Chapter 8.

The public emergence of international religiously based terrorism in 2001 added regional volatility and set in motion new forces and actors in the region. The most obvious addition to the mix was the United States as the direct victim of the 9/11 terrorist attacks by Al Qaeda (AQ). The United States had been a politico-military collaborator with Iran prior to the revolution, but that role changed to protection of oil access previously secured by the Shah from the new regime that, among other things, seized and occupied the American embassy in Teheran for 444 days. Once the hostage crisis was resolved, relations were broken with Iran, and the United States moved to an oil route–protecting role that placed it in close alignment with the Gulf oil states—and especially Saudi Arabia. In the process, it created a de facto alignment with the Sunni states that had most of the petroleum. It returned in force in 1990 when Iraq invaded and occupied Kuwait and stood menacingly at the Saudi border, a short dash from the oil industry that the Saudis could not protect by themselves. The result was Operation Desert Storm, which ended with Iraqi banishment from Kuwait.

The terrorist attacks of 9/11 had an enormous impact on U.S. national security policy in the region, expanding that presence from a mandate to protect the American and Allied oil supply to a question of national security from attack. The response has largely framed U.S. policy since, augmented by a strong tilt toward Israel since 2017.

The reaction to the carnage and rubble was swift and emotional. President George H. W. Bush ascended the rubble in lower Manhattan and strongly pronounced the intention of his administration to bring the AQ perpetrators to justice. AQ, many of whose members and leaders had been part of the resistance to the Soviet occupation of Afghanistan in the 1980s, had planned the attacks from safe havens on Afghan soil and enjoyed a protected status from the Taliban government that held power in Kabul. They denied U.S. demands to surrender AQ and its leader Osama bin Laden to American custody, and the United States replied with a failed physical intrusion when the Afghans refused to remand the perpetrators to U.S. control. The United States is still in that country. In 2003, accusations circulated through the government that the Iraqi government of Saddam Hussein was somehow cooperating with AQ and might provide the terrorists with nuclear or chemical weapons. These accusations have never been authenticated, but helped provide the rationale for invading Iraq, a commitment from which the United States has yet totally to extract itself. Much of the argument about endless wars has its genesis in this period.

One of the most striking and arguably anomalous features of the post-9/11 period is that it did not include a negative reaction to Saudi Arabia or a detailed examination of who in that country may have had a role in the attack. The Saudis and the Americans had long been petroleum-based partners, and the United States led the defense of Saudi oil assets in 1990. At the same time, the AQ-Saudi connection was manifest. Bin Laden is a Saudi (his family immigrated from Yemen), and seventeen of the twenty-one terrorists involved in the 9/11 attack were Saudi nationals. These facts were not publicized in 2001 and have only become widely known in very recent years. One can only speculate how or whether the trajectory of U.S. national security preferences in the region might have been different had they been.

The Arab Spring seemed to offer a ray of hope in the more byzantine and arguably medieval politics of the region. It began as a series of uprisings in Tunisia largely led by students demanding an end to autocratic rule in Muslim countries and advocating democratization of their country. The Tunisian movement was initially quite successful and extracted major concessions from the country's rulers. Emboldened by this success, the Spring movement spread across northern Africa to the Atlantic Ocean and eastward as far as Iraq. As already noted, one of the places where it gained traction was in Syria in the form of demands against the Assad regime, and it was the regime's brutal repression of Arab Spring supporters that helped lead to the civil war.

The Arab Spring was widely applauded in the West and especially by the Obama administration in an area where political participation has traditionally been limited to elites, normally embracing religious precepts and deeply opposed to and suspicious of populist appeals. Despite its early appearance of promise, the Spring's record of instituting more representative governance was, at best, mixed. Arab Spring movements did result in regime change in a few regional states like Tunisia, Libya, Yemen, and Egypt, but not all these were positive in the long run. The Egyptians, for instance, managed to force eighty-four-year-old Hosni Mubarak from the presidency, but the country has been in such chaos since that it is no longer the major regional power it had historically been. Movements in other countries were repressed: in Bahrain, Sudan, and most importantly for present purposes, Syria. It has largely receded as a force in the politics of the Middle East. Its most lasting monument may be the ongoing chaos in Syria.

The promise of the Arab Spring was replaced by the spectacular introduction of the Islamic State (IS). The IS emerged in 2014 as the reincarnation of Al Qaeda in Iraq (AQI) as part of the Sunni resistance to the Assad regime. It quickly escaped that tether and began its rampage across northeastern Syria and into the Kurdish and Sunni regions of Iraq, coming within a shockingly close distance of the Iraqi capital of Baghdad. Its militant Salafism was intent on reestablishing the caliphate and raised fears of its terrorist intentions toward the West and the overthrow of regimes in the Crescent, notably Shi'a majority countries like Iraq. Western, including American, aid flowed into the region in response. Much of this assistance was acquired by the Kurdish pesh merga, on whose lands many of the IS atrocities were focused. These Kurdish territorial militias were successful in turning the military tide and causing an IS retreat.

The shadow of IS remains part of Crescent dynamics. First, its success would have radically altered the map of the Crescent, particularly in anti-Shia terms (the IS credo is militantly fundamentalist Sunni). IS has retreated but could revive, a specter with major intra-Muslim implications. Second, IS and the campaign against it enlivened the movement surrounding Kurdish statehood, as discussed in Chapter 5, and its return would have an impact on that aspect of Crescent dynamism. Third, IS could act as a stimulus for broader territorial, religious change. As noted in Chapter 2, the overall region has been analogized with the chaotic change of the Thirty Years' War in Europe, and the resurgence of IS in the Crescent could exacerbate a similar process. Fourth, IS represents the basic anomaly of the Saudi position in the region. Private Wahhabi citizens in the kingdom were almost certainly a primary source of IS funding and recruitment, but as the 1979 Mosque crisis revealed, the Saudi political-religious establishment opposes evangelical, and especially Salafist, interlopers who might challenge its national and regional position. Thus, the survival and revival of IS ultimately is a problem for the Saudis as well as virtually everyone else.

THE CRESCENT AND U.S. INTERESTS

As first introduced in Chapter 1, interests are a bedrock concept in determining and guiding a country's foreign policy. Controversy arises because different observers view what is and is not in the national interest differently and because they place contrasting assessments on how important the pursuit and achievement of those interests are to national priorities and ultimately safety. Because of those kinds of assessments, people advocate different, and often contradictory, views of what policy should be and how to react to events. These determinations are always difficult and contentious. In an area like the Crescent, making and reconciling interests is made more difficult because there are multiple sovereign actors with contrasting visions that must somehow be reconciled, and where any given advocacy and outcome may have negative or unpredictable impacts on others. If this sounds complicated and even confusing, the reason is that it is both.

The kerfuffle between President Donald J. Trump and his former National Security Advisor (NSA) John Bolton, revealed in his 2020 book about his White House experience, illustrates some of this context. The two men come from widely varying backgrounds. Although they are nearly the same age (Trump was 74, Bolton 71 in 2020), they have very different backgrounds and experiences. Trump was a real estate developer and entertainer with no foreign policy experience or known interests before running for president; Bolton has been a national security advisor to presidents dating back to George H. W. Bush and has held various positions in Republican administrations since. Bolton self-describes himself in his 2020 book as a conservative Republican whose philosophy predisposes him to a pro-military orientation toward matters of national interests, both in terms of content and solution. Trump's pre-presidential national security orientation is less clear but was less militarily oriented.

These differences were reflected in how the two men approached American interests in the Crescent. Bolton argued that the United States has important interests in the region that he does not go so far as to typify as vital but as crucial enough to require a continuing military commitment to Syria, for instance. He emphasized opposition to Iran and minimizing Russian presence and influence as priorities. Trump entered office as an effective dove regarding the Crescent who bemoaned the problem of "endless war" and thus downplayed an American military role. He vowed to extricate American forces from the region, a position Bolton found inappropriate and dangerous. Trump's major Crescent-related interest was in Israel and in assisting the Netanyahu policy of expanding Greater Israel through actions like moving the U.S. Embassy to Jerusalem and recognizing the annexation of territory by Israel (positions Bolton basically endorsed). Bolton's basic purview included a belief there are sufficient U.S. interests in the region generally that the United States must retain some forces there to protect those interests. Trump's view was more parochial and confined to support for Israel's continuing expansionism.

How do these contrasting positions relate to the traditional troika of U.S. interests as they are applied to the Crescent? The events that have had an impact on the Crescent have affected the United States in different ways, and their cumulative effect has been a receding of American activism and influence in the region. Part of the reason is that the Crescent has historically not been a major concern in terms of the three pillars of American regional policy. Because Israel is contiguous to two Crescent states (Lebanon and Syria), the Crescent is of some interest in American policy because of support for the Jewish state, but it is a problem the Israelis have largely nullified since 1967. Lebanese Hezbollah fighters are an annoyance to Israel but not a basic threat. Access to Persian Gulf oil has never been an important concern from the Crescent with the limited exception of Iranian interference with the flow of that oil through the Persian Gulf. Syria provided a foothold for the Soviets in the Crescent and for Russia today, but the degree of that threat is debatable. The reluctance of the United States to become directly involved was first articulated by the Obama administration and was reinforced by Trump. Not involving the country directly in the Syrian conflict stands as the clearest example of the contemporary American posture.

Because Lebanon and Syria are contiguous to Israel and contain elements that oppose Israel and especially its expansion, there has always been a built-in American concern based in the guarantee of Israeli security and survival pillar of policy. Since the establishment of the Israeli state, this concern has tended to focus on Syria, which has been one of the larger Islamic states directly opposing Israel. The bellwether of that concern has always been the Syrian Golan Heights as a key staging area for Syrian attacks. Before the 1967 war and occupation, the issue focused on Syrian use of the Heights as a platform for launching artillery strikes against Israeli settlements in the valleys shadowed by Golan, and one of the Israeli rationales for occupation was to remove this physical threat to Israeli soil and people. Since 1967, the core of the issue has been the Israeli occupation and more recently the colonization and annexation of Golan by the Netanyahu government as part of the general expansion of Israel and to reinforce Israeli security. An adjustment of the territorial situation will almost certainly be a primary objective of whatever Syrian regime emerges from the civil war, although Israeli annexation may have rendered such efforts moot (which was part of the reason for annexation). In addition, the Assad regime has provided unofficial permission to Iranian-sponsored insurgents to operate from Syrian soil against the Israelis as part of the collaboration between the two countries. Although these incursions do not threaten Israeli national security in any direct way, they are an annoyance the Israelis would like to eliminate.

Lebanon, the other Crescent state that borders Israel, is a special state. The smallest member of the Crescent, it has an area about one-third the size of Maryland and a population of about 5.5 million. It is a special place, with a current population divided almost equally between Sunni and Shia Muslims and Christians, with small minorities of Alawites and Druze. It was designed as a multiconfessional state with leadership positions divided by religious affiliation. It has long had border disputes with Israel and Syria, and the country was physically occupied by the Syrian military from 1976 to 2005. The insurgent/terrorist group Hezbollah is indigenous to Lebanon, and Hezbollah raids into Israel precipitated a brief war between the two states in 2006.

Historically, Lebanon has served as the financial center of the region from its capital of Beirut, a position that leads it to try to be neutral in regional conflicts. Its border differences with Israel and its historically contentious relations with Syria will be affected by whatever leadership emerges from the Syrian war. As a multicommunal country with a tradition of tolerance, it has been a major destination for the flow of Middle Eastern refugees. It currently houses about 1.5 million Syrian and Palestinian refugees. Both groups are affected by regional and Crescent politics: the Palestinians by the conflict centering on Israeli expansionism and the Syrians on postwar conditions that would allow them to return home.

CRESCENT WILD CARDS: IRAN, THE AFTERMATH OF THE SYRIAN CIVIL WAR, AND THE KURDS

The Crescent area is clearly one of the most unstable, changeable parts of a Middle East region that displays both characteristics vividly. This part of the Middle East has known virtually constant upheaval and instability for much of recorded history, and the process begun with the breakup of the Ottoman Empire is still working its way out in the area. Peace and stability are unlikely to break out in the Crescent anytime soon.

The current witches' brew of Crescent politics has three basic foci, each of which is of some interest to the United States and none of which is moving toward an early or stable conclusion. The key actor is Iran. Without the shadow of Iran hanging over and defining the interactions of the members, there would likely be no Crescent designation, and it is Iran and its quest for broader international recognition and status that largely define the Crescent as a geopolitical entity. The Syrian civil war has raged in the western Crescent for nearly a decade and is moving toward a conclusion. What happens to Syria after the killing stops will have a great deal of salience for the region and its international politics. One of the dynamics that is largely located in the Crescent are the non-Shia Kurds. Three of the four states that potentially contribute territory and population for Kurdistan are part of the Crescent (Turkey is the exception), and the secession of the Kurds could influence greatly the fate of all Crescent countries. Moreover, the most "obvious" solution for the Kurdish direct lack of access to the outside world (its landlocked status) would be a corridor across Syria and possibly part of Lebanon.

Iran is clearly the 800-pound gorilla in all these dynamics. Since the 1979 Iranian Revolution, the sectarian takeover of Iran's government has produced an expansionist regime that has broken formal ties with Western countries like the United States and has pursued greater power and sway in the region. In terms introduced earlier, Iran is reprising its regional role as the pivotal state in the extended Crescent, a "regional power that by virtue of history, size, self-sense, and a variety of other measures" makes it "the most important state within the geographic region," as this author described it in a 2018 book. Persia has been such a state in the region, as has Egypt and more recently Saudi Arabia and Israel. Pivotal states are often at odds with outside great powers that do not fully accept the pivotal state's status and treat it as an ordinary state. Iran's status was secure when the Shah was effectively aligned with the United States; when that bond was severed, Iran's revolutionary government elected to reassert its role.

The change has taken leadership in forming and leading the Crescent and opposing pretenders to its role, notably the oil-besotted Saudis and the expansionist Israelis. Given the dynamics of this kind of state with the world and the special relationship with Israel, it is not unsurprising that the United States finds itself at odds with Iran (see Chapter 8). Whether the relationship needs to be as toxic as it has become is a different matter. Within the Crescent, this effort significantly has included Iranian efforts in organizing, training, and directing the efforts of anti-Israeli insurgents on behalf of the Palestinians.

This has been a source of conflict between the Iranians and the Israelis. Iranian major general Qasem Soleimani, who directed and coordinated much of this effort as commander of the Quds, was assassinated in an American "targeted drone strike" on January 3, 2020, in Baghdad and was the symbol of much of this effort. If reports of imminent Israeli annexation of most of the West Bank that surfaced in June 2020 are true, they would add an additional combustible element to the mix.

The outcome of the Syrian civil war represents the key to the short-term to midterm status of the Crescent region. The civil war seemed to be nearing a conclusion in 2020, although it was not entirely clear what that outcome would be and how it would affect postwar Syria, notably including the rebuilding of the country and related crises like the COVID-19 impact on Syrians. In a geopolitical sense, the shape of that outcome will have numerous geopolitical impacts, including the integrity of the Syrian state and the constitution and nature of a possible dissolution of the highly artificial Syrian polity (including its relationship to the sectarian divide in the country, how a reconstituted series of successor states will deal with Russia, and what impact the breakup of artificial Syria might have on equally artificial Iraq). Different outcomes affect other states in the region differentially, thus complicating postwar calculations for others like Turkey and the United States.

Who wins has consequences across the region. The victory of Assad certainly benefits the Alawite minority and thus is supported by Shiite Iran as the western anchor of the Crescent as well as a "highway" across Syria for support of Lebanon and for other anti-Israeli activities. Likewise, the current power hierarchy clearly benefits the Russians, providing them with a foothold and source of presence it would likely not have otherwise anywhere else in the region. Moreover, Syria's western shores are washed by the Mediterranean, thereby providing a base for the Russian navy at Tartus.

That calculus may change when the war is over. The overwhelming burden of rebuilding Syria (including treating the pandemic) is estimated in the trillions of dollars, and neither Iran nor Russia is in any position to provide it. The obvious alternate source of funding is the oil riches of the Persian Gulf states, but they are unlikely to provide it for a Shiite Assad regime that has suppressed the 70 percent of the Syrian population that is Sunni. The Syrian government or a successor (possibly of a reconfigured state) will have to choose between the ideological and geopolitical support provided by Iran and Russia and the possible reconstruction dollars the Gulf states might provide a Sunni successor regime. These calculations are further muddied by the uncertainty that COVID-19 recovery will have on funds available from anywhere for dealing with rebuilding what is left of Syria. Repatriation and resettlement of the internal and external refugees is no small portion of both the pandemic and reconstruction calculi.

The possibility that Syria will splinter into two or more states adds to the uncertainty. If Assad's forces prevail, there will be retribution against those who opposed them, creating another potential wave of violence that might only worsen matters. Since Syria is in fact an artificial state, there is logic to a partition. One possibility is for the country to divide into three states: an Alawite state along the northern coast, a central Sunni state encompassing most of the developed interior and anchored by Aleppo and Damascus, and the Kurdish state/province of Rojava in the east. A possible Druze micro-state in the south is also a possibility. Partition might solve some internal differences and bitterness, but it has costs. The Alawites would oppose a Sunni state because most current Syrian wealth is concentrated there. The Turks, as they showed in December 2019, would strongly oppose Rojava as the stalking horse for a Kurdish state that would have ambitions in Turkey (see Chapter 5), and Iran would be left with a diminished Alawite ally. Nothing is ever simple in the Crescent.

The fate of the Kurds is the third wild card. Particularly since they played such a pivotal role in containing the IS threat, they have become much more difficult to ignore than before. The turmoil in the Crescent may alter the map enough to make dreams of self-determination more realistic than before, but not necessarily. The partition of both Syria and Iraq would facilitate the Kurdish areas of those countries in their efforts to break away and form the core of Kurdistan by uniting these contiguous territories. Doing so, of course, is fundamentally opposed by Turkey, which probably rightly fears a united Iraqi-Syrian based Kurdish state would be the staging ground for incursions and subversions of Kurdish areas of Turkey. It is also not clear that the Iranians would grant independence to the Kurdish area of Iran, where the second largest number of Kurds reside.

The prospects of Kurdistan in the middle of the Crescent creates contradictory possible dynamics. If the purpose of the Crescent is to create an Iranian-based and -dominated Shia region, a Sunni Kurdistan upsets that outcome. At the same time, the Kurds and the Iranians are the largest non-Arab peoples south of Turkey, and if the purpose is to reduce Arab dominance, Kurdistan could add to that result. Like other parts of the region, any change creates ambivalent outcomes and prospects for those involved, and those possible impacts play a major part in determining how outsiders like the United States should respond to the possible impact of different outcomes on various American interests.

CHOOSING POLICY: IMPACTS ON THE UNITED STATES

Determining American interests and crafting appropriate strategies and policies for the Shia Crescent as a whole is ultimately a futile gesture because the idea of the Crescent is essentially a contrived name for a part of the Middle East whose major commonality is that its members have significant Shia populations. Some, like Iran, Iraq, and Bahrain, have overwhelming Shia majorities; in others Shia are minorities that may or may not represent pluralities. Some are Arab, others are not. They are a diverse group with different interests and roles, not a monolith.

Policy impacts must thus be fashioned on a country-by-country basis. Anyone looking for a common U.S. Shia Crescent policy will likely labor in vain. There are, however, two clear, interrelated anchors to the region and its environs that form the ongoing basis of American policy concern: Iran and Israel. These countries have been at odds since the 1979 Iranian Revolution and the Israeli ascendancy of an expansionist Israeli regime a decade ago. Ultimately, the focus of that conflict is the West Bank and its alternative futures either as an independent Palestinian state or as part of Israel. The United States is in the middle of that dispute.

Although the Crescent idea was first floated by the Jordanian monarch, the dynamics of the Crescent are clearly an Iranian construct the purpose of which is largely the promotion of Teheran's quest to reassert its position as the pivotal power in the region. There are three major pillars of Iranian policy radiating from that motivation: support for the Shia Alawite regime in Syria, promotion of Shia power in Iraq, and the use of Crescent territory as a staging ground for insurgent harassment of Israel's expansionist policies.

The three policy priorities are in roughly ascending order of priority. A Shia-based government in Baghdad is the anchor of the operational western extension of the Crescent. In addition to increasing the geopolitical extent of the Crescent, the transit issue of providing a safe route for Iranian aid transmission for use against Israel is greatly facilitated by a friendly Syrian government (which coincidentally shares the Iranian interest in reversing Israeli expansion at their expense). Shiite control of the majority of Iraq aids this transit and increases the size of the Crescent region. Dealing with Sunni and Kurdish regions of Iraq remains a problem, especially if the breakup of Syria stimulates the existing secessionist sentiment in Iraq. Finally, there is the question of Israel. Since 1967, Israel has become a (some would argue the) geopolitical force in the Crescent region, especially since the fall of the Shah. The reassertion of a pivotal Iranian state is best served by a restrained Israel. The two outcomes are closely related. Greater Israel as the Netanyahu regime (and many Israelis) see it and the recognition of Iran as the regional pivotal state are basically incompatible. Among other related consequences are the convergence of Israeli and Gulf States (especially Saudi) interests in effectively containing Iran. It is a geopolitical marriage of convenience, not goodwill.

There are three related policy problem areas for the United States arising from this construct: Syria, Iraq, and Israel. Throughout its merciless near decade of fighting, the Syrian civil war has been an international embarrassment for everyone. The United States has largely joined most major countries in avoiding direct involvement in the tragedy out of fear of another endless war. When the fighting began, the United States tried to find a way to aid anti-Assad rebels by providing military and humanitarian assistance, but the military effort was hamstrung by the inability to identify a reliable faction that had widespread public support, seemed capable of challenging the government on the battlefield, and could be trusted not to allow military aid to slip into the hands of IS. These kinds of inhibitions did not hamstring the Turkish and Russian governments from interfering in the fighting to protect interests like the Turkish-Syrian boundary and the Russian naval base at Tartus. The United States simply has lacked a sufficiently large interest to justify a more activist policy.

Will that situation change when the war ends? The answer depends on at least two factors. One is how much residual influence the Russians maintain. Should Assad fall, a non-Alawite successor would have little need or desire for the Russians. Should Syria dissemble into several sovereign jurisdictions, the Russians would also be affected, although if one of the successor states was in the Alawite region, its naval position might be secure. A Sunni Syrian successor in the central area would not keep the Russians around, especially since its presence could impede the flow of Arab financial assistance for rebuilding. Russia has a clear interest in an Assad victory and consolidation of the country. The United States does not.

The second factor is the physical form postwar Syria takes. If the country is partitioned, the likely successors include an Alawite state in the north, a Sunni state in the middle, and a Kurdish state in the east. The United States would be under a good bit of pressure from the Kurds to sponsor or assert an independent Rojava; doing so would further strain relations with Turkey. How that conflict of interests would be resolved is uncertain and would be affected by the outcome of the 2020 presidential election in the United States.

From an American vantage point, Iraq creates the most ambivalence. American popular opinion would not favor much activism in support of involvement in that country. There is a residual American military presence in Iraq justified as a counterweight to possible Iranian activism there, but the expansion of American activity would be politically problematic for any American administration that proposed or supported it. Iraq is an inherently unstable, artificial state that has teetered on the edge of fracturing for decades, and a Syrian collapse could easily spread into Iraq and leave that country split into three sovereign jurisdictions: a Shiite south, a Sunni center, and a Kurdish north. The outcome the United States most opposes is an independent Shiite country that is unduly influenced by Iran. Interest in Iraq is as a part of the jigsaw puzzle minimizing Iranian influence in the Crescent, not an inherent interest in stabilizing the chaos its 2003 invasion created.

Israel is, in important ways, the important lynchpin of American interest in the Shiite Crescent because of Israeli-Iranian competition for regional geopolitical sway in the Middle East. During the Trump administration, the promotion of Netanyahu's activism and expansion was the backbone of American policy, and changes in American policy were largely measured against the impact on the Israelis.

A regional concern with Israel is one of the three historical core interests of the United States in the Middle East, and it currently finds its most obvious expression in the Crescent, both because of Israeli incursions into one Crescent state (the Syrian Golan) and periodic skirmishes with another (the Lebanese Hezbollah). Israeli assurances regarding military security are at heart based on the uncertainty that others in the region have about the circumstances under which Israel might threaten or employ nuclear weapons. Israeli security is premised on the nuclear monopoly it has enjoyed since 1968, and only Iran has the realistic possibility of being able to negate this advantage by obtaining these weapons themselves. The militancy of the post-1979 Iranian government in its advocacy of Palestine adds to a bilateral relationship that was cooperative and nonconfrontational prior to 1979.

It has always been an underlying premise of U.S. Middle Eastern policy that American interests are best achieved in an atmosphere of peace and maximum tranquility in the region, and it is the conflict between Israel and Iran that has eclipsed the old Arab-Israeli confrontation as the primary challenge to that peace. The dynamics of that relationship are clear. Iran aspires to being recognized as the pivotal Muslim state in the region, a position that is opposed by most Islamic states because the Iranians are neither Sunni nor Arab. The Iranians have made the promotion of Palestinian statehood their signature regional issue, which in turn has translated into advocacy of the Crescent. This militant position, of course, brings them into direct conflict with the equally militant Greater Israel policy of the Netanyahu government. Israel's obstinacy is based on the solidification of exclusive nuclear-based Israeli security.

The region, as exemplified in the Crescent, will remain conflictual and sometimes confrontational if the two countries continue to pursue aggressively these initiatives at the expense of the other. In that circumstance, the

American preference for regional tranquility will be frustrated. Before 1967, Israel and Iran were pillars of the American goal of stability in the region; now both countries frustrate that goal. Since 1979, the Iranians have been the prime opponents of the United States, which has—especially under Trump—tilted decisively in support of Israel. If these conditions continue to hold, tranquility will remain elusive.

Is this the best policy for the United States? Events in the Crescent are likely to destabilize even further in the next few years, with repercussions for basic Iranian-Israeli relations: the two countries, for instance, have very different visions for postwar Syria or its successor states. These matters are unlikely to heal without outside political intervention—which may or may not work. Much of this dynamic revolves around Iran and its evolving role in the region, which is examined in Chapter 8. What do you think the Americans can or should do?

BIBLIOGRAPHY

Alawi, Ali. *Iran and Palestine: Past, Future*. New York and London: Routledge, 2019.

Armajani, John. *Shia Islam and Politics: Iran, Iraq, and Lebanon*. Lanham, MD: Lexington Books, 2020.

Bolton, John. *The Room Where It Happened: A White House Memoir*. New York: Simon & Schuster, 2020.

Daher, Joseph. *Syria after the Uprisings: The Political Economy of State Resilience*. Chicago: Haymarket Books, 2019.

Friedman, Thomas L. *From Beirut to Jerusalem*. New York: Picador, 2012.

Fromkin, David. *A Peace to End All Peace: The Fall of the Ottoman Empire and the Creation of the Modern Middle East*. Twentieth Anniversary Ed. New York: Holt, 2009.

Haass, Mark L., and David W. Lesch (eds.). *The Arab Spring: The Hope and Reality of the Uprisings*. Second Ed. New York: Routledge, 2016.

Halm, Heinz. *Shi'a Islam: From Rebellion to Revolution*. Princeton Series on the Middle East. Princeton, NJ: Princeton University Press, 1996.

———, Janet Watson, et al. *Shiism*. Second Ed. New York: Columbia University Press, 2004.

Heern, Zackery M. *The Emergence of Modern Shiism: Islamic Reform in Iraq and Iran*. London: Oneworld Academics, 2015.

Hinnebush, Raymond. *The War for Syria: Regional and International Dimensions of the Syrian Uprising*. London: Routledge/St. Andrews Syrian Studies Series, 2019.

Hitchcock, Mark. *Israel and Iran: Wars and Rumors of Wars*. Irvine, CA: Harvest House, 2013.

Katz, Yaakov, and Yoaz Hendel. *Israel vs. Iran: The Shadow War.* Washington, DC: Potomac Books, 2012.

Levitt, Matthew. *Hezbollah: The Global Footprint of Lebanon's Party of God.* Washington, DC: Georgetown University Press, 2015.

Lynch, Marc. *The New Arab Wars: Uprisings and Anarchy in the Middle East.* Reprint Ed. New York: PublicAffairs, 2017.

Mansbach, Richard W., and Kristen Taylor. *Challenges for America in the Middle East.* Washington, DC: CQ Press, 2016.

Matar, Linda, and Ali Kadri. *Syria: From National Independence to Proxy War.* London: Palgrave Macmillan, 2018.

Norton, Richard. *Hezbollah: A Short History.* Third Ed. Princeton, NJ: Princeton University Press, 2018.

Ottoway, David, and Marina Ottoway. *A Tale of Four Worlds: The Arab Region after the Uprisings.* New York: Hurst, 2019.

Phillips, Christopher. *The Battle for Syria: International Rivalry in the New Middle East.* New Haven, CT: Yale University Press, 2016.

Riedel, Bruce. *Beirut 1958: How America's Wars in the Middle East Began.* Washington, DC: Brookings Institution Press, 2019.

Snow, Donald M. *The Case Against Military Intervention: Why We Do It and Why It Fails.* London: Routledge, 2016.

———. *Regional Cases in U.S. Foreign Policy.* Second Ed. Lanham, MD: Rowman & Littlefield, 2018.

Stoker, Donald. *Limited War and US Strategy from the Korean War to the Present.* Cambridge, UK: Cambridge University Press, 2019.

Trenin, Dmitri. *What Is Russia Up to in the Middle East?* Washington, DC: Potomac Books, 2017.

Uskowi, Nader. *Temperature Rising: Iran's Revolutionary Guards and Wars in the Middle East.* Lanham, MD: Rowman & Littlefield, 2018.

Von Dam, Nikolaus. *Destroying a Nation: The Civil War in Syria.* London: I. B. Tauris, 2017.

Weiland, Carsten. *A Decade of Last Chances: Repression and Revolution from Damascus Spring to Arab Spring.* Seattle, WA: Cune, 2012.

Worth, Robert F. *A Rage for Order: The Middle East in Turmoil, from Tahrir Square to ISIS.* New York: Farrar, Straus and Giroux, 2016.

Zahlan, Rosemarie Said. *The Making of the Modern Gulf States: Kuwait, Bahrain, Qatar, the United Arab Emirates, and Oman.* New York: Routledge, 2016.

8

The Mini Cold War Struggle
Iran and Saudi Arabia

In addition to the multiple subregional conflicts in the Middle East, a geopolitical struggle has emerged and intensified between the two physically largest states in the core region—Iran and Saudi Arabia. It pits two of the region's leading powers and the acknowledged centers of Sunni and Shia Islam, one of the most important cleavages in the Middle East. The difference is also ethnic. Saudi Arabia is the properly acknowledged central physical center of the Arab world. Being an Arab is considered of paramount importance to the claim of attachment to the Prophet Muhammad, who was what would later be called a Saudi, and multiple people with questionable empirical claims proudly declare themselves to be Arabs. The Persian Iranians are ethnically, physically, and linguistically distinct from the Arabs. The two groups speak different basic languages (Arabic versus Persian) and profess different communal ties.

The current dynamic began with upheavals within the two principal countries in 1979. That year produced fundamental political challenges and responses in both Teheran and Riyadh that have helped create the atmosphere in which this "mini cold war" was born and how it has evolved. Ethno-religious differences stand at the base of the crisis, and they have been both cause and effect of the geopolitical rivalry. Iranian activism unleashed by the revolution has made that country more aggressive/assertive than it had been under Shah Reza Pahlavi, manifested both in the anti-Westernism that had underlain much of the revolution and thus its support for more confrontational relations with countries like Israel and the United States. Other countries reciprocated Iran's animosity, which has evolved into something of an "alliance of convenience" that has extended to relations between Israel, Saudi Arabia, and the United Arab Emirates. The United States has become more partisan in this process: the United States and Iran have had a love-hate relationship that has ebbed and flowed since the immediate post–World War II period and has hardened into virulent opposition to Teheran since the Shah was expelled and Iranian radicals occupied the American embassy in Teheran and held its personnel hostage between 1979 and 1981. Especially under the Trump administration, American opposition to the Teheran regime hardened, as has virtually unquestioned support for Israel. American-Saudi relations have been somewhat more ambivalent, but the United States remains basically supportive of a Saudi government in transition.

This is a complex, confusing set of relationships and dynamics, but it has much wider potential ramifications that make grasping it necessary to understanding the region and beyond. Although it has not been the historical case, Iran and Saudi Arabia are major competitors for leadership in the modern Middle East, and the basis of that relationship is communal, ethnic, and political. Understanding the basis and contours of the mini cold war that, when combined with the prospects of a regional nuclear arms race, must begin by comparing these central players.

IRAN AND SAUDI ARABIA: A COMPARISON

These two countries rose into international prominence in the immediate post–Cold War competition for Middle East petroleum that was, along with the fate of Europe, the primary basis of the Cold War geopolitical competition between East and West. One of the first hot spots of what became the Cold War was the 1946 Soviet occupation of the Iranian province of Azerbaijan, which prompted an American response that triggered both the Cold War and the rocky, schizophrenic relationship between the United States and Iran. With what were considered at the time the world's largest oil reserves, Saudi Arabia became a progressively central power as the world's addiction to "black gold" ballooned. Iran's reserves are the fourth largest in the world, as reported by the *CIA World Factbook*, 2019–2020.

The two countries provide ample points of contrast and similarity. Geography is a prime part of that comparison. Both countries are large physically: Iran has about three-quarters the physical territory of Saudi Arabia. The Kingdom is the fourteenth largest country in the world in land mass, while Iran is nineteenth. They sit directly across from one another, separated by the relatively narrow Persian (or Arabian, depending on ethnic preference) Gulf, separated by only about 125 miles at the narrowest point. The Gulf is the primary shipping route for petroleum exiting the Gulf littoral, making its control of great geopolitical significance and the source of conflict between the two parties. Before the Iranian Revolution of 1979, the Iranians, acting as effective agents for the Americans, controlled the Gulf and assured the unimpeded flow of Gulf petroleum to the rest of the world. The breakdown of that condominium is one of the major sources of contemporary tension.

The demographic comparison extends to questions of population and wealth. The population of Iran is more than twice that of Saudi Arabia (about 83 million Iranians, compared to 33 million Saudis), and a measure of the combination of population and physical size reflects the difference: the number of Iranians per square mile is about three times that of Saudi Arabia (130 to 41). This disparity is also reflected in comparisons of military size and potential. The Iranian armed forces are over twice the size of their Saudi counterparts (563,000 to 251,500 in the Saudi forces), according to the International Institute for Strategy Studies (IISS) figures for 2017. Moreover, the heart of the Iranian forces was tested during the 1980–1988 Iran-Iraq War and in asymmetrical warfare support for various insurgencies in the area (notably Syria and Lebanon). By contrast, most of the experience of the Saudis has been in their conflict with Yemen since 2015, and many Saudi military members are foreign mercenaries whose loyalty and effectiveness may be suspect. The Saudis invest nearly 10 percent of their GDP on defense, compared to about one-fourth that percentage for the Iranians.

Economic comparisons are distorted by U.S.-led sanctions against Iran, for which there are no Saudi equivalents. The Saudi GDP measured in terms of purchasing power parity is larger than Iran's, and by that measure the Kingdom ranks sixteenth compared to Iran's eighteenth. In per capita GDP, the Saudis rank twenty-second in the world at $54,500, whereas Iran is eighty-ninth at $19,600. Were sanctions to be lifted against Iran, this gap would shrink, a point of ongoing contention between Teheran and Washington. The Saudis spend nearly $70 billion on defense (a sizable part of which comes in the form of arms purchases from the United States), compared to about $6.3 billion by the Iranians. These figures are worth noting in terms of the comparative military strength of the two countries.

Islamic faith is the other great commonality of the two countries, but the sectarian gap between Sunni and Shia is also the basis of much of their disagreement. The liturgical differences between the two sects are not great, dating back to the question of succession to Islamic leadership after the Prophet died and failed to leave a male heir, who would have been the logical leader of the religion. Both sects have both liberal and conservative traditions, including questions of interpretation of Quranic culture, heritage, and the role of early regional culture in modern life (e.g., how literally to apply seventh-century sharia law). If theological debates were the true underlying base of division, it would, however, not be profound. The Sunni-Shia split is more a political divide phrased in liturgical terms than it is a religious cleavage as such.

A final point of comparison is historical, touching upon the geopolitical motives and aspirations of the two countries. Iran is the world's second oldest continuous civilization after China. The original Persian Empire is conventionally dated back to Cyrus the Great in 550 BC, and the country has been the source of major participation in the region since. After World War I dismantled Ottoman control of much of the Middle East, one of the major changes was the declaration of a new Persian dynasty under the rule of the shahs, a phenomenon that lasted (with interruptions) until the overthrow of Shah Reza Pahlavi in 1979.

The Arabian Peninsula, of which Saudi Arabia is the largest tenant, has a different and less unified past. For most of its history, the peninsula was ruled by shifting groups of nomadic tribesmen who held sway over different parts of the desert landscape. Saudi Arabia began to emerge as a modern state in the early twentieth century as the Al Saud tribe (the current ruling family) gradually consolidated their control over the area, declaring the Kingdom of Saudi Arabia. In the process, the royal family gained control of the two major assets of the area: Islam's holiest sites at Mecca and Medina and the vast petroleum assets under the sand. One major aspect of that consolidation was the confirmation of an abiding relationship with the Wahhabis, the very conservative Sunni faction that predominates the peninsula, in return for acquiescence to rule by the royal family, reflecting a condominium dating back to 1744. The preeminence of the Wahhabis and their conservative value system is a major factor in assessing the Kingdom's actions in the international realm. The Kingdom of Saudi Arabia was declared in 1930.

The historical contrast between the two countries helps explain the differences between them. Iran considers itself the region's pivotal state based largely on its preeminent position over time. Cyrus, after all, came to power in Persia over 2,500 years ago, and Iran/Persia has considered itself the cornerstone of the eastern Middle East ever since, a status that has been periodically suspended but never forgotten. The Saudis, on the other hand, are geopolitical newcomers who want to become a pivotal state by virtue of their wealth and position. As the two geographically largest states in the region, some rivalry between them is likely under any circumstances. Ethnicity and confession add to and help define their differences.

THE EVOLVING RELATIONSHIP

For much of the post–World War II period, relations between the two Persian Gulf giants were correct, if not necessarily close. Ethnic and confessional differences were present, but they were largely sublimated to the great wealth being generated by the exploitation and sale of oil to the West. During the period of the Shah's reign, Saudi Arabia and Iran had a condominium in support of the maximum exploitation of that lucrative commodity, whereby the vastly larger and more capable Iranian military (and notably the navy) patrolled the Persian Gulf to ensure unimpeded flow with the tacit approval of their partners across the Gulf on the Arabian Peninsula. Since it relieved the United States of the personal need to commit major resources to protect that flow, the United States was a willing partner in this arrangement and enjoyed friendly relations with both sides. The houses of Saud and Pahlavi carried on normal formal relations, and while these were more correct than convivial, the result was a situation where both sides enjoyed substantial benefits.

The process that collapsed this tranquil condition began to emerge in the latter 1970s, and it has gradually transformed the region to its current geopolitical status. The most obvious events occurred independently in the two countries in 1979. The Iranian Revolution succeeded in toppling the Shah and replacing his government with a much more militant, fundamentalist regime that, among other things, has been antagonistic toward the United States. A less well publicized event occurred in Saudi Arabia with the seizure by religious opponents of the regime of the Grand Mosque in Mecca for two weeks in November and December of that year, resulting in a crackdown by the Saudi regime and the imposition of stricter sharia law than had previously existed.

These two events transformed the countries and began the process of competition that has resulted in the current confrontation between them. Although not so often emphasized in this regard, at least two other events and trends have also contributed. One has been the greater activism and militancy of the Saudis, particularly connected to the trauma of the Iraqi invasion of neighboring Kuwait. Major expressions of this trend have been the Saudi war against neighboring Yemen and the controversial rise of Mohammad bin Salman (MBS) as crown prince and thus heir apparent to the throne. The other has been the gradual emergence of Israeli-Saudi condominium in opposition to Iran, a phenomenon with roots and implications surrounding the Israeli nuclear arsenal, including the connection between that arsenal and the possibility of Iranian nuclear weapons.

These events are arguably only snapshots of the geopolitical drama being played out in the region, and other dynamics could doubtless be included in it. The examples listed here have, however, been particularly important in defining the evolving American position and role toward the mini cold war, and they are thus emphasized because they relate to American perceptions and the American regional debate over appropriate strategy and policy.

Chapter 8

THE IRANIAN REVOLUTION

The overthrow of the Shah's Peacock Kingdom set in motion what is arguably the central dynamic of the current competition. Moreover, it was the culminating event in the highly schizophrenic relationship between the United States and Iran, which I have elsewhere typified as "the clash of the Great Satans" (see *The Middle East, Oil, and the U.S. National Security Policy*).

The relationship between the two countries has been tumultuous since the United States became an active participant in Iranian politics after World War II. In the latter 1940s, the American interest in Iran was in obtaining guaranteed, economical access to Iranian oil and to thwart Soviet attempts to penetrate Iranian Azerbaijan to gain access to Iranian and Gulf petroleum. This initially manifested itself in support for a young and inexperienced Reza Pahlavi. That sponsorship was temporarily derailed with the election of Dr. Mohammed Mossadegh, the only fully democratically elected president in Iranian history, who committed the political sin of nationalizing the Iranian oil industry to ensure Iran reaped the maximum benefit from its exploitation. It also meant wresting control of that industry from American and other European oil companies. With assistance from the Central Intelligence Agency, a coup removed Mossadegh from office and restored Pahlavi. The schizophrenic path to current Iranian and American relations was set in motion.

For a quarter century, Iran and the United States were close collaborators and enjoyed warm and cordial intergovernmental and interpersonal relations. Iranian students, military officers, and scientists were regular parts of the American physical scene, and many Americans—mostly engaged in developmental efforts of the Iranian government—were present in Teheran. The Shah was fervently pro-Western, and his positive policies extended to regional states like Israel, with whom the Iranian government cooperated in matters such as providing petroleum to Israel during its crises with the Arab states.

Each country had something to offer the other. The Shah provided the United States with a secure, reliable source of petroleum independent of reliance on the vicissitudes of Arab politics: Iranian oil, for instance, continued to flow during Arab-Israeli crises like the Arab boycott after the 1973 Yom Kippur War. The Iranian Navy patrolled and regulated activity in the Persian Gulf.

The Shah's underlying goal was to modernize and secularize Iran to make it powerful enough to reassert itself as the region's pivotal state, and he found a willing partner in the United States for that aspiration. The Iranian military was modernized and built up with American weapons that Iran purchased largely with oil revenues. Central to the Shah's goal was to transform the country into a highly Westernized, advanced state that could compete with and be a prominent part of the contemporary global order. His vehicle for this enterprise was the White Revolution, a comprehensive effort to tear down the traditional Muslim society and replace it with a Western-style society. Reza Pahlavi was the architect of this dream; the United States was the vessel to implement that transformation through the provision of economic, technical, and social reform.

The White Revolution was the quintessence of the Shah's vision. He was not, however, an ardent enthusiast of political democracy, and his regime was noticeably authoritarian and even totalitarian. The symbol of political reality for many Iranian dissenters was SAVAK, the Shah's secret police force, which stifled dissent and killed and tortured those who opposed the Shah.

The result was to crystallize the schizophrenia that has marked U.S.-Iranian relations ever since. The effects of the White Revolution were very different for different Iranians. For many Iranians who had overseas experience and wanted Iran to become a modern power, the White Revolution was the vehicle for their aspiration. Particularly in and around Teheran, Iran was transformed into a modern Western metropolis with a technological base and a rising, Westernized middle class who benefited from the Shah's reforms and the transformation of Iranian society from a conservative, rural-dominated theocracy to a Westernized worldview (sans political democracy, of course). Unfortunately, not all Iranians shared that view and either did not benefit from the White Revolution reforms or were injured by them. They progressively opposed the Shah and sought his overthrow.

Ayatollahs suffered from White Revolution reforms. Traditionally, for instance, the clergy held title to much rural property, and the Shah's government stripped them of much of this land and the revenue it produced. The religious hierarchy also performed functions in the administrative system akin to civil law in Western societies, and they lost these powers as well. Their resentment built, and they shared it with their peasant base. There were effectively two societies in Iran: a large, traditionally religious rural peasantry in the countryside who looked to the conservative religious hierarchy for leadership and a rapidly secularizing and Westernizing urban class centered in and around Teheran. This class was highly urbanized, many of its members had traveled abroad (especially to the United States, in which many of them studied), and they were prodemocratic. They shared the technologically produced wealth and prestige the regime provided, but the Shah's regime was strictly authoritarian and politically repressive, making the alliance imperfect.

The United States was firmly aligned with the government. Americans advised both the government and private enterprise in the further Westernization of the country. This alliance proceeded blissfully until the mid-1970s, as American intelligence accepted representations by the Shah's SAVAK of contentment and support from the people. It proved to be more illusion than reality.

The clash between the Shah's supporters and other factions began to congeal in the early 1970s. The rural peasantry and their religious mentors suffered the most upheaval under the Shah's reforms, and many had to migrate to urban centers, where they suffered grinding poverty in the urban slums that popped up in the cities. The ayatollahs and other religious leaders railed against Western-style profligacy. The anti-Shah movement grew during the early 1970s, but the government did not forcibly suppress it, much to the surprise of Western observers.

The Shah's rule weakened throughout the 1970s as his health declined. The growing powder keg ignited in early 1979. On January 16, 1979, the Shah announced he would leave the country to pursue treatment for the cancer that had been debilitating him and from which he would die. His medical condition had been a closely guarded secret, but the debilitation it caused helped explain why the Shah had not acted vigorously to suppress the growing wave of anti-Shah activity. It was widely assumed (correctly) that he was in fact abdicating and leaving the country for permanent exile. Within two weeks of his departure, Ayatollah Ruhollah Khomeini, the leading Iranian cleric and inspirational leader of the resistance, returned from Paris exile to a hero's welcome. The Peacock Empire was effectively gone, and the question was what would happen next.

As the period evolved, two related events shaped both the evolution of the revolution and the future or relations between the United States and Iran. The first was the realization of the Shah's cancer and his treatment for it in New York. When it became known that the Shah's cancer was likely terminal, any possibility of his return to power disappeared. As the succession struggle raged and intensified, however, there was increasing sentiment in Teheran to force his return to the country to stand trial for his regime's excesses. The demand was an effective death sentence, and the Shah's American hosts and allies refused the request. This response infuriated many Iranians, triggering the second, and in terms of long-term relations between the two countries more consequential, event. On November 4, 1979, Iranian "students" assaulted and captured the American embassy in Teheran, including its staff. Their underlying demand, not widely publicized at the time, was to return the Shah to Iran in return for the end of the embassy occupation and the release of its personnel. The United States refused, and the occupation lasted until January 20, 1981. The United States broke all relations with Iran. Most of the animosity and distrust between the two countries and certainly American hostility toward its former regional partner are the direct result of these actions.

REVOLUTIONARY IRAN AND THE TWO "GREAT SATANS"

Post–Peacock Empire Iran has become a radical theocratic state. The 1979 revolution was a synergistic political and religious event, the implications of which are still evolving. Epitomized by Ayatollah Khomeini, the regime that emerged from the postrevolutionary struggle was a clear victory for militant Shiism and a rebuke for the Westernized pretenders who grossly overestimated their own skill and appeal and underestimated the attraction and organization of the religious "rubes" and their fiery, charismatic leaders.

Revolutionary Iran has been built broadly on two principles: religious purification, evangelism, and its export and the expansion of Iranian power to its former role as the region's pivotal state. Internal purification was accomplished by ruthlessly suppressing former supporters of the Shah who were not lucky enough to escape the country. The moderate middle class fared slightly better. The result has been an ongoing tension and competition between the remaining secularist elements and the clergy. This division is manifested in a split government: an elected, secular regime and system of which Hassan Rohani is president, and the religious hierarchy currently headed by Ayatollah Ali Khamenei—the Supreme Leader. Much day-to-day governance is conducted by the Rohani government, and when moderate positions emerge from Teheran, they are normally associated with the Rohani government. Khamenei and his religious council have an effective veto on government decisions, and when a more moderate position emerges from Teheran that is subsequently reversed, it is normally because of action from Khamenei and his officials. Effectively having two governments, one secular and the other sectarian, complicates understanding Iranian policy and creates opportunities for those who support or revile the Iranians.

The other forbidding aspect of dealing with Iran is Iranian military power and potential, and this is particularly a problem for the Saudis. According to figures from the 2016 IISS Military Balance, the Iranian armed forces are the eighth largest in the world and Saudi forces are twentieth. The Iranian advantage is particularly great in ground and naval forces. Their forces are twice as large as Saudi Arabia's, and many have been battle tested. The contrast is especially stark in naval vessels that can be used in the Persian Gulf: the 2016 figures are particularly vivid for patrol boats (194–11) and submarines (21–0). The Iranians also have an advantage in asymmetrical and guerrilla manpower and experience through entities like the Quds force formerly led by General Soleimani and the revolutionary guards.

The one area where Iran is regionally uncompetitive is in nuclear weapons. Iran has the scientific and technical capability to develop these weapons but has refrained to this point. Should they reverse course, they would destroy the Israeli regional monopoly, and thus the Israelis are the most virulent and vocal opponents of Iran in the region to prevent Iran from reactivating its nuclear weapons program.

The mutuality of Satanism suggested in the section heading between the Americans and the Iranians comes from these factors. For the Americans, regime radicalism by the Shiite power structure has made them satanic, and this indictment extends to Iranian policy supporting anti-Israeli expansionism. The possibility of Iranian nuclearization adds to the hysterical tone of that rhetoric and further reinforces the demonic depiction of the Iranians. Given the schizophrenic nature of U.S. involvement in that country and its current implacable opposition to the Iranian system and its policies, it is also not hard for the Iranians to think of the Americans as great Satans.

THE SAUDI SIDE OF THE EQUATION

Iran and Saudi Arabia are sharply contrasting places. They share a common religion in Islam but from different sectarian perspectives (Sunni versus Shia). They both share global importance thanks to huge petroleum deposits beneath their soil and economies based largely in exploitation of that resource. With the historically largest known reserves, the Saudis have ranked first in the world (a status eclipsed by discoveries in Venezuelan fields) and a dominant political position among the smaller oil-rich states of the Persian Gulf and have been the symbolic leaders and spokesmen for Middle Eastern oil. Iran ranks fourth in proven reserves but has been unable to sell much of its oil in recent years due to American-led economic sanctions.

They have important differences. The most obvious and enduring is political. Saudi Arabia is the world's largest and most consequential absolute monarchy, and the foundation of the sway of the Saud extended family is its long-term close working relationship with the conservative Sunni members of the Wahhabi sect, which is the largest religious group in the country. This relationship is tight and mutually reinforcing and has historical roots going back to the eighteenth century when the leaders of the new Wahhabi sect of Sunnism and the House of Saud formed an alliance in their communities located in the desert not far from Riyadh. This arrangement has been the enduring dynamic of Saudi existence since that alliance was formed in 1744. It remains the foundation both of life within the country and in its relations with the world, including the United States.

Enormous oil wealth and the unique absolute theocratic nature of the Saudi system are the Kingdom's most salient characteristics. Without the oil of the Persian Gulf littoral, of course, hardly anyone would pay much attention to the Arabian Peninsula beyond its symbolic location as the place where Mohammed had his revelations and Islam was born. The oil provides the Saudis and their government with enormous wealth and the influence it brings. The fact that Mecca and Medina, the holiest sites of Islam, are within Saudi boundaries creates a religious significance it would not otherwise have since all Muslims are required to try to travel to the holiest spots at least once in their lifetimes (the hajj). Access to the sites is controlled by the government. The oil is on the Persian Gulf side of the peninsula; the holy sites are nearer the Red Sea. Without these bookends, Saudi Arabia would be much more lightly regarded.

SAUDI ARABIA AS ACTOR AND ANACHRONISM

The experience of Saudi Arabia stands in sharp contrast to that of Iran. For most of Middle Eastern history, the Arabian Peninsula was a relatively unimportant piece of real estate except for its prominence as the birthplace of Islam in the seventh century AD. Most of the peninsula is a desert, and it was sparsely populated by nomadic tribesmen until the Prophet's revelations ignited a revolution that ultimately led to the conquest of much of the Mediterranean world in the name of Allah in the eighth century and beyond. At the time, nobody knew about the value of petroleum or that a disproportionate amount of that black gold lay beneath the desert sands and the Persian Gulf littoral.

What has become contemporary Saudi Arabia began in earnest in the eighteenth century in the Najd region of central Saudi Arabia, not far from the current capital of Riyadh. The vehicle for this dynamic was the interaction and alliance between two forces, one political and one religious. The political movement was the House of Saud, and its clan leader, Muhammad ibn Saud, who was the founder of the family that has ruled the country ever since. The religious element was dominated by Muhammad ibn Abd al-Wahhab, the eighteenth-century Islamic scholar, theologian, and activist whose religious teaching forms the basis of the state religion of contemporary Saudi Arabia. In 1744, the two leaders reached an agreement whereby Ibn Saud agreed to protect and help spread Wahhabi sectarianism, in return for which Wahhab and his followers would support and provide religious legitimacy for rule by the House of Saud. That basic agreement remains the cornerstone of the theocratic absolutist monarchy of Saudi Arabia, which formally joined the family of sovereign states in 1930.

The two forces are synergistic and form the core to understanding what, by most contemporary criteria, is one of the most anachronistic, anomalous regimes in the world. The Wahhabist doctrine is very conservative, reflecting conformance to the literal pronouncements of Muhammad in the seventh century as an indication of virtue and as the definitional guide to behavior and societal rectitude. The most frequently cited example is a belief in a literal interpretation of sharia law, which includes summary forms of punishment and contrition that are considered primitive, and even barbaric, in many other—and notably Western—cultures. The Wahhabi faith is evangelical—seeking to spread belief in what it considers the real and "true" interpretation of Islam—and autocratic, with interpretation of Quranic meaning reserved for highly conservative elders. Within Sunnism, Wahhabism competes with more liberal (moderate) belief systems. Shiism has a similar continuum of sects, including the conservative sect that holds power in Iran. What distinguishes Wahhabism is that it happens to be the state religion of one of the richest oil-producing states in the world.

The code of social organization associated with Wahhabism is, to put it mildly, at odds with the premises of almost all other contemporary countries and societies. Possibly the most publicized example is its rigid male patriarchism, by which all rights and freedoms are restricted to males and in which women are essentially powerless and societally repressed. These forms of treatment are widely ridiculed and condemned in the rest of the world—the public stoning of women is a particularly egregious and highly publicized example—and have helped create a global depiction of Saudi Arabia as an anachronistic, medieval society.

The religious and political aspects of Saudi sovereignty are synergistic. Politically, Saudi Arabia is one of a handful of states in the world that are still classified as absolutist monarchies. This form of government, prevalent in Europe during much of the Middle Ages, refers to a sovereign state in which all power and authority resides with a single individual. This individual, who is designated as the "sovereign," has absolute power and authority, and no individual or group within the sovereign's territory can exercise power independent of the sovereign. This notion has been eclipsed in most of the world by some variation of the idea of popular sovereignty (sovereignty resides in individuals within the state). There are a few remaining monarchies in Europe and elsewhere, but they are generally symbolic historical holdovers with no real power or authority in political life.

Saudi Arabia is the world's most prominent exception. All power and authority are held by the member of the Saud family who holds the title of king. There are only a few other similar systems. Three are fellow Gulf Sunni regimes: Oman, Qatar, and the United Arab Emirates. Other absolutist states include Brunei, Swaziland, and Vatican City. The combination of its form of rule and religious connection is symbolized by the fact that the formal title of the king is "Custodian of the Holy Mosques."

The combination of Saud absolutist rule based largely in terms of the Wahhabi religious philosophy defines contemporary Saudi society, its place among the world countries, and challenges to the regime, including the question of internal modernization and change and the competition for power and recognition in the region and beyond. Since his elevation to the position of heir apparent to the throne in 2015, those questions have tended to center on Mohammed bin Salman (MBS). Collectively, they also tend to define the position of Saudi Arabia in the region and beyond and American relations with the country. This entire complex is conditioned by the declining dominance of petroleum as an effective source of power and influence in the world and the continuing controversy over Saudi military actions toward neighboring Yemen.

THE CONTEMPORARY SAUDI MIX

Saudi Arabia has enjoyed a privileged and reasonably tranquil existence for most of the postwar period. The engine for that position, of course, has been the fabulous wealth that oil has bestowed upon the regime. Although the fruits of that privilege have, for the most part, been limited to native-born males, the regime has spread the wealth around to other residents and selectively to other regional actors. Political rights have been strictly reserved for native Saudis (no person of foreign birth can become a citizen), hardly any rights extend to females, and dissent has been blunted by a draconian system of sharia law and its enforcement. Other countries, including the United States, have been dependent on Saudi oil to the point of feeling the need to avert their gaze from the most blatant, medieval authoritarianism practiced in the Kingdom. When Saudi was faced with the prospect of an invasion by Iraq their forces were incapable of repelling, foreign countries, led by the United States, fell all over themselves coming to Saudi aid. Checkbook diplomacy and control of oil were the bases of Saudi foreign and national security policy.

Things are changing. Politically, the Kingdom is in a process of change, although its outcome is uncertain. The current king, Salman bin Abdulaziz al-Saud, ascended to the throne when his predecessor died in 2015. The new king was seventy-nine years old at the time he was elevated, and while the passage of sovereignty from one wing of the extended Saud family to another was not necessarily momentous in itself, it came at a time when Saudi Arabia was under some strain from declines in the price of oil and global pressures to move away from carbon-based energy that potentially threatened the long-term base of Saudi's opulent wealth. The emergence of the COVID pandemic as a problem in Saudi Arabia has added to internal concerns. The relationship with Iran (see below) was also showing strain, most dramatically illustrated by the proxy civil conflict in Yemen with opposing elements supported by both countries. Most dramatically, the new king brought one of his sons, Mohammed bin Salman (MBS), into the inner circle in 2015 as Minister of Defense and Deputy Crown Prince. He was elevated to Crown Prince—the heir apparent to the throne—on June 20, 2017, two months shy of his thirty-second birthday. He has become the focus of attention for both reform within the Kingdom and controversy in the domestic and foreign policy arenas and was a favorite figure within the Trump White House.

He burst upon the scene as an apparent beacon of light within the anachronistic Saudi system, an impression he nurtured but which has faded. He became a celebrity by visiting the White House where, among other things, he developed a relationship with President Trump and his son-in-law Jared Kushner, who remained a supporter when he was named Crown Prince. He became a global figure by leading a limited reform program that included increased rights for women (e.g., removing the ban on driving a car and allowing increased participation in the economic life of the country) and even putting some limits on the religious police. These actions were more symbolic than fundamental, but they earned MBS a reputation in the West as a reformer. It was at least partly an illusion.

His reputation has been tarnished, and along with it some Western support for the regime. MBS was a leading figure in the Saudi intervention in the Yemen civil war in 2015, leading the effort against the Houthi rebels and, in the process, helping organize and implement a brutal campaign that has left many opposition Yemenis dead or suffering. The campaign has not gone well, causing Gause to assert in August 2020 that there is "no reasonable chance" for the Saudis and their Sunni Yemeni allies "to defeat the Houthis." Among other things, the underperformance of Saudi forces has reinforced international perceptions of the limits of Saudi military forces. MBS has also been tainted by his complicity in the assassination of Saudi-born American journalist Jamal Khashoggi, who was killed and famously dismembered by Saudis. Despite Trump administration continued support, his reputation as a modernizing reformer has essentially disappeared in the United States, especially among Democrats. In addition, drops in oil prices have put some strains on the Saudi largesse that has been the basis of much of their regional reputation, and the COVID pandemic has hit Saudi hard. Gause, for instance, asserts that over 280,000 Saudis had been infected by August 2020, "more, by far, than have been recorded in any other Arab country."

THE IRANIAN-SAUDI CONFLICT

The conflict between the two largest Gulf states exists within this context. As a geopolitical competition, it is neither symmetrical nor even. By any measure other possibly than wealth, Iran is clearly the larger, more powerful, and generally consequential of the two. It has over twice the population of its rival, has a long history as both an entity and regional geopolitical actor, and has a military force that essentially all observers agree is superior to its Saudi counterpart. Saudi Arabia has historically had the larger checkbook, but until recently it has invested little of that wealth in diversifying the economic base to allow it to compete in a future environment in which petroleum is a less central part of economic prosperity and prominence. To his credit, MBS seems to understand the need to invest and diversify, but his other missteps have dulled an appreciation for this insight. Iran, on the other hand, continues to suffer from the effects of the American-led economic sanctions that began in the wake of the hostage crisis.

The mini cold war in the Gulf exists within this complex of factors. Iran has been the politically more aggressive participant, exporting military assistance to states with large Shiite populations in places like Yemen and opposing Israeli expansionism in the occupied territories. Effectively, its current activism is in the Shiite Crescent and Yemen. Both areas are of interest to Israel (especially the West Bank and thus the Palestinians) and the Saudis (mostly Yemen), which helps explain the emergence of the condominium between them in recent years. These interests are geopolitical, based in religious affiliation. Iran is clearly interested in providing the leadership for the Shia region and thus as head of one side in this cold war. The Saudis, and especially MBS, have clear aspirations to lead a Sunni coalition, its claim based in the religious symbolism of Mecca and Medina and Saudi wealth. The sectarian differences between the rivals are not so great as to produce a very intense, militarized confrontation.

One factor exists that conditions the Iran-Saudi axis and the broader region: nuclear weapons. Israel, of course, is the only nuclear weapons possessing state in the region and wants desperately to remain so, providing a level of interest that would not otherwise be present. Iran, of course, is the country most physically capable of breaking that monopoly, creating two regional security dynamics. First, Israel and Saudi Arabia both oppose an Iranian nuclear weapon, if for different reasons. From a Saudi perspective, a nuclear Iran would place them in an untenable power position with the Iranians and essentially cede hegemony over the Gulf to their Shiite, non-Arab rivals. As a regional power, in other words, an Iranian bomb relegates Saudi Arabia to being a second-class regional power, a situation they find intolerable. Second, that possession would end the Israeli monopoly and thus military hegemony in the region, with ripple effects on areas like physical expansion. These factors largely explain the basis for Israeli-Saudi rapprochement.

Third, and of potentially far greater international significance, is the likelihood that Iranian possession of nuclear weapons could spark a regional arms race in this highly emotional, volatile region. An Iranian weapon, for instance, would almost certainly result in a Saudi attempt to get a weapon of its own, probably purchased from Pakistan. A Saudi and Iranian nuclear competition is a contingency nobody wants to see. Horror scenarios about weapons spread to unstable regimes are particularly vivid in this area: the image of MBS with his finger on the nuclear button is especially chilling. A cold war between nonnuclear Iran and Saudi is one thing; the same dynamic with nuclear weapons added to the mix is something much more ominous for the area and the international system.

CHOOSING AMERICAN POLICY: IRAQ, SAUDI ARABIA, BOTH, OR NEITHER?

What should the United States position be? Before the Iranian Revolution, the United States was basically neutral, with cordial or at least correct relations with all the major parties. After the hostage crisis ended, American relations with Iran were ended and have not been revived, leaving the Americans as supporters of the Saudis by default and by virtue of the Saudi position as the largest purchasers of American armaments. Israel has always been a centerpiece of U.S. policy, and animosity between Iran and Israel reinforced estrangement with the Iranians. The attachment between the United States and Saudi Arabia increased under Trump.

The rivalry between Saudi Arabia and Iran is the centerpiece of conflict in the Gulf region, and most sources of conflict and violence have some basis in the competition between the leading Sunni and Shiite states. That rivalry is asymmetrical: Iran is clearly the more powerful of the two states by any measure other than gross wealth. The gap is particularly great in military terms: Iran has a much larger military force that has been tested in combat. The closest Saudi Arabia has to an equivalent is its campaign in Yemen, and it has been largely a failure. The Saudis can only pose a military threat to Iran with considerable outside assistance.

The wild card in the regional balance is nuclear weapons, and this makes Israel a factor in Gulf geopolitics in a way it would not otherwise be. The real military danger in the Gulf arises from the possible introduction of nuclear weapons into the calculus. That introduction could happen in two ways, neither desirable for regional for global peace. One possibility is an expansion and formalization of the Saudi-Israeli relationship by which Israel offers a guarantee of Saudi integrity, which inevitably would have an implicit nuclear component. The August 2020 announcement of impending relations between the United Arab Emirates (UAE) and Israel could lead to a further realignment with unknown repercussions. Israel agreed to "suspend" but not rescind annexing the West Bank, the UAE got access to American F-35 fighter jets, and, as usual, the Palestinians lost, leaving continued Iranian support of their cause.

The second, and more likely, possibility is if Iran feels forced to rebuke its historic pledge not to go nuclear and fabricates a weapon either to enhance its position as a key regional actor or to deter Israel. Preventing the Iranians from reaching that decision has been a keystone of U.S. policy in the region, but it is not entirely clear that it can succeed indefinitely. The components of that policy—especially under Trump—have included threats and sanctions and withdrawal from the treaty Iran signed with the United States and five of its European allies by which Iran committed itself from abstention. It is not clear how long the current policy can succeed, especially since the Americans and their allies are at odds.

Nuclearization of the region is the clearest and most dangerous threat the countries pose to one another and to the rest of the world. Should Iran fabricate weapons, it would precipitate a dangerous confrontation with Israel and almost certainly cause the Saudis to buy weapons of their own. The region is emotional: India and Pakistan have managed to control their vitriol toward one another for over two decades of mutual possession: Could Iran and Saudi Arabia do the same? No one knows or wants to find out. The key element in the region is clearly avoiding a nuclear spiral. Other conflicts like that in Yemen are annoying and upsetting; the possibility of a nuclear Gulf is qualitatively different.

Robert Malley, in a 2019 article, framed the broad contours of U.S. regional policy in this area. "The question is how the United States should choose to engage: diplomatically or militarily, by exacerbating divides or mitigating them; and by aligning itself with one side or the other or seeking to achieve a sort of balance." The United States has made itself a partisan force under Trump and other predecessors: Is that how we should proceed in a new decade? Where do American interests truly lie?

BIBLIOGRAPHY

Abrahamian, Ervand. *A History of Modern Iran.* Revised and Updated Second Ed. Cambridge, UK: Cambridge University Press, 2018.

Amanat, Abbas, Derek Perkins, et al. *Iran: A Modern History*. New Haven, CT: Yale University Press, 2019.

Axworthy, Michael. *A History of Iran: Empire of the Mind*. New York: Basic Books, 2016.

———. *Revolutionary Iran: A History of the Islamic Republic*. Oxford, UK: Oxford University Press, 2013.

Blumi, Isa. *Destroying Yemen: What Chaos in Arabia Tells Us about the World*. Berkeley: University of California Press, 2018.

Central Intelligence Agency. *The World Factbook*, 2019–2020. New York: Skyhorse Publishing, 2019.

Central Intelligence Agency. *The World Factbook*, 2020–2021. New York: Skyhorse Publications, 2020.

Commins, David. *The Wahhabi Mission and Saudi Arabia*. London: I. B. Tauris, 2009.

Cordesman, Anthony. "Military Spending: The Other Side of Saudi Security." Washington, DC: Center for Strategic and International Studies, 2018.

———. *Western Strategic Interests in Saudi Arabia*. London: Routledge, 2020.

Ehteshami, Anoushiravan. "The Middle East's New Power Dynamic." *Current History* 108 (December 2009), 395–401.

Firro, Tarik. *Wahhabism and the Rise of the House of Saud*. Sussex, UK: Sussex Academic Press, 2018.

Fraihart, Ibrahim. *Iran and Saudi Arabia: Taming a Chaotic Conflict*. Edinburgh, UK: Edinburgh University Press, 2020.

Frantzman, Seth. *After ISIS: America, Iran, and the Struggle for the Middle East*. Jerusalem: Gefen Publishing House, 2019.

Gause, F. Gregory III. "The End of Saudi Arabia's Ambitions: MBS Must Cut His Losses to Avoid Catastrophe." *Foreign Affairs* (online), August 4, 2020.

Ghattas, Kim. *Black Wave: Saudi Arabia, Iran, and the Forty-Year Rivalry That Unraveled the Culture, Religion, and Collective Memory in the Middle East*. New York: Henry Holt, 2019.

Goldberg, Jeffrey. "How Iran Could Save the Middle East." *The Atlantic* 304 (July/August 2009), 66–68.

Gonzalez, Nathan. *Engaging Iran: The Rise of a Middle Eastern Power and America's Strategic Choice*. Westport, CT: Praeger Security International, 2007.

Hill, Ginny. *Yemen Endures: Civil War, Saudi Adventurism, and the Future of Arabia*. Oxford, UK: University of Oxford Press, 2017.

Hiro, Dilip. *Cold War in the Islamic World: Saudi Arabia, Iran, and the Struggle for Supremacy*. Oxford, UK: Oxford University Press, 2019.

Hope, Bradley, and Justin Schenk. *Blood and Oil: Mohammed bin Salman's Ruthless Quest for Global Power*. Paris: Hachette, 2020.

Hubbard, Ben. *MBS: The Rise to Power of Mohammad bin Salman*. New York: Tom Duggan Books, 2020.

International Institute for Strategic Studies. *IISS Military Balance 2016 and 2017*.

Kamrava, Mehran. *Routledge Handbook of Persian Gulf Politics*. New York: Routledge, 2020.

Kaplan, Robert D. "Living with a Nuclear Iran." *The Atlantic* 306, no. 2 (September 2010), 70–72.

Kazemzedeh, Massoud. *Iran's Foreign Policy: Elite Factionalism, Ideology, the Nuclear Weapons Program, and the United States.* New York: Routledge, 2020.

Keynoush, Banafsheh. *Saudi Arabia and Iran: Friends or Foes?* London: Palgrave Macmillan, 2016.

Kinzer, Stephen. *All the Shah's Men: An American Coup and the Roots of Middle Eastern Terror.* New York: Wiley, 2008.

———. *The Brothers: John Foster Dulles, Allen Dulles, and Their Secret World War.* New York: Times Books, 2013.

Louer, Laurence. Translated by Ethan Rundell. *Sunnis and Shia: A Political History.* Princeton, NJ: Princeton University Press, 2019.

Mabron, Simon. *Saudi Arabia and Iran: Power and Rivalry in the Middle East.* London: I. B. Tauris, 2015.

Mackintosh-Smith, Tim. *Arabs: A 3,000 Year History of Peoples, Tribes, and Empires.* New Haven, CT: Yale University Press, 2019.

Malley, Robert. "The Unwanted Wars: Why the Middle East Is More Combustible than Ever." *Foreign Affairs* 98, 6 (November/December 2019).

Marcus, Jonathan. "Why Saudi Arabia and Iran Are Bitter Rivals." BBC News (online), September 16, 2019.

Nahouza, Namira. *Wahhabism and the Rise of the New Salafists: Theology, Power, and Sunni Islam.* Library of Modern Religion. London: I. B. Tauris, 2018.

Parsi, Trita. *Treacherous Alliance: The Secret Dealings of Israel, Iran, and the United States.* New Haven, CT: Yale University Press, 2008.

Polk, William R. *Understanding Iran: Everything You Need to Know, From Persia to the Islamic Republic, From Cyrus to Khomeini.* New York: St. Martin's Press, 2009.

Razoux, Pierre, and Nicholas Elliott. *The Iran-Iraq War.* Translation Ed. Cambridge, MA: Harvard University Press, 2015.

Riedel, Bruce. *Kings and Presidents: Saudi Arabia and the United States Since FDR.* Updated Ed. Washington, DC: Brookings Institution Press, 2019.

Rundell, David. *Vision or Mirage: Saudi Arabia at the Crossroads.* London: I. B. Tauris, 2020.

Sick, Gary G. *All Fall Down: America's Tragic Encounter with Iran.* New York: Random House, 1985.

Snow, Donald M. *The Case Against Military Intervention: Why We Do It and Why It Fails.* New York: Routledge, 2016.

———. *Cases in International Relations.* Sixth Ed. Chapter 7, "Pivotal States: Confronting and Accommodating Iran" (pp. 125–144). New York: Pearson, 2015.

———. *Cases in International Relations: Principles and Applications.* Eighth Ed. Lanham, MD: Rowman & Littlefield, 2020.

———. *The Middle East, Oil, and the U.S. National Security Policy.* Lanham, MD: Rowman & Littlefield, 2016.

Valentine, Simon Ross. *Force and Fanaticism: Wahhabism in Saudi Arabia and Beyond.* London: Hurst, 2015.

Vatanka, Alex. *The Battle of the Ayatollahs: The United States, Foreign Policy, and Rivalry Since 1979.* London: I. B. Tauris, 2021.

Wald, Ellen R. *Saudi, Inc.: The Arabian Kingdom's Pursuit of Profit and Power.* New York: Pegasus Books, 2018.

Waltz, Kenneth N. "Why Iran Should Get the Bomb." *Foreign Affairs* 91, 4 (July/August 2012), 2–5.

Ward, Terence. *The Wahhabi Code: How the Saudis Spread Extremism Globally.* New York: Skyhorse Publishing Arcade, 2018.

9

The Forever Wars
Iraq and Afghanistan

Much of the controversy over the American involvement in the Middle East today has its roots in two military excursions that were (or at least were argued to be at the time) direct consequences of the 9/11 terrorist attacks against New York and Washington. American military intervention in Afghanistan began mere weeks after Al Qaeda (AQ) launched attacks on the United States mainland. The intervention was a response to American demands that the AQ perpetrators who enjoyed protection from the government in Afghanistan be turned over to American officials in order to try them for their crimes. The request was denied by the Taliban rulers in Kabul. The United States intervened militarily to capture the AQ terrorists as they fled across the Tora Bora mountains into Pakistan, where many still reside. The United States remained in the country as part of the resistance to the Taliban after this October 2001 failure. They are still there twenty years later.

The United States invaded and occupied Iraq in 2003. The action was largely justified as part of the ongoing response to 9/11. It was argued by the George W. Bush administration that the government of Saddam Hussein was cooperating with AQ and that they might even be planning to provide the terrorists with weapons of mass destruction (WMD) for use against Americans. Neither charge has ever been proven, but the United States completed the invasion and was the occupying government of the country until 2011, when it completed the withdrawal of the bulk of its forces. The Americans never left completely, and there is a residue of American force presence in 2021.

These involvements are the two longest wars in American history. Both have become highly controversial for a variety of reasons, including whether they should have occurred and why they have lasted so long. They have become the prototypes of what is known as endless wars or forever wars.

The major questions that surround them include how and why the United States became so involved in these conflicts in countries of historical insignificance to the United States, how to extricate the country from them, and how to avoid repeating the mistakes that led to them and arguably continue to be made in prosecuting them. In the 2020 presidential election, incumbent Trump referred to them as "endless" wars; challenger Biden coined the phrase "forever" wars in a 2020 *Foreign Affairs* article. The imputation in both depictions is that American involvement was not a good idea and is to be avoided in the future.

It is important to examine each as an American national security problem for two reasons. First, both wars have been failures, and if the United States is to learn from them, we must understand why. The answer is different for each war; what they share is that the United States entered both with only vague ideas of what it sought to accomplish, those objectives were largely unattainable and hence quixotic, and the military and geopolitical underpinnings were much different and more difficult than the United States envisaged when it undertook the missions. More succinctly, both were essentially bad ideas conditioned by America's mistaken analysis of the situations and the region. Second, both have been not only lengthy, but physically draining of American blood and treasure, and these losses will only continue to grow until they end.

A commonality of both situations is the proximity of both countries to Iran, with which the two countries have different relations. Iran and Afghanistan have had generally friendly formal relations since the 1930s, and the peoples of the two countries have considerable attachments, including languages with common roots and cultural ties. Iran backed those who came to power in 2001 in Afghanistan, despite the fact that the Iranians are overwhelmingly Shia and most Afghans are Sunni. Iranian relations are closer with Iraq, which is also majority Shiite. One of the American objectives in overthrowing the Sunni-dominated minority government of Saddam Hussein was the hope that a Shiite Arab regime in Baghdad would be independent of and resistant to Persian Shiite Iran. Most observers believe just the opposite has occurred.

Understanding how the United States got mired into seemingly endless involvement in these two countries is important to American national security policy generally and specifically to regional policy. The discussion pivots on both the forever war sentiment versus the asserted need to maintain American ability to influence world events. Both strands of advocacy are exemplified by the long wars in Afghanistan and Iraq.

The rest of the chapter will examine these questions. For both the Afghanistan and Iraq cases, it will begin by looking at the objectives the United States had, focusing on the sufficiency and accuracy of perceived interests.

The second question in each case is the importance and attainability of those objectives: Were they important enough to pursue and could we reach them? Following that assessment, the third question is why has the United States failed to attain its objectives in either, resulting in forever wars?

THE AFGHAN WAR

The causal chain of American major military involvement in the Middle East in the twenty-first century begins in the remote central Asian country of Afghanistan. The cause is clear. AQ, the terrorist group that mounted the 9/11 attacks, lived in Afghanistan as the protected guests of the Taliban government. The connection between the Taliban and AQ goes back to the 1970s Afghan campaign to expel the Soviet Union occupiers of the country. Many members of the Taliban were native Afghans who had fought in that resistance, and many of the Al Qaeda members (including founder Osama bin Laden) were foreigners who also joined that resistance, creating the bond between them.

Prior to 9/11, American involvement in Afghanistan was minimal and marginal. There are several reasons for this marginality. The first is geographic. The forty-second largest country in the world in land mass (about the size of Texas), Afghanistan is literally halfway around the world from the United States. It is a rugged, arid, mountainous land, and forbidding topography has separated the various clans that populate the country and help form the basis for Afghan culture and political structure. Geopolitically, the country is important mostly because major trade routes transverse it: east-west routes from the Orient to Asia Minor and Europe, and north-south routes from Central Asia and Europe to the Indian subcontinent. The east-west routes have attracted invaders like the Mongol Hordes; the north-south routes have attracted numerous intruders from Alexander the Great to the British and the Russians. Without these intrusions, Afghanistan would largely have been left alone, which its clans prefer.

The people reflect this geography. Like virtually everything about Afghanistan, they are a diverse and often contentious lot. Of the estimated (July 2020 estimate in *CIA World Factbook*) 36,643,815 Afghans, the largest ethnic group is the Pashtuns. This tribe has numerous subclans and is subdivided into urban and rural branches and has historically constituted a majority in the country that has ruled when Afghanistan has a truly national government. Although reliable figures are not available, their percentage of the population today probably is about 42 percent; many Taliban, for instance, are rural Pashtuns who fled to Pakistan (where they are the second largest ethnic group) before the current civil war broke out. Rural Pashtuns are the backbone of the Taliban, whereas urban Pashtuns (former President Hamid Karzai is a prime example) have tended to lead governments based in Kabul. Other major clan/ethnic groups include the Tajiks, Hazara, Uzbeks, Baloch, Turkmen, Nuristani, Arabs, and others as recognized in the 2004 constitution. Almost all are Sunnis, and official languages include Afghan Persian Dari and Pashto. Most of these tribes come into conflict, sometimes violently, at one time or another. It is sometimes said of the Afghans that when there is an outside invader, they unite and repulse the intruder; when there is no outside threat, they fight among themselves.

Two cultural artifacts have particularly affected the American effort. The first comes from the Pashtun culture and, more specifically, the code of Pashtunwali. It has two relevant aspects. The first is hospitality: if someone or a group is one's guest, that individual or group is accorded the maximum security by the Pashtun host. Former Soviet-resisting AQ allies of the Taliban enjoyed this status, and it is an important part of the reason the Pashtun-dominated Taliban government refused to turn their AQ guests over to American control in 2001. The second cultural artifact is more general but no less potent, and it was part of the Taliban appeal. As Malkasian explains it, "The Taliban exemplified an idea that runs deep in Afghan culture that . . . in the eyes of many Afghans defines an individual's worth. In simple terms, that idea is resistance to occupation."

Afghan attitudes toward government also mirror the people and their physical environment. Afghan tribes and their members are intensely individualistic and distrustful of others, including foreigners and even other tribal groups, and this is reflected in a general suspicion and opposition to government, and especially centralized Kabul-based governments. The traditional preference for Afghans and specifically rural, Pashtun-dominated tribes, is for minimal government that is, at most, confederal in structure and authority. The historic expression of this preference has been government by loya jirga, periodic gatherings of clan elders where common problems are discussed and resolved, with essential anarchy at other times that is mediated when necessary. A strong central government is an aspiration associated with the large metropolitan areas and notably the government supported by U.S. policy. A prime artifact is the Afghan national army.

SUFFICIENCY AND SALIENCE OF OBJECTIVES

Why did the United States intervene in Afghanistan? It began with a simple and understandable American desire for revenge against the terrorist organization that had carried out the 9/11 attacks expressed as a desire to apprehend and bring those international criminals to justice. It was clearly in the American national interest—arguably a vital interest—to demonstrate to potential future enemies the consequences of potential acts. Had this occurred, the mission would have been an inarguable major success. Unfortunately, that did not happen, and in the process the mission—and its purpose—changed with the result of the forever war that has gone on ever since.

What went wrong? From a strategic vantage point, the answer is virtually everything. First, the Taliban refused to hand over their guests to American control in September 2001, a traditional Pashtunwali response that the Americans did not anticipate. When that happened, the United States organized an armed attack on the Tora Bora region of eastern Afghanistan to which AQ had retired after the attack. The Americans pursued them, but with the help of sympathetic rural tribesmen, AQ slipped through the planned encirclement of Operation Anaconda and snuck into exile in Pakistan, from which many of them still operate.

At this point, the Americans faced a decision point, and the determination they reached has resulted in the current morass. In early 2002, the United States had two choices. One was to withdraw its troops and continue its pursuit of AQ in other ways such as clandestine, special forces operations, placing pressure on Pakistan to turn them over, or finding AQ hideaways and obliterating them with air strikes—three popular options at the time. The other was to leave the troops in place, which inevitably created a de facto alliance between the Americans and the coalition of opponents of the Taliban known as the Northern Alliance that ultimately prevailed with American support. The result was to create a relationship and interest with the Northern Alliance as it became the Karzai government and thus to involve the United States in the Afghan civil war that has raged ever since. The commitment was unprecedented in U.S.-Afghan relations and represented no important historical American interest. No detailed explanation for this decision has become public beyond a generalized belief among some Americans that AQ would try again in 2002.

The result was a contrast. In October 2001, the United States reached a determination to enter Afghanistan based on a clearly stated desire for retribution the importance of which was universally supported. When the United States did not capture AQ, its accomplishment of that objective had failed. Early the next year, the United States decided not to withdraw and left a force in the country that became aligned with one element in the country's internal struggle. The United States became an occupier and the enemy of many Afghans, notably the Taliban. The objective for this has never been crystalline, nor has the vitality of its achievement. The forever war was engaged without any consensual American objective.

IMPORTANCE AND ATTAINABILITY OF THE OBJECTIVE

Whether Afghanistan was important enough to warrant a major American military effort depends on which American objective one is assessing. The original October 2001 purpose of suppressing AQ (and by extension, other international terrorist organizations) clearly met the criterion of worthiness and responded to the rage the American people felt at the atrocious acts that had been committed. Preventing a reprise certainly met the test of vitality and political importance. Had the Taliban remanded Al Qaeda to American control, the Afghan experience would have been an undeniable success, and there would have been no Afghan War from the American perspective (the civil war between the Taliban and the Northern Alliance presumably would have continued). The United States would have had no long-term commitment to that country, and the episode would have been a footnote in American security, not a central controversy.

That, of course, is not what happened, and instead Afghanistan has become synonymous with the forever war. What is remarkable about the transformation of the American involvement is that it was done essentially by accident. The Americans entered Afghanistan in the waning months of 2001 to achieve a concrete objective, and they failed. But they did not leave; instead they stayed, and it was not clear then and is not clear today why.

LESSONS OF AFGHANISTAN

Judging the Afghanistan war in terms of success and failure and thus what lessons should be taken from it is difficult, confusing, and controversial. Nineteen years after the initial American deployment occurred, less than 4,000 American forces, many special forces trainers there instructing the Afghan army, remain. President Trump vowed early on to end this "endless" commitment, and former Vice President Biden decried Afghanistan as the quintessential "forever" war and thus an episode to be concluded. At the other end of the spectrum, many hawkish observers maintain a continued minimal presence is necessary to prevent a Taliban victory in the long civil war and thus open the possibility for AQ to return or an organization like the Islamic State (IS). Is that reason enough to continue an involvement that cost over a trillion American dollars and several thousand American lives? Have we achieved the goals we set out to accomplish? Are we on the way to somehow "winning" this conflict? How will we know if we have fulfilled our mission?

The frustration of answering the question is that it was not clear at the time exactly what we were trying to accomplish. The initial goal was clear: capture, try, and punish the AQ terrorists who had attacked New York and Washington. If that goal had been achieved, we could have saluted briskly, loudly proclaimed "mission accomplished," and left the country to fend for itself in its civil war. The problem, of course, was that we did not achieve the goal, but we also did not leave. We had little if any vested interest in whether the Northern Alliance or the Taliban won the civil conflict beyond the possibility a Taliban victory would create a more hospitable terrorist environment. Was that reason enough for the longest war in U.S. history? A more compelling set of articulated objectives was not widely shared publicly at the time. How could we measure then or now whether an unarticulated objective was worthy or could be achieved?

Our confusion was facilitated both by the political and military situations into which we placed ourselves. Prior to the terrorist attacks of 9/11, relations between the two countries were minimal. Located half the world apart, the only major source of contention was the heroin pipeline from the Afghan countryside to the United States. The United States provided arms to the Afghan rebels combatting the Soviet Union in the 1970s, but that action was motivated to compound problems for the Soviets, not out of any bond with the Afghans. In 2001, the United States had little interest in the outcome of the civil war until the Taliban regime's refusal to remand AQ to American control created an interest for them.

The fear of another AQ attack devised from Afghanistan drove the American deepening involvement in the country. The government's refusal to accede to American demands made them the de facto enemy and the Northern Alliance the American "ally," and that confluence led to American support for the Karzai regime that emerged from the civil war when the Taliban fled temporarily to Pakistan. At that point, the mission of the United States and its allies became keeping the Taliban and especially AQ from returning and regaining power. They did return and resume the active civil war in 2003. That war is still ongoing, reflecting deep divisions among Afghans and the unpopularity and corruption of the government in Kabul.

The presidential election of 2020 was held nineteen years and a month after the United States first deployed in Afghanistan. After they failed to capture AQ, there was no dramatic announcement or debate on what the ultimate objective was: When could the United States declare mission accomplished (victory) and come home? The war just continues; no one declares progress toward "victory." The response from Afghanistan apologists is that the

United States has (normally undefined) interests and that it would harm those interests should the Taliban emerge victorious in the civil war. What the presence of a few troops (mostly trainers) does to prevent this outcome generally goes unexplained.

The adequacy of the objective to justify a continuing military presence in Afghanistan is the first, primary flaw in the American presence: it means success is unmeasurable in any precise way. How do we know when we have won? When can we declare victory? Do we need an "Aiken victory" (named after a Vermont senator during Vietnam), who suggested we simply declare victory, come home, and let the world figure out what victory means?

That leads to the second problem: Was victory in any military sense ever attainable at acceptable cost? Or did the United States so totally misunderstand the situation that it undertook a mission impossible? Afghanistan, "the graveyard of empires" in the title of a book on the country, is a difficult place to fight and prevail. Many, from Alexander the Great to the Soviet Union, have tried, and the tough Afghans have become very adept at repulsing them. A bleak, forbidding topography and climate have combined with a very tough, unyielding character among the contentious tribesmen. Malkasian, as noted, has summarized it: virtue in Afghan eyes is based on "resistance to occupiers." Historically, it does not matter who the invaders are or why they intrude on the country: Afghans will resent their presence and unite enough to resist. Combined with the historic hatred many Afghans have for a central, urban-based government that may impinge on their autonomy (and with whom the Americans have allied themselves), the United States set itself up for failure over objectives, which, after AQ escaped Operation Anaconda, were simply not worth it. It is not clear the Americans understood this when they decided to send forces into the country originally, but they should have when they decided to stay.

The Afghan tribesmen are extremely difficult to defeat on the ground. A rugged, harsh topography with which they but not their opponents are familiar is a tremendous advantage that they ruthlessly exploit, and they are fierce, even savage warriors. Accepting bounties for killed enemies (as alleged in 2020) is not surprising for people whose purpose is to drive enemies from their land by making it too awful for them to stay and is part of the tradition. Moreover, the Afghans are masters of what is now called "asymmetrical war" (see Chapter 10), which is well suited to the Afghan landscape and credo, but this has not historically been an American strength. The Americans should have understood this when deciding on their course of action, but there is no indication they did. As a result, the United States created an impossible situation for themselves, from which, as the 2020 presidential election was impending, it had been unable to admit its error and follow the lead of innumerable intruders before packing up and leaving the Afghans to themselves.

THE IRAQ WAR

Many observers of U.S. national security policy in the Middle East do not believe that Afghanistan was the worst decision the country has made in this century. That distinction is generally reserved for the other prototypical forever war in Iraq, the action that began with the American invasion and conquest of that country in May 2003. Ben Rhodes, Deputy National Security Advisor under Obama, mirrors the conclusion of most policy analysts by describing the invasion as "the single most catastrophic foreign policy decision of my lifetime." It was certainly the most perplexing and, in the estimation of most national security professionals, the least successful use of American force in the region.

The Iraq War shares the common root of the American reaction to 9/11 as the precipitant. In the case of Afghanistan, the initial connection was clear and popularly defensible; it was subsequent actions (staying for so long after failing to accomplish the initial objective) that have been controversial. The Iraq adventure is different: the rationale for taking down the Saddam Hussein government and acting as the effective occupying power for the next eight years was controversial at the time and has remained so. The Iraq War was also shorter: American forces officially withdrew at the end of 2011, but remnants have remained to this day. Before the general election of 2020, for instance, President Trump announced that he would reduce the American presence from 5,200 to 3,500 troops. Iraq remains a forever war.

American relations with Iraq have been short but tumultuous. Iraq is a classic artificial state that did not come into existence until 1932, and U.S.-Iraqi relations were minimal until 1979, meaning, among other things, that there were few discernible long-term American interests there around which to form a basis for future involvement. That changed in 1979 for two reasons. First, an internationally unknown Iraqi army colonel with broad regional ambitions named Saddam Hussein came to power in Baghdad, consolidating control by the country's Sunni minority. Second, the general tumult of the Gulf area discussed in Chapter 8 brought a radical Shiite regime to power in neighboring Iran.

The Iranian Revolution created palpitations throughout the region as well as instability in Iran, and Hussein sought to exploit both for Iraqi and personal reasons. With American diplomats still hostage in Teheran, Hussein invaded Iran in 1980. He was undoubtedly influenced by perceived weakness in the Iranian military caused by purges of an officer corps that had been loyal to the Shah, and he believed Iraq could achieve a quick victory that would, among other things, make him a hero of a Sunni world frightened by events in Iran and, at best, even elevate him personally as the successor of Gamal Abdul Nasser as titular leader of the Arab world.

His calculation of Iranian weakness proved wrong. The Iranians rebounded from early setbacks, and the war became an inconclusive contest that continued until 1988. The United States had its first real involvement with Iraq during this period, supporting the Iraqi military effort against the Iranians. On paper, the war was a mismatch, with Iran having a population and military twice the size of Iraq's, and as the war dragged on, the Iraqi government gradually bankrupted itself. After it ended, Saddam Hussein went to the Sunni states he had allegedly helped by protecting them from Iran and asked for forgiveness of loans he had been given by them. Iraq's leading creditors were oil-rich neighbor Kuwait and Saudi Arabia. Both refused Saddam's request.

In August 1990, Saddam invaded and rapidly conquered Kuwait to force compliance with his demands. After a lightning campaign the Iraqi forces stood at the Kuwaiti-Saudi border, a short dash from the Saudi refining facilities that Saudi forces were totally incapable of defending. Fearing a repeat of the conquest of Kuwait, the Saudis accepted an American offer to come to their assistance, in the process rejecting an offer by a then-obscure veteran of the Soviet-Afghanistan War named Osama bin Laden and sparking an undying hatred for Americans among his AQ followers. The United States quickly assembled a coalition to evict the Iraqis from Kuwait, an action successfully executed during the Persian Gulf War of January–February 1991. One consequence was to transform Iraq and Hussein from an erstwhile partner in the opposition to Iran into an implacable foe who would need dispatching as well.

The Iraqi-American relationship festered for over a decade. Some American analysts believed that coalition forces should have marched into Iraq to complete the 1991 campaign, an option President George H. W. Bush presciently rejected as likely to lead to a long civil war against the occupiers. The prospect disappeared from public view during the Clinton administration, but it resurfaced as part of the reaction to 9/11.

The precipitants were reports in 2002 and 2003, largely from a hawkish Republican faction known as the neoconservatives (or neocons) of Iraqi connivance with AQ. These reports included two unlikely, linked claims. The first was that Saddam Hussein was building WMDs, notably chemical and biological weapons, that he might make available. The plausibility of this arose from the second accusation—that the Iraqi dictator and AQ were cooperating against the United States. No plausible evidence was ever produced to substantiate either claim. Saddam had abandoned his chemical weapons program in the 1990s, and despite extensive efforts to find evidence of a renewed effort after the American occupation was in place, no conclusive supporting evidence was ever found. The claim of an alliance between the Iraqis and AQ was simply ludicrous: the two forces were enemies with strikingly different religious beliefs. At the time they were made, however, the United States was still in the throes of antiterrorist hysteria reinforced by an almost total lack of knowledge of Iraq, and so they were not seriously challenged in public. They formed the public basis for the American invasion.

The invasion and conquest of Iraq were a walkover. The Iraqi armed forces had been smashed in 1991 by American forces in Kuwait, and the Iraqis offered only a token resistance that was easily brushed aside. Instead, they quit the field and went underground, where they waged an asymmetrical, guerrilla-style resistance against the Americans that was effective in frustrating the occupiers, prolonging the conflict, and eventually alienating the Americans to the point that they largely left the country. It is also largely the military approach of the Taliban in Afghanistan and is a strategy for which the United States lacks a satisfactory counterstrategy.

SUFFICIENCY AND SALIENCE OF THE OBJECTIVES

When the United States invaded Iraq in 2003, it did have one remaining interest that dated back to 1991. After the war ended, Saddam Hussein turned to exacting revenge against those Iraqi groups that had not supported the war effort, notably the Kurds and the Shiites. His vengeance against the Kurds was especially savage, including chemical weapons attacks on Kurdish villages. Many Kurds panicked and fled across the border into southern Turkey, where they were decidedly unwelcome by the government. The question was how to get them to return to Iraq, and the United States devised a plan to do so. Called Operation Provide Comfort (later Northern Watch), it declared that the Kurdish areas would be off limits to Iraqi armed forces, a declaration to be enforced by American and other allied armed forces.

It also created a problem. Given Saddam's vengefulness, the safety it provided would only last for as long as enforcement continued, making it open-ended. If the United States left, the situation would revert. The ban was extended to the Shiites (Operation Southern Watch), and it remained in force until the 2003 invasion. With Saddam's government overthrown and the dictator eventually captured and executed, the guarantee was no longer relevant, and the operation ceased. The invasion thus solved one problem.

The problem of the objective has plagued the operation ever since. If one rejects the official accusations of WMDs and connivance with AQ (which many did at the time and almost everyone does now), with what is one left to justify the invasion and conquest? Saddam was a ruthless despot whose Sunni-dominated government (29–34 percent of the population) dominated the rest of the population virtually totally, but there are numerous other regimes which were as reprehensible by American standards that got a pass from the United States. In the end, it has been difficult to delineate any geopolitically important objective to justify the action, making it impossible to tell for sure if it was accomplished. The best answer to "did we achieve the objective?" may be "what objective?"

IMPORTANCE AND ATTAINABILITY OF THE OBJECTIVE

The lack of a clear reason for invading and occupying Iraq contributed to what almost all observers view as a botched effort. Once the regime had fallen, the American command disbanded the Iraqi armed forces and the government. The intent was to remove the supporters of the tyranny from power; the effect was to strip both the government and the military of nearly all their expertise and to leave those official Iraqis bitter, unemployed, and even less happy than they would have been otherwise. One of the ironies of the effects was that many former Iraqi military officers became leaders of IS as it tried to overthrow the Shiite-dominated Iraqi state. It also created a ready manpower pool for the resistance to American occupation. Unintended consequences were a hallmark of the occupation.

The United States removed its last remaining combat forces in 2011 (some trainers and guards remained) and turned governance over to an Iraqi government dominated by the Shiites who, in the words of U.S. advisor Emma Sky, embraced the goal as "a nation at peace with itself, a participant in the global market of goods and ideas, and an ally against violent extremists." These were noble goals for a country that had experienced over eight years of occupation and occasionally violent resistance to foreign rule, and they provided at least some evidence of accomplishment of some objectives. Unfortunately, the conditions were more difficult to meet, at least partially because the intergroup (Sunni-Shia-Kurd) cooperation on which they were premised were easier to state than to implement. The Kurdish region acted increasingly autonomously from Baghdad, and resistance was especially great among the Sunnis in the area known as the Sunni Triangle wedged between the Shiite South and the Kurdish north. The most important example accompanied the emergence and prairie fire-like rise and spread of IS, which also delayed a total American withdrawal of the American military presence in the country.

Ironically, the emergence of IS as a regional and possibly wider threat provided a more plausible threat and rationale for American involvement in including Iraq than did the situation in 2003. As IS swept apparently unstoppable across eastern Syria and northern Iraq in 2014 and maps showed more of the area turning IS black, there was growing fear that the evangelical backers of the Caliphate would pose a terrorist threat greater than that presented by AQ in the previous decade. The Caliphate's forces came within striking distance of Baghdad. Their campaign posed a level of national security threat that had not existed in 2003.

LESSONS OF IRAQ

The situation was further ironic because the negative reaction to the long occupation made it politically impossible for the United States to contemplate a major effort to stop IS with American forces. Fortunately for the Americans, much of the IS campaign occurred in Kurdish areas, and Kurdish militias (the pesh merga) responded, stopped, and reversed the march of IS. The United States provided material assistance to the Kurds as its contribution to achieving their mutual interest in containing IS. In 2003, the situation arguably did not justify a major U.S. military action, but one occurred. In 2014, such an effort was probably justifiable but was impossible to sell because of the folly of the first action. The bogus fear of Iraqi involvement in terrorism in 2003 created the illusion of a threat to basic U.S. security that was marginal at best and led to the current morass of forever wars. The threat was at least potentially real in 2014, but the folly of 2003 made decisive response politically impossible in the United States.

There are three major lessons of the Iraq experience. The first is determining the adequacy of the objective as a justification for dispatching American forces into what became an open-ended commitment that clearly exceeded any objective assessment of vital interest engagement. The neocons who pushed for the invasion argued that the criterion of vital interest involvement to permit the use of force was too high, that nefarious actions by Saddam endangered American interests, and even that the successful overthrow of his regime could lead to the establishment of a model political democracy in the country that could be an example for the region. Numerous critics, many included in the bibliography for this chapter, rejected (or even ridiculed) these assumptions, and they were largely proven correct. They carried the day in the Bush White House, however.

The second lesson is that one must clearly understand the nature of the situation into which one proposes to insinuate one's self. Saddam's Iraq was a ruthless dictatorship where one of its major groups (the Sunni Arabs) had essentially all power that they applied to suppress the other groups (the Shia and the Kurds). When the Americans asserted themselves, they stripped the Sunnis of all their power. Among the effects of doing so was to create a power vacuum that left the country without experienced personnel to run it. The Kurds exploited the chaos to act virtually autonomously in their zone, but the Shiites were clearly not capable of organizing a viable government. Running the country fell to the Americans, who were not prepared for the task, and their rule created even more unrest, including a rebellion by many Sunnis. The Americans had entered Iraq expecting a short and decisive operation. In May 2003, U.S. Secretary of Defense Donald Rumsfeld predicted almost all forces could be withdrawn by Labor Day of that year. The Americans not only had an inadequate reason to invade Iraq; they also had little idea what to do once they were there and in charge.

The third lesson is understanding the kinds of wars that occur in places that can become forever involvements for the United States. Two characteristics, elaborated in Chapter 10, stand out. First, these involvements occur in developing world states that are multinational, featuring political, ethnic, and often religious cleavages that are internal in nature. The wars that occur are what are generically called "civil wars," and among the most salient characteristics of these conflicts is that they are inherently desperate, with high stakes that can rarely be reconciled through political compromise. I have called these situations developing world internal conflicts (DWICs) elsewhere (see *National Security*, Seventh Ed.) and have argued outside interventions to resolve these rarely succeed, especially if the outsiders do not know what they are getting into. Second, the issues that divide the parties are inherently more important to the internal parties than they are to the intervening power. As a result, those internal powers will persist long after the intervener either bores of or becomes frustrated by the endlessness and lack of progress of the effort and leaves. For the internal powers, dealing with the outsiders means maximizing the frustration of the interveners. Dragging out endless wars is part of that strategy.

CHOOSING POLICY: AVOIDING ENDLESS WARS

The forever wars in Afghanistan and Iraq are prime examples of the dynamics described immediately above. The Afghan civil war began well before the United States intervened and will probably continue long after the Americans leave. In Iraq, the United States in effect created the civil war and unrest among internal factions. The internal groups have not been able to resolve their differences, and the Americans have not been much help in that process. What has become crystal clear, however, is that the American public (like the publics in most democracies) dislikes these kinds of involvements and that, like the period after a similar involvement in Vietnam a half century ago, is likely to be politically prohibitively suspicious of any possible action that could have a similar result. The possibility of future forever wars is political poison.

What should the United States do? The short and easy answer is that the country should pack its bags and leave both countries with as much dignity as possible, which is essentially what it tried to do in Southeast Asia. That solution, however, had costs then, and it probably would now. In 1975, the cost was an inward turning that probably handcuffed much foreign activism, and some of it was probably justified. Retreating from the possibility of forever wars would connote failure to many Americans and would make it more difficult to act for some time to come. Would foreign adversaries like Russia exploit the perception of American reluctance to compete in the Middle East, where they seek to increase their influence? They almost certainly would.

As with virtually all the problems already discussed in this volume, there are pros and cons to any solution. If the problem in both Iraq and Afghanistan was rushing into situations where we did not fully understand the situation and where success neither served vital interests nor was attainable anyway, then leaving and articulating more cautionary criteria for assessing possible future activism is not a bad general guidepost. The problem, of course, is always in the unique factors that surround any situation, especially in as complex an area as the Middle East. The devil, as always, is in the details, but one thing seems clear: just as the Southeast Asian war resulted in a clarion cry for "no more Vietnams," the response to Iraq and Afghanistan will spawn a "no more forever wars" response. What exactly that might mean will be the subject of Chapter 10.

BIBLIOGRAPHY

Ansary, Tamim. *Game Without Rules: The Often-Interrupted History of Afghanistan.* New York: Public Affairs, 2012.

Bacevich, Andrew J. *America's War for the Greater Middle East: A Military History.* New York: Random House Home Trade Paperbacks, 2017.

Bailey, Beth, and Richard H. Immerman. *Understanding the U.S. Wars in Iraq and Afghanistan.* New York: New York University Press, 2015.

Barfield, Thomas. *Afghanistan: A Cultural and Political History.* Princeton, NJ: Princeton University Press, 2013.

Barnett, Roger W. *Asymmetrical Warfare: Today's Challenge to U.S. Military Power.* Washington, DC: Potomac Books, 2013.

Belasco, Amy. *The Cost of Iraq, Afghanistan, and Other Terrorist Operations Since 9/11.* Washington, DC: Congressional Research Service, December 8, 2014.

Biddle, Stephen, Fotini Christia, and Alexander Thier. "Defining Success in Afghanistan: What Can the United States Expect?" *Foreign Affairs* 89, 4 (July/August 2010), 58–60.

Brisard, Jean Jacques. *Zarqawi: The New Face of Al-Qaeda.* New York: Other Press, 2005.

Central Intelligence Agency. *CIA World Factbook, 2020–2021.* New York: Skyhorse, 2020.

Chandrasekaran, Rajiv. *Imperial Life in the Emerald City: Inside Iraq's Green Zone.* New York: Alfred A. Knopf, 2007.

Cockburn, Patrick. *The Rise of the Islamic State: ISIS and the New Sunni Revolution.* London: Verso, 2015.

Coll, Steve. *Directorate S: The CIA and America's Secret Wars in Afghanistan and Pakistan.* New York: Penguin Books, 2018.

Cronin, Audrey Kurth. "ISIS Is Not a Terrorist Group: Why Counterterrorism Won't Stop the Latest Jihadi Group." *Foreign Affairs* 94, 3 (March/April 2015), 87–98.

Draper, Robert. *To Start a War: How the Bush Administration Took America into War.* New York: Penguin Books, 2020.

Ewens, Martin. *Afghanistan: A Short History of Its People and Politics.* New York: HarperPerennials, 2002.

Gallagher, Brendan R. *The Day After: Why America Wins the War but Loses the Peace.* Ithaca, NY: Cornell University Press, 2019.

Goldberg, Jeffrey. "After Iraq." *The Atlantic* 301, 1 (January/February 2008), 68–79.

Haass, Richard. *Wars of Necessity, Wars of Choice: A Memoir of Two Iraq Wars.* New York: Simon & Schuster, 2009.

Isikoff, Michael, and David Corn. *Hubris: The Inside Story of Spin, Scandal, and the Selling of the Iraq War.* New York: Three Rivers, 2007.

Jalil, Ali Ahmed. *A Military History of Afghanistan: From the Great Game to the Global War on Terror.* Lawrence: University of Kansas Press, 2017.

Johnson, Robert. *The Afghan Way of War: How and Why They Fight.* Oxford, UK: Oxford University Press, 2011.

Jones, Seth G. "How Trump Should Manage Afghanistan: A Realistic Set of Goals for the New Administration." *Foreign Affairs* (online), March 21, 2017.

———. *In the Graveyard of Empires: America's War in Afghanistan.* New York: W. W. Norton, 2009.

Lee, Jonathan L. *Afghanistan: A History from 1620 to the Present.* London: Reaktion Books, 2019.

Malkasian, Carter. "How the Good War Went Bad: America's Slow-Motion Failure in Afghanistan." *Foreign Affairs* 99, 2 (March/April 2020), 77–91.

———. *War Comes to Garmser: Thirty Years of Conflict on the Afghan Frontier.* Oxford, UK: Oxford University Press, 2013.

McCants, William. *The ISIS Apocalypse: The History, Strategy, and Doomsday Vision of the Islamic State.* New York: St. Martin's Press, 2015.

O'Connell, Aaron B. (ed.). *Our Latest Longest War: Losing Hearts and Minds in Afghanistan.* Chicago: University of Chicago Press, 2017.

Packer, George. *The Assassin's Gate: America in Iraq.* New York: Farrar, Straus and Giroux, 2005.

Polk, William R. *Understanding Iraq.* New York: HarperPerennials, 2005.

Pollack, Kenneth M. *The Threatening Storm: The Case for Invading Iraq.* A Council on Foreign Relations Book. New York: Random House, 2002.

Rhodes, Ben. "The Democratic Renewal: What It Will Take to Fix U.S. Foreign Policy." *Foreign Affairs* 99, 5 (September/October 2020), 46–56.

Ricks, Thomas E. *Fiasco: The American Adventure in Iraq.* New York: Penguin Books, 2006.

Sadat, Kosh, and Stanley McChrystal. "Staying the Course in Afghanistan: How to Fight the Longest War." *Foreign Affairs* 96, 6 (November/December, 2017), 2–8.

Shahrani, M. Nafiz (ed.). *Modern Afghanistan: The Impact of Forty Years of War.* Bloomington: Indiana University Press, 2018.

Sky, Emma. "Iraq: From Surge to Sovereignty." *Foreign Affairs* 90, 2 (March/April 2011), 117–127.

Snow, Donald M. *The Case Against Military Intervention: Why We Do It and Why It Fails.* New York: Routledge, 2016.

———. *Cases in International Relations: Principles and Applications.* Eighth Ed. Lanham, MD: Rowman & Littlefield, 2020.

———. *The Middle East, Oil, and the U.S. National Security Policy: Intractable Conflicts, Impossible Solutions.* Lanham, MD: Rowman & Littlefield, 2016.

———. *National Security.* Seventh Ed. New York: Routledge, 2020.

———. *Regional Cases in U. S. Foreign Policy.* Second Ed. Lanham, MD: Rowman & Littlefield, 2018.

———. *What After Iraq?* New York: Pearson Longman, 2009.

———, and Dennis M. Drew. *From Lexington to Desert Storm and Beyond.* Third Ed. Armonk, NY: M.E. Sharpe, 2010.

Stern, Jessica, and J. M. Berger. *ISIS: The State of Terror.* New York: Ecco, 2015.

Tanner, Stephen. *Afghanistan: A Military History from Alexander the Great to the War against the Taliban.* Boston: Da Capo Press, 2009.

Tomsen, Peter. *The Wars of Afghanistan: Messianic Terrorism, Tribal Conflicts, and the Failure of Great Powers.* New York: PublicAffairs, 2013.

U.S. Army and U.S. Marine Corps. *Counterinsurgency Field Manual* (U.S. Army Field Manual 3-24) (U.S. Marine Warfighting Publication 3-3.35). Chicago: University of Chicago Press, 2007.

U.S. Marine Corps. *Afghanistan: Operational Culture for Deploying Personnel.* Quantico, VA: Center for Advanced Operational Cultural Learning, 2009.

Weiss, Michael, and Hassan Hassan. *ISIS: Inside the Army of Terror.* Updated Ed. New York: Regan Arts, 2016.

Weston, J. Kael. *The Mirror Test: America at War in Iraq and Afghanistan.* New York: Vintage Books, 2016.

Wood, Graeme. "What ISIS Really Wants." *The Atlantic* 321, 2 (March 2015), 78–90.

10

Navigating the Geopolitical Spider's Web

American national security policy has been more fully engaged in the Middle East than in any other part of the world since the turn of the century. The country has always had an energy-driven stake in that part of the world, but those forces have expanded. The precipitant, of course, was 9/11 and the shock wave of anger, fear, and demand for retribution it created in the population. The reaction led to two of the longest and most controversial military actions in U.S. history. Both continue to command resources and take American lives. Attempts at extraction have proven unsuccessful.

Although both campaigns for the presidency in 2020 vowed leaving Iraq and Afghanistan and hinted at a more restrained assessment of American interests and their pursuit, it is not clear how that goal will be implemented. Candidate Biden was more explicit in his vow to reduce American commitments. In a 2020 *Foreign Affairs* article, he said "It is past time to end the forever wars. We should narrowly define our [Middle East] mission as defeating Al Qaeda and the Islamic State." Incumbent Trump also emphasized concluding what he called the "endless wars," but his overall policy orientation (which Indyk calls his "accidental diplomacy"), centered heavily around support for Israel and its expansionist policies and a higher level of activism in the region generally. Trump and his son-in-law Jared Kushner have been major instigators of U.S. policy both toward Israel and between Israel and other regional states like the United Arab Emirates (UAE; the so-called Abraham Accord). The stated intent of both candidates was to reduce the military presence of the United States in the region. It has been easier said than done.

The preceding analysis suggests that the key to American Middle East policy will revolve around relations with three principal states: Israel, Saudi Arabia, and Iran. The Israeli foundation of that policy rests on two questions: American acceptance, promotion, or opposition to Israeli territorial expansionism, and the plight of the Palestinians and the Palestinian state. The Trump administration clearly supported expansion and without admitting opposing Palestinian self-determination by supporting Israeli territorial annexation of parts of the West Bank. Support for a Palestinian state (the two-state solution) has been a Democratic Party touchstone for years. Saudi Arabia policy has been complicated by two major factors: one is the rise of the highly controversial Mohammed bin Salman (MBS) as crown prince and heir apparent to the Saudi throne. MBS has been controversial on human rights (e.g., the murder of Jamal Khashoggi) and foreign policy, notably his sponsorship of the Saudi undeclared war in Yemen. Democrats have been decidedly cooler toward the Kingdom than the Trump administration. Second, the warming of relations between Israel and Saudi Arabia, a clear marriage of convenience arising from a shared opposition to Iran, is a further irritant. The third state is Iran. The non-Arab, Shiite Iranians represent the largest state in the region and feel they are the pivotal state in the area. They are opposed by the other two major regional powers and the United States. A major common interest of regional states and the United States is the possibility that Iran will accelerate its nuclear program and become a nuclear power, an outcome that would represent the most traumatic and potentially destabilizing influence in the region.

THE CURRENT BALANCE

The relationships between the three major regional states and the United States is complicated and conflicting. Moreover, aspects of the triangular (or rectangular if the United States is included) relationship spill over into other parts of the region and their troubles. Traditionally, each country has been important for the United States, if in different ways. The architecture of American regional interests and commitments is, however, changing, making a reassessment of each relationship worthwhile.

Israel. The guarantee of Israel's security and continued existence remains the cornerstone of American security policy in the region. Before the 1967 war and Israeli acquisition of nuclear weapons in 1968, that condition was at least sometimes problematical. The need for the guarantee was important or essential, as Israel's Muslim neighbors had periodically attacked the Israeli state with the stated purpose of driving the Israelis into the sea or at least of establishing a Palestinian state on the West Bank. Particularly after the Israelis threatened to arm their nuclear weapons in 1973 when they were in some danger of losing the Yom Kippur War, that problem has been rendered moot: for over fifty years, the Israelis have been quite capable of taking care of themselves as long as the regional security architecture does not change. The American interest in Israel's survival remains important/vital; the Israelis themselves have, however, created a security structure that guarantees their personal ability to protect themselves. The American guarantee is now a backup reassurance, not the core to survival, a situation the Israelis must prefer. Their actions, however, create problems for the region and for a United States that is publicly not unrecognized or unaddressed in American national security discussions.

The Israelis face two potential threats that could endanger their security. From the vantage point of unilateral Israeli policy in the region and toward the world, each reaction is justifiable and has the support of many, even most, Israelis. Both responses, however, have potential ramifications that could weaken the Israeli position and certainly could put themselves at odds with the traditional American national interests in the region. Under Trump, these possibilities had been hidden by the tight alignment between that administration's policies with and acceptance of the Netanyahu government in Jerusalem/Tel Aviv (whether the United States should recognize Jerusalem as Israel's legal capital is part of the controversy).

The two key elements of the Israelis' long campaign to establish self-enforced security are their nuclear monopoly and their physical expansionism. In principle, both represent policy positions the United States opposes in the world at large. The United States has been a long-term supporter of nuclear nonproliferation, although it has not forcefully condemned the acquisition of these weapons by either North Korea or Israel. The premise of opposition to proliferation is that the more "fingers on the nuclear button," the more countries can initiate nuclear war. The Israelis disavow any intention to use these weapons except in the direst retaliatory role, but can any state at whom they might be aimed afford to believe that admonition? Can the regularly demonized state of Iran accept the situation indefinitely? For that matter, can one think of a part of the world other than the Middle East where nuclear weapons possession is more problematical? The Israeli obsession with security and survival is certainly understandable, but is the effect of its response acceptable? The United States government has taken no public position on whether Israel has these weapons (they do not admit nor deny it officially), and this ambiguity has allowed the United States to avoid calling for the Israelis to decommission their nuclear force (which is the U.S. position toward all other proliferators).

The other controversial element is Israeli expansionism beyond its traditional boundaries. It is also a policy that may be justifiable from a strictly Israeli vantage point: it secures territory that had previously been used to attack Israel. The Golan Heights is the prime example; the Sinai Peninsula had a similar effect before the 1973 War and subsequent peace treaty with Egypt solidified Israel's southern flank, thereby allowing concentration of its resources on its other neighbors. Occupation and annexation of Golan similarly relieves Israel of the need to protect itself from Syrian artillery shells raining down on kibbutzes in Israel.

The two outcomes were achieved differently. Israel neutralized Sinai by negotiating recognition with Egypt: a diplomatic solution aided by Israel's 1973 military victory. To this point, the Netanyahu regime has eschewed diplomacy regarding Golan and has simply imposed annexation (with Trump's blessing) over the area, converting it into an Israeli resort area by displacing the Syrian inhabitants. Because of its civil war, Syria has been unable to object effectively to that expansion. A post–civil war regime will have restoration of Golan to its sovereign control as a prime goal.

The elephant in the room, of course, is Palestine. The Israeli government has offered, with American encouragement and support for Netanyahu's Greater Israel policy, to annex most of the West Bank to make any pretense of a Palestinian state a sham. He is unlikely to reverse course without significant U.S. pressure. The other Arab states have been remarkably silent on this annexation and its effects on the Palestinians. The Palestinian state was a unifying rallying cry for the Arab world before the Israelis acquired the nuclear capability to vaporize them. It has been muted since 1968. Is that coincidental?

The two threads of Israeli security policy dovetail with Israel's recent initiatives in the region. Nuclear hegemony has made Israel immune from attack by its former enemies, who fear any success they might enjoy in opposing the Israelis could lead to their vaporization. Israeli hegemony could be endangered in only one of two ways: a concerted American campaign aimed at nuclear disarmament, which is highly unlikely, or by the acquisition of nuclear capability by someone else. Territorial expansion creates a much higher level of tactical safety for the Israelis from attack. These factors also help explain the Israeli-Saudi–led peace initiative that has begun to encompass other Gulf states because the maintenance of nuclear hegemony and nonopposition to expansionism are both opposed by the major, non-Arab state in the region, Iran. Much Israeli policy can be attributed to an Israeli desire to contain its only real rival in the area, the Iranians. Among other things, this means that a major tenet in Israeli policy also has to be ensuring American opposition to Iran.

Iran. The enmity between Iran and Israel and between Iran and the United States is enigmatic. Cyrus the Great of Persia was the first to recognize a Jewish state of Israel over a millennium ago, and during the reign of the

Shah, Iran was about the only Islamic country that recognized Israel and, for instance, provided Israel with access to oil during the various Arab-Israeli conflicts. Relations between Iran and the United States are a bit more complicated. Since Iran is the arguable pivotal state in the region, there has been some natural rivalry as the United States sought to increase its influence in the area. The two reached condominium during the quarter-century rule of the Shah, but the overthrow of Mossadegh created "antipathy toward the United States for empowering the dictatorial shah and led to virulent anti-Americanism that endures to this day," according to Gordon. Especially since the 1979 revolution, the United States has sided increasingly with Arab Sunni states in the region against Persian Shiite Iran. This places the United States on the Arab side of the sectarian power competition. Israeli relations with the states of the Gulf add to the attempt to encircle and isolate the Iranians.

The United States and Iran have had a rocky, occasionally schizophrenic relationship. Iranians, for instance, are fond of reminding Americans that the CIA was an instrumental force in overthrowing the only fully democratic leader (Mossadegh) in the country's history for the "sin" of nationalizing the Iranian oil industry and thus depriving private oil companies of control and huge profits. Those Iranians suppressed by the Shah remember the United States was the chief supporter of his autocratic rule and the source of his protection after his de facto abdication in 1979. Americans principally remember the embassy hostage case and the militancy of the current regime. The major ongoing reason for enmity is the competition between the global power and the regional power and influence. The United States has clearly come down on the side of anti-Iranian contestants in the region, but it is not entirely clear what gains accrue from this partisan commitment or whether issues like the Iranian nuclear program could not be managed more effectively in a more positive atmosphere between the two countries.

Saudi Arabia. The Kingdom of Saudi Arabia is clearly at the beginning of a wrenching adjustment to the contemporary world. The pillar of Saudi prominence, oil, is under challenge as a source of leverage, and a leadership controversy is underway. When the dust has settled, the Saudis will have a different position in the Middle East and the world. Whether that position is enhanced or reduced is not clear, nor is the capacity of the Saudi leadership to influence the outcomes decisively.

The drop in oil prices and the global trend toward reduced fossil fuel consumption are combining to make the world look at the Saudis differently and to make toleration of the anachronism of absolute monarchy in the twenty-first century more anomalous. This situation also applies to several of the small Persian Gulf states and threatens to discredit the rationale on which their peculiarities has been based. The rise of MBS, who initially seemed a liberating reformer by virtue of symbolic actions like allowing women to drive, has given way to a darker, more primitive worldview that includes the killing and dismemberment of a Saudi-born Western journalist and the brutal war against Yemen's Houthis.

Much recent Saudi security policy gains extra meaning to burnish its reputation among the world's countries. The Saudi royal family (and notably MBS) seeks a larger place in the international community, not just as a fabulously rich oil spigot. Much emphasis has centered on a greater, and more varied, geopolitical position in the region, notably as an Arab Sunni counterweight to the Iranians. The Saudis have spent large amounts of money on arms (much of their appeal to U.S. suppliers), but it is not clear how effectively Saudi forces—many of whom are mercenaries—would fight. More concretely, the Saudis have tried to help engineer the encirclement of Iran among Arab states, and their recent initiatives with Israel represent a marriage of convenience expanding on a long-standing clandestine relationship.

It is not clear whether Saudi assertiveness will work. The symbol of the problem of adaptation to modernity in the post-petroleum world is symbolized by the rise of MBS. In the view of Hubbard, he has simply accentuated the shortcomings of a medieval regime seeking to keep itself intact: traditions like vast corruption, extreme nepotism manifested in widespread incompetence in governance, and "almost infinite entitlement" for the inheritors of the Saud-Wahhab condominium of the eighteenth century. The assassination of Khashoggi symbolizes how far the Saudis must go before they fully join the modern system of states. MBS may mature and change, or his ascension may be stopped by modernizers, in which case the Saudis may move to join the modern world. If these possibilities do not transpire and the role of oil continues to decline, it is hard to envision Saudi Arabia as a long-term regional power and force for stability. Barring the reemergence of some Sunni state like Egypt as the leader of the Arab world, Iran is the most likely candidate for recognition as the pivotal regional state, a status to which they aspire and which, since 1980, the United States has sought to deny.

The recent Israeli-Saudi warming of relations reflects the situation. There is no love lost between the two countries, but there is some potential benefit for each. Saudi Arabia may be headed for decline, but its coffers remain overflowing with resources the Israelis desire, and the Saudis can benefit from Israeli expertise if they decide to take a chance on modernization. Both countries see Iran as their primary regional rival and impediment, and their physical accommodation is particularly augmented by accord with places like the UAE and Bahrain. That accord also mutes Arab advocacy for the Palestinians. At the same time, the relationship is fragile: the two countries have, after all, been sworn enemies since the establishment of Israel in 1948. The

UAE may have decreed that Abu Dhabi restaurants have to add kosher dishes to their menus to celebrate accord; that does not mean they will remain long-term friends. The Trump administration led the cheerleading for agreements between Saudi and the Israelis; it is not clear how much there is to cheer about.

Convergence. The major, overwhelmingly most dangerous, but least discussed problem of the region is the potential spread of nuclear weapons capability beyond Israel. It is not the only troubling problem in the region, of course. In a geopolitical sense, several of the regional dynamics are troublesome and engage the important interests of both Middle Eastern and global powers. Access to petroleum and religiously based terrorism are the two most obvious examples.

Access to oil has been the greater international issue historically. Everyone needs oil, secure and reliable access is not available to all countries, and the dynamics have some of the characteristics of a zero-sum game: gains for one claimant are losses for someone else. Those dynamics remain but have decreased as demand has decreased and other sources of large amounts of reserves have provided alternatives that lessen dependence on the Middle East. Until the transition away from carbon-based energy is complete, the issue will remain relevant, but it will decreasingly be the source of global conflict. Terrorism has been the background rationale for much interest since the turn of the century. 9/11 was the obvious catalyst, but the possible dynamic of terrorist involvement is prominent in most other discussions. Examples include the rise of ISIS and the Syrian civil war and Iraqi politics, accusations of Iranian suborning of terrorists in the Shiite Crescent, Saudi private bankrolling of terrorists, and Israeli rationales for heightened security measures. For the foreseeable future, possible terrorist activity in or emanating from the region will remain a standard part of discourse.

These factors help frame the major policy/strategic issues in the region. The nuclear weapons issue lurks in the shadows of public discussion but is pivotal to regional stability and peace, the proclaimed American goal. The situation is stable and highly desirable from a partisan Israeli vantage point. It makes Israel the major military power in the region, a clear and understandable (at least from an Israeli viewpoint), but it also creates a power imbalance that is especially galling to Iran. The Iranians have said repeatedly that they do not want to build these weapons, but Iran is also dedicated to reestablishing its status as the recognized premier state in the region. Its aspiration and Israel's continuing status are incompatible, and that makes the establishment of condominium and restraint on Iranian programs incompatible. Israel has instead decided to align itself with the Sunni Gulf states, Iran's other rivals. This may make Israelis feel more secure; it makes little geopolitical sense.

Likewise, Israeli expansionism at the expense of its neighbors may make territorial sense for the near term but it also assures the list of potential Israeli enemies will not contract.

The current power configuration also leaves much unsettled. The Middle East is a fractious, unstable place politically. Most states are multinational and centripetal politically, and the current lack of stabilization from inside or outside the region promotes continuing cleavage and instability. Syria and Iraq are prime candidates for disintegration into more ethnically pure countries, and successful secessionist movements would almost certainly trigger activation of the movement to establish the Kurdish state, a development with major regional implications: Kurdistan would be a major regional actor, and Turkish opposition—possibly violent—could open a whole new area of instability in the region. Iraq and Afghanistan remain unsettled. The Palestine issue is not going away.

THE UNITED STATES AND THE MIDDLE EAST: INTERESTS AND RESPONSES

When the Cold War imploded, one desirable outcome was supposed to be a reduction of the heavy military emphasis that had largely defined the relationship. In the 1990s, American enthusiasts loudly argued there would be a "peace dividend" that would also wash over the Middle East.

American military activism did decrease during the decade of the 1990s, although it certainly did not disappear altogether. The decade began with the first Iraq War (Operation Desert Storm), and it continued with smaller deployments in places like Haiti and Kosovo as the twentieth century moved toward a conclusion. The attacks of 9/11 reversed what turned out to have been the illusion of peace and a dividend in its name.

Andrew Bacevich, who has been a major chronicler of American military activism, summarized the result in a 2020 article. "In the last three decades, the flag of the United States Army has accumulated 34 additional streamers—each for a discreet campaign conducted by U.S. troops," he said. "Unfortunately, the frenetic pace of military activity has seldom produced positive outcomes." What it has "produced" are the forever/endless wars in places like Iraq and Afghanistan.

One consequence of a movement away from a geopolitical focus on the east–west confrontation was to allow a redirection of that focus to one of the theaters in which the Cold War played out, the Middle East. The Cold War was a high octane environment: the confrontation between the superpowers and their allies clearly involved the most important interests of both sides, and that meant the military instrument as the means to realize or secure interests was frequently invoked and always in the background. The major restraint on the competition was the danger that if a clash between them got out of hand, the result could be their mutual (assured) destruction.

That atmosphere was transferred into the contemporary system in enigmatic ways. The tendency to look to military solutions to national security concerns survived, even if the vital interests that underpinned militarization in the last century were questionably present. One signature example of this phenomenon surrounded American participation in the Iraq War. Cold War realists counseled not to go to war because adequately vital U.S. interests were not threatened; enthusiasts of engagement argued the criterion of vitality was too restrictive and should be relaxed. These neocons carried the day. The post–Cold War world has also not had the daunting prospect of possible nuclear escalation as a brake on proposed action. It has been easier to invoke force because the consequences are not potentially as apocalyptic as before. The only nuclear possessors in the Middle East, after all, are the Israelis, who are not going to attack the United States with them. Terrorists pose a real threat, but it is nowhere near so extensive. The structure of inhibition and reluctance has been a victim of these changes.

WHERE WE ARE: A SUMMARY

The situation remains unsettled, with major issues and conflicts dotting the landscape. Israel continued to gobble more land, with enthusiastic support from the Trump administration. The past four years were a bonanza for Netanyahu and his supporters, annexing and transforming the surrounding geopolitical landscape. Syrian Golan is now an Israeli resort area, Jerusalem is now the de facto capital of Israel, and the Israeli government seeks to add more of the West Bank to its territory under the guise of a peace settlement with the Palestinians. Trump's "bromance" with Netanyahu contributed to the change. Among the Islamic states, Iran is the major champion of the Palestinian cause, even though the Palestinians are Arab and Sunni, and they are neither. The Arab states sit on the sideline.

Centripetal conflict haunts the geographic ends of the Shiite Crescent. Regardless of who "wins" the Syrian civil war, there will be considerable pressure from dissident elements (Sunni Arabs and Kurds most prominently) to break up Alawite dominance and arguably the state after the dust settles. To the east, Iraq always teeters on the edge of breakup into three states, one Sunni, one Shiite, and one Kurdish. Developments in Syria and Iraq could form the vital center of gravity for a concerted Kurdish drive for statehood, with enormous potential regional geopolitical consequences. The redrawing of political maps stimulated by multinationalism and nationalist sentiment could easily reignite international and regional momentum for the Palestinians, an event that would clash with Israeli regional aspirations.

There are geopolitical overlays. The strongest is attempts by fractious Sunni states to blunt or reverse the geopolitical assertiveness of Shiite Iran as the regional pivotal state. The countries west of Suez (notably Egypt) have opted out of that effort due to internal problems, and Saudi Arabia is trying to play the role of leader of the opposition to Iranian ambitions. That country is not up to the task, and MBS is not the answer to the problem. As an example, Gause points out MBS announced something he called "Vision 2030" that, in addition to other things, Saudi could "live without oil" by 2020, hardly a vision that has been realized. The Saudis still have overflowing cash reserves that they can devote to burnishing their image, but they are hardly a geopolitical match for the Iranians.

WHERE WE WANT TO GO: A MENU

Have traditional American interests in the Middle East changed greatly, or have the circumstances in which those interests must compete with other actors changed? The interests that emerged during the long Cold War (the sanctity of the Israeli state, guaranteed access to Middle East petroleum at a reasonable price, and Soviet exclusion) were not entirely consistent with one another. The Arab states with the oil were at least rhetorically committed to the destruction of Israel (and by extension supported a Palestinian state), creating a contradiction in which policy that served one end often came at the expense of the other. Opposition to Soviet influence was one theater of the broader Cold War, and the Soviet appeal was somewhat vitiated by the fundamental incompatibility of atheistic ("godless communism") and Islamic religiosity, especially among the conservative monarchies that had most of the oil. The promotion of American interests was consensually agreed to be the promotion of regional peace and stability.

The structure of that environment has changed, and although the interests of the United States remain akin to those in the past, their pursuit is different, arguably more difficult. Events in three years have been especially noteworthy. The Iranian Revolution of 1979 partially undermined the security of America's oil access by removing the Shah's regime, which had enforced that security from the board. Late in that year, the Saudi mosque occupation upset the torpor of that country and set it on a more activist international path. In 1991, the Soviet Union imploded, ending the Cold War and knocking Russia out of regional competitiveness for a decade. In addition, the United States turned militarily assertive that year, leading the coalition that evicted Iraq from Kuwait and thus intensifying its presence in the region. In 2001, the AQ terrorist attacks of 9/11 cemented American military activism.

The United States has been deeply committed and exposed ever since. The forever wars in Iraq and Afghanistan are the most dramatic and enduring symbol, and they have been reinforced by the emergence of an IS threat that is currently dormant but could reignite. That possibility justifies ongoing military presence in the region. Trump's virtual alignment with Netanyahu added a partisan element to American policy in the Mediterranean. Involvements and interests in situations like Syria and the Kurdish quest for territory along its border with Turkey add to the spider's web.

The traditional pillars of the three-legged stool of American interests has changed. American dependence on Persian Gulf oil has lessened and will continue to decrease as Americans continue to use less oil and turn to other sources like American shale oil. The Middle East oil security pillar is less important than it was, and relations with those producers is less based on American petroleum needs. Except for embargoing Iranian oil, American regional policy has been slow to recognize or exploit this reality. The United States is no longer the energy hostage of the leaders of the anachronistic regimes of the Gulf kingdoms. Israeli nuclear weapons have transformed the Jewish state from David to Goliath, with the spinoff consequence of empowering regional imperialists among the Israelis. The Russians remain present in Syria thanks to their naval base at Tartus. Their appeal elsewhere in the region is modest. The three legs of the policy stool are decidedly different than they were when that construct was constructed. But does policy reflect these changes?

CONCLUSION: THE CHOICES AHEAD

The politics and instabilities of the Middle East have arguably occupied a disproportionate amount of American time, energies, and resources since the end of World War II and especially during the twenty-first century. That level of attention has historically been justified by the need to protect the integrity of Israel and secure access to Persian Gulf energy. Prior to 1991, the Soviet Union added to the threat to those interests. The protection of oil access and Israeli security represented consensually agreed upon vital interests for the United States, and Soviet intrusion was one aspect of the global vital interest in opposing the spread of communism.

All three historical mandates have changed, and those changes raise legitimate questions of whether they form the most useful troika of American vital interests for the future, notably engagement of American armed forces. Middle Eastern oil is a declining factor for Americans (if not Europeans), and Israeli nuclear weapons maker them quite capable of defending themselves. Despite the activism of Vladimir Putin and his "bromance" with Donald Trump, Russia is increasingly a Potemkin Village, a partially fraudulent front obscuring significant prospects for shrinking power and influence (see my *Regional Cases in U.S. Foreign Policy*, Second Edition, for a discussion). At the same time, the region seethes with internal conflicts and violence that has drawn in American attention, resources, and even troops.

Is it time to reassess the hierarchy of American Middle East national security interests? Raising that question exposes two underlying assessments. The first is the intensity of those interests: Which are vital and demand attention, including force, and which are less important and warrant more restrained American attention? And what should be the intensity of American interest pursuit in the region?

Given the diversity of the region, different observers will have different answers to these related questions, but the answers are crucial to the framing of a coherent national security approach to the region. My own are probably controversial and somewhat unorthodox, but I share them for exemplary purposes. The reader can accept, reject, or modify them.

There is an old saying in security circles that interests do not change much, but that threat to those interests do, and that observation is relevant to thinking about the Middle East. It is one of the global enigmas that the Middle East, one of the first world civilizations and the incubating crib of three of the world's great monotheistic religions, is also one of the world's most contentious, violent, and even savage places. The process of modernization has been slower in the region than in most parts of the world, and many of the underlying cleavages and violence-producing divisions among the many conflicting, largely tribal communities would have been basically familiar to people who lived there thousands of years ago. For a large part of history, these anomalies proceeded without major outside intervention or mediation. The discovery of "black gold" in enormous amounts produced a level of interest in the area it had not previously had, but it did little to moderate the underlying incivility, instability, and violence. The reign of petroleum-based fossil fuel energy has reached, possibly passed, the tipping point. What does that mean? What do we want the region to be like?

America's interests are best served in the creation of peace and stability in the region. The United States still wants peace and safety for Israel, access to remaining oil reserves, and the minimization of outside influence. American dissatisfaction with a prominent military role for the country is most vividly articulated as a demand for an end to the forever, endless wars of this century.

If the area stays in turmoil, which it likely will, the temptations to interfere will remain; what the region wants and serves the U.S. basic interest is stability. The question is how to achieve that end.

Three key actors and the relationship between them must change if stability is to emerge. Those countries are Israel, Iran, and Saudi Arabia. In a stable Middle East, the three should have a peaceful, proper relationship that is not necessarily highly cooperative, which is probably impossible given real differences and conflicts of interest. However, the conflictual, confrontational, generally negative tone and content of their current relationship virtually guarantees continued regional instability that at times can become violent. They may be incapable of a broad, comprehensive condominium, but that does not mean they cannot cool their antagonism enough to coexist in a way that will stabilize the region and avoid a regional war.

Given the highly conflictual relationship that has prevailed among them, such a change may seem utopian and unattainable, but it is not. At various times in the not distant past and the present, they have had proper, nonconfrontational relationships. The original Israeli state was first recognized by Cyrus the Great of Iran, and under the rule of the Shah, Iran was as close to an Islamic friend as the Israelis had. Likewise, the relationship between the Shah's regime and the Saudis was formal and correct, with the Shah visiting Riyadh upon occasion. In the last year or so, Saudi Arabia and Israel have formalized relations.

There are formidable sources of division among the three that have dominated the contemporary environment and that would have to be improved before change occurs. The three states have bilateral issues that divide them and on which a reduction in difference is necessary for some accord to develop. The divisions are sharpest and most consequential in Iran-Israeli relations. There are two major chasms between them, each of which must be moderated to allow a viable framework of regional peace.

The first, and in an international (including American) sense most consequential issue, is the nuclear question. Israel uses its arsenal as a cudgel to guarantee that its security is unchallenged. Given the unique Jewish history of the twentieth century, Israel's concern is understandable and must be satisfied if there is to be any form of peace, but the threat of the Samson Option can only be destabilizing in a crisis. A major regional state like Iran can only find the threat demeaning and its consequences (i.e., being at the mercy of a state with a population less than 10 percent of its own) ultimately intolerable. Iran says it does not want to field its own arsenal, but Israel's arsenal collides with its pretension as the pivotal regional state. Is it only a matter of time until the Iranians find the situation intolerable and begin to field their own arsenal? If the Israelis got wind of such a development, would they move to destroy it, possibly with a nuclear strike (they have destroyed nascent programs in Iraq and Syria in the past)? This is the single worst case in the region. The only stabilizing solution is peace between the two parties. The problem is how to achieve it.

The other issue is Palestine. The Iranians have trained, bankrolled, and equipped various insurgent/terrorist groups, and they become the primary regional champions of the Palestinian state cause. The marriage is an anomaly: the Palestinians are overwhelmingly Sunni and Arab, a combination normally associated with the opponents of Iran. The connection thus has different geopolitical bases. The Arab states have shown little more than occasional rhetorical support for the Palestinians; recent evidence includes the willingness of Saudi Arabia and other Gulf states to embrace Israel with hardly a murmur about Palestinians. The opportunity is thus there. Sponsorship and assistance enhance Iranian presence and leverage in the Shiite Crescent, primacy over which is clearly an Iranian goal. It also creates some concern within Israel that reciprocates Iranian discomfort with the Israeli nuclear threat they perceive. In tandem, the two issues provide a small opening for negotiations. Although both countries have issues with the other, war avoidance must be at the top of both lists for the sake of the region.

The other bilateral parts of the triangle are less problematical. Saudi opposition to Israel has always been more rhetorical and economic than military: the Saudis write checks; they do not fight. That said, the Saudis and Israel are at policy odds about Palestine. As Indyk (2019) points out, King Salman has "repeatedly stated, Saudi Arabia will not support a Middle East settlement without Palestine." This position has been sublimated in light of publicly improved Israeli-Saudi relations, but it exists in the overall regional dynamic. Similarly, the fissures between the Saudis and the Iranians have been manageable in the past, and a cooling of the rhetoric would serve the interests of both. Reaching some accord on freedom of the Persian Gulf would seem a good starting point.

A lowering of the geopolitical temperature clearly serves American interests. The centerpiece of making the region less threatening is some form of agreement about nuclear weapons. If the shadow of the mushroom-shaped cloud continues to hang over the region, a stable accommodation is probably impossible. These weapons underpin Israeli security calculations and have given them a sense of security they did not possess before 1968. Nuclear weapons inoculate Israel from their Muslim enemies, and they will remain extremely resistant to anything that might alter that dynamic.

Unfortunately, the price of Israel's security is everyone else's insecurity. Clearly, this is true for Israel's traditional Arab opponents, and it extends to Iran. It also affects external powers with an interest in the region, notably the

United States. In essence, a lowering of regional tensions and thus greater stability has two roots, without which stabilization will remain elusive. Those two issues are nuclear weapons and Palestine.

Nuclear weapons have liberated Israel's regional strategy, providing a shield behind which Israeli territorial expansion and denial of an acceptable Palestinian state have proceeded. In essence, the Israelis can tell those states that oppose "Greater Israel" that their resistance is empty rhetoric. This reality has effectively stifled Arab opposition to Israeli policies, and especially Palestine and other territories adjacent to the pre-1967 Israeli state. This change has certainly improved the sense of safety felt by Israelis, but has the price been worth it in terms of overall regional stability? Without the nuclear threat, much of this Israeli "success" would have been impossible.

Iran stands in the way. Its opposition begins from its perceived need to be recognized as the "big kid on the block," a status Israeli nuclear weapons deny. A nuclear Iran could effectively deter the Israeli threat and thus reduce Israel's sense of safety. Palestine becomes the key ground for the contest and assertion of what Benjamin and Simon argue is Iran's security goal: "maximizing its security in a deeply hostile environment." Israeli and Iranian pretensions are the core of the dilemma: the Saudis are essentially along for the ride.

Since 2016, American policy emphasized virtually total support for Israeli positions and hence opposition to Iran. American-Iranian animus has been ongoing for most of the post-1945 period, symbolized by American complicity in the overthrow of Mossadegh and support of the Shah and the Iran hostage crisis. It is a mutually held and nurtured hatred. As Ewers et al. put it, "a legacy of deep distrust divides Washington and Tehran" and is expressed most clearly by opponents in the United States and region by a coalition of "Israel, Saudi Arabia, and congressional Republicans."

Is that situation viable or likely to succeed to produce peace? Should the United States continue to support the Israelis and Saudis (and their cooperation) in lavish terms while vilifying the Iranians as heinous villains? One need not argue that the United States should in effect change sides in who it supports, but would a more evenhanded approach enhance the ability to create a modus vivendi in the region between the major antagonists? Should the United States return to a strong advocacy of the two-state solution on Palestine? What about putting some reins on the Israeli nuclear weapons program? Is a nuclear-armed Israel and its resultant claim to hegemony truly in American interests?

The Iranians and the Israelis have the strongest positions from which to negotiate a more peaceful regional framework and thus to start a process of accommodation. Israel, for instance, wants and even needs a cessation of

Iranian-backed attacks on Israeli soil, and Iran wants controls on Israeli nuclear posture and expansionism. Is there an opening for compromise in their positions? What are the two countries willing to sacrifice to gain their most important goals? The Saudis are supporting actors, but if Riyadh wants to remain a major power in an environment where its oil does not guarantee that status, how much must it reform? Can Iran and Israel help in that transition?

These are questions for the reader to contemplate. They are only part of the swirl of issues and conflicts that ravage the region and ensnare the United States. The futures of Iraq and Syria are major questions with potentially great importance for the region and U.S. interests. Terrorism, which originally drew the United States into its long military involvements, remains a force lying just below the surface that keeps America active in regional politics. The Kurds are a pivotal, and in some ways, tragic factor: Will Kurdistan ever come to be, and what will that mean? The list goes on.

The book began with the problem of forever wars, and one prominent way to end them and to limit the likelihood is to withdraw wholly or partly from the Middle East. Would such a solution make the regional situation better or worse for Middle Eastern countries involved and the United States? The answer is neither easy to formulate nor to predict the likelihood of achieving. One ends with the old saw that "for every complicated, complex question, there is an answer that is simple, straightforward, and wrong!"

BIBLIOGRAPHY

Anderson, Scott. *Lawrence in Arabia: War, Deceit, Imperial Folly, and the Making of the Modern Middle East*. New York: Anchor Books, 2013.

Bacevich, Andrew. "The Endless Fantasy of American Power: Neither Trump Nor Biden Aims to Demilitarize American Policy." *Foreign Affairs* (online), September 18, 2020.

———. *Washington Rules: America's Path to Permanent War*. New York: Henry Holt and Company, 2010.

Benaim, Daniel, and Jake Sullivan. "America's Opportunity in the Middle East: Diplomacy Could Succeed Where Military Force Has Failed." *Foreign Affairs* (online), August 23, 2020.

Benjamin, Daniel, and Steven Simon. "America's Great Satan: The 40-Year Obsession with Iran." *Foreign Affairs* 89, 6 (November/December 2019), 56–66.

Betts, Richard K. "Pick Your Battles: Ending America's Permanent State of War." *Foreign Affairs* 93, 6 (November/December 2014), 15–24.

Biden, Joseph R. Jr. "Why America Must Lead Again: Rescuing U.S. Foreign Policy After Trump." *Foreign Affairs* 99, 2 (March/April 2020), 64–76.

Bolton, John. *The Room Where It Happened: A White House Memoir*. New York: Simon & Schuster, 2020.

Ewers, Ilisa Catalono, Ilan Goldenburg, and Kaleigh Thomas. "On Iran, the Next Administration Must Break with the Past." *Foreign Affairs* (online), October 1, 2020.

Farrow, Ronan. *War on Peace: The End of Diplomacy and the Decline of American Influence.* New York: W. W. Norton, 2018.

Firro, Tarik. *Wahhabism and the Rise of the House of Saud.* Eastbourne, UK: Sussex Academic Press, 2018.

Fontaine, Richard. "The Nonintervention Delusion: What War Is Good For." *Foreign Affairs* 89, 6 (November/December 2019), 84–98.

Gates, Robert M. *Exercise of Power: American Failures, Successes, and a New Path Forward in the Post-Cold War World.* New York: Alfred A. Knopf, 2020.

———. "The Overmilitarization of American Foreign Policy: The United States Must Recover the Full Range of Its Power." *Foreign Affairs* 99, 4 (July/August 2000).

Gause, Gregory III. "The End of Saudi Ambitions: MBS Must Cut His Losses to Avoid Catastrophe." *Foreign Affairs* (online), August 4, 2020.

George, Roger, Harvey Rishikoff, and Brent Scowcroft (eds.). *The National Security Enterprise: Navigating the Labyrinth.* Second Ed. Washington, DC: Georgetown University Press, 2017.

Gordon, Philip H. "The False Promise of Regime Change: Why Washington Keeps Failing in the Middle East." *Foreign Affairs* (online), October 7, 2020.

Haass, Richard. "Present at the Disruption: How Trump Unmade U.S. Foreign Policy." *Foreign Affairs* 99, 5 (September/October 2020).

———. *Wars of Necessity, Wars of Choice: A Memoir of Two Iraq Wars.* New York: Simon & Schuster, 2010.

Hitchcock, Mark. *Showdown with Iran: Nuclear Iran and the Future of Israel, the Middle East, the United States in Biblical Prophecy.* Edinburgh, UK: Thomas Nelson, 2020.

Indyk, Martin. "Disaster in the Desert: Why Trump's Middle East Plan Can't Work." *Foreign Affairs* 89, 6 (November/December 2019), 10–20.

———. "The Middle East Isn't Worth It Anymore." *Wall Street Journal*, January 17, 2020.

———. "Trump's Accidental Diplomacy in the Middle East: How a Botched Peace Plan Produced the Abraham Accord." *Foreign Affairs* (online), August 19, 2020.

Jabar, Faleh A., et al. *Tribes and Power: Nationalism and Ethnicity in the Middle East.* London: Saqi Books, 2002.

Jarmon, Jack. *The New Era in U.S. National Security: An Introduction to Emerging Threats and Challenges.* Lanham, MD: Rowman & Littlefield, 2014.

Kaplan, Robert D. "The Art of Avoiding War." *The Atlantic* 313, 5 (June 2015), 12–33.

Katz, Yaakov, and Yoaz Hendel. *Israel versus Iran: The Shadow of War.* Washington, DC: Potomac Books, 2012.

Kessler, Ronald. *The Trump White House: Changing the Rules of the Game.* New York: Crown Forum, 2018.

Kotkin, Stephen. "Realist World: The Players Change, but the Game Remains." *Foreign Affairs* 97, 4 (July/August 2018), 10–15.

Lewis, Bernard. *The Multiple Identities of the Middle East.* Berlin: Schocken, 2003.

Louer, Laurence, and Ethan Rundell. *Sunnis and Shi's: A Political History.* Princeton, NJ: Princeton University Press, 2020.

Meacham, Jon. *The Soul of America: The Battle for Our Better Angels.* New York: Random House, 2018.

Merhavy, Menahem. *National Symbols in Modern Iran: Ethnicity and Collective Memory.* Syracuse, NY: Syracuse University Press, 2020.

Osman, Tarek, and Michael S. Doran. "Will Power Shifts in the Middle East Revive 'Land for Peace?'" *Foreign Affairs* 99, 3 (May/June 2020) (online).

Parsi, Trita. *Treacherous Alliance: The Secret Dealings of Israel, Iran, and the United States.* New Haven, CT: Yale University Press, 2019.

Rand, Dafna H., and Andrew P. Miller (eds.). *Re-Engaging the Middle East: A New Vision for U.S. Policy.* Washington, DC: Brookings Institution Press, 2020.

Reidel, Bruce. *Kings and Presidents: Saudi Arabia and the United States Since FDR.* Geopolitics in the Twenty-First Century. Washington, DC: Brookings, 2017.

Reveron, Derek S., and Nikolas Gvosdev. *The Oxford Handbook of U.S. National Security.* Oxford, UK: Oxford University Press, 2018.

Robinson, Kali. "What Is U.S. Policy in the Israeli-Palestinian Conflict?" New York: Council on Foreign Relations. CFR Backgrounder, September 15, 2020.

Singh, Michael. "Conflict with Small Powers Derails U.S. Foreign Policy: The Case for Strategic Discipline." *Foreign Affairs* (online), August 12, 2020.

Snow, Donald M. *The Case Against Military Intervention: Why We Do It and Why It Fails.* New York: Routledge, 2016.

———. *The Middle East, Oil, and the U.S. National Security Policy: Intractable Problems, Impossible Solutions.* Lanham, MD: Rowman & Littlefield, 2016.

———. *National Security.* Seventh Ed. New York and London: Routledge, 2020.

———. *Regional Cases in U.S. Foreign Policy.* Second Ed. Lanham, MD: Rowman & Littlefield, 2018.

———. *The Shadow of the Mushroom-Shaped Cloud.* Columbus, OH: Consortium for International Studies Education, 1978.

Sternfeld, Lior B. *Between Iran and Zion: Jewish Histories of Twentieth Century Iran.* Palo Alto, CA: Stanford University Press, 2020.

Stoessinger, John G. *Why Nations Go to War.* Eleventh Ed. New York: Simon & Schuster, 2018.

Tajbakhsh, Kian. "Getting Real About Iran: It's Not an Existential Threat or an Ally in the Offing." *Foreign Affairs* (online), March 19, 2019.

Talwar, Puneet. "Iran and the United States Can't See One Another Clearly." *Foreign Affairs* (online), June 29, 2020.

Vine, David. *The United States of War: A Global History of America's Endless Conflicts, From Columbus to the Islamic State.* Berkeley: University of California Press, 2020.

Ward, Terence. *The Wahhabi Code: How the Saudis Spread Extremism Globally.* Baltimore, MD: Arcade Press, 2018.

11

Challenges for the New Administration

The COVID pandemic dominated the 2020 election agenda to the point that matters of national security, including those surrounding the Middle East and American policy toward the major aspects of that tumultuous relationship received little attention. Based on the analysis contained in the first ten chapters of this book, however, it is possible to organize how the Biden administration will approach the three pillars of the basic dynamics of the region (Israel, Iran, and Saudi Arabia and the relations among them), and how those relations will radiate to and influence other aspects of the region, from the Syrian civil war to the Palestinian and Kurdish questions and beyond.

The change begins with basic philosophical differences between the outgoing and incoming administrations about how they see international relations and America's position in the world order. It is rooted in a philosophical difference between those who believe U.S. interests are best achieved by close cooperative efforts with other states (multilateralism) and those who believe the United States should act on its own to protect and promote its interests (unilateralism). The Trump administration's mantra of "America first" was the quintessential expression of unilateralism, whereas the Biden call for an American return to active collaboration with the world ("America is back" as its initial cry to other countries) represents the internationalist position that has dominated most of the post–World War II system. It is a good place to begin looking at the likely trajectory of change.

The Biden direction was publicly proclaimed on the late November 2020 day when the then president-elect introduced the core of his foreign/national security policy leadership team. As she was accepting Biden's nomination to be U.S. Ambassador to the United Nations on November 24, 2020, veteran Foreign Service officer Linda Thomas-Greenfield exulted that "Multilateralism is back!" Biden added that a major goal of the transition to the Biden presidency would be to let world leaders know that "America is ready to lead" in the active pursuit of international goals.

Translating that determination into policy that will shape future U.S national security in the Middle East will not be easy or straightforward. Much of the national security effort during the Trump incumbency centered on controversial policies advocated and pursued by the Netanyahu administration in Israel like the consolidation of regional territorial expansion in areas contiguous to pre-1967 Israel. These actions included annexation of parts of the Golan Heights from Syria and moving to change the rules of governance on the West Bank that made any pretense of granting independence to the Palestinians a hollow gesture, at least from the Palestinian viewpoint. The crowning symbolic aspect of the Trump "tilt" toward the Netanyahu position (engineered by Trump son-in-law and Netanyahu family friend Jared Kushner) was American recognition of Jerusalem as the legal capital of Israel and moving the U.S. Embassy from Tel Aviv to the newly claimed capital. These positions all contravened international opinion and the provisions of UN-sponsored resolutions condemning them and were thus the most dramatic regional examples of Trump's "America first" unilateralism.

Trump unilateralism left its mark on the other two elements of critical concern as well. The Trump administration was also deeply critical of and antagonistic toward policy toward Iran, and especially the Iranian nuclear program. One of Trump's early decisions in the region was to remove the United States from the nonproliferation agreement between Iran, the United States, and five European allies by which Iran eschewed the pursuit of nuclear weaponry. The grounds were that the Iranians were cheating on provisions (a staple of the Israeli position). One of the great ironies of this position is that it never even mentions the Israeli regional nuclear monopoly (a status that neither the Israelis nor the Americans ever acknowledged). The assassination of Iranian nuclear physicist Mohsen Fakhrizadeh after the American election allegedly by Israeli agents similarly evoked no visible condemnation from the Trump team.

These policies are all reflections of the Netanyahu position, and it was often impossible to distinguish between the policies pursued by Trump and by Netanyahu (or, for that matter, whether the source of those policies was Washington or Tel Aviv/Jerusalem). Without acknowledging that there is a "bomb in the basement" to describe Israeli nuclear hegemony in the region, the Israeli government argued, with implicit Trump administration acquiescence, that the prospect of an Iranian bomb was highly destabilizing without mentioning the Israelis "nuclearized" the region in 1968 and that a basic element of their regional security strategy is the possibility of regional (and possibly global) nuclear Armageddon. The United States remains totally mute on this anomaly.

Israeli actions in the Persian Gulf are the third element of the Trump legacy. The geopolitics of the Israeli diplomatic initiative toward Saudi Arabia and the other Arab Gulf states, that likely has two major purposes. The first is as a device to further isolate and "contain" the Iranians and thus to build a more extensive network of those resisting Iranian expansionism. Given the military insignificance of most of the Gulf States, the gesture is more symbolic than physical. The second purpose is probably to gain access to some of the great oil wealth that those states possess. In geopolitical terms, the initiative is of fairly minor significance, but it was enthusiastically promoted by the Trump administration, and especially Secretary of State Mike Pompeo, in the waning months of the Trump incumbency.

The Trump legacy also includes the further, deeper demonization of Iran, a policy at odds with past administrations and likely to be reviewed and moderated by the Biden team. The most dramatic example is removal of the United States from the treaty arrangement by which Iran binds itself not to develop nuclear weapons. The Joint Comprehensive Plan of Action (JCPOA) was originally signed in 2015 with the United States as a signatory along with Iran, the five members of the permanent members of the U.S. Security Council, and Germany. Citing Iranian cheating on its provisions (a not unusual Trump charge), he withdrew the United States in 2017, a move applauded by Israel. With the United States on the outside, Iranian nuclear activity has probably predictably increased, much to the alarm of the Israelis (also a predictable, if hypocritical consequence).

The Trump impact also extends to Saudi Arabia and several of the conservative Sunni monarchies of the Persian Gulf littoral. The thrust has featured closer cooperation with these states, beginning with Saudi Arabia. It began with the courtship of Mohammed bin Salman (MBS) after his ascent to the position of crown prince (designated heir to the Saudi throne) in 2017. In his early thirties at the time, he was extolled as a reforming force and was an honored guest at the White House. His luster disappeared when his complicity in the Khashoggi assassination was revealed and the White House reluctantly distanced itself from him. The courtship of the House of Saud and its close kindred neighboring states has continued, with the Trump administration acting as an informal sponsor and champion of Israeli initiatives. It has been a marriage of convenience aimed at further encirclement and isolation of Iran (which sits across the Persian Gulf from these monarchies). What to do regarding these arrangements will be part of the Biden agenda.

In addition, many of these actions involving the central players extend to other regional situations examined in these pages and in which the United

States has some arguably ongoing interest. An obvious example is the impact of the end of the Syrian civil war. Although Israel has occupied the Syrian Golan Heights since 1967, the expansion of that occupation to annexation of these areas (and their commercial development) accelerated after the civil war broke out, an event that effectively suspended Syrian efforts to reclaim these territories. What will happen when the war ends and some semblance of national governance returns to Syria is an open question. If Trump had been reelected, he probably would have continued support for Israeli actions; it is doubtful that Biden will. This same logic applies to the Palestinian question. The outcome in Syria will also affect the Kurdish self-determination question, and Iraq and Afghanistan remain lingering issues not resolved under Trump.

THE CHALLENGE AGENDA

As the Biden administration was inaugurated on January 20, 2020, the basic dynamic dominating and roiling Middle East geopolitics is a bipolar cold war between the two major military powers of the region, Israel and Iran. Although not phrased in the kinds of terms used during the Cold War competition of the last century, the heart of this competition is which state will occupy the dominant role in the region: which one will be, in language used throughout this book, the regional recognized major player, the regional pivotal player. It is a competition that has been growing since the Iranian Revolution of 1979, although part of its roots date to the earlier Israeli acquisition of nuclear weapons. Each country has different reasons for wanting to wear the mantle of pivotal power: Iran because it is the largest state in the effective Middle East and the major Shiite power; it feels history and gravitas make it deserving of the recognition among both the majority Sunni states and Israel. The Israeli claim is based in its nuclear hegemony, its military power, and the realization of the Netanyahu policy of "Greater Israel" that has justified both territorial expansionism and immigration to Israel (a prospect made possible largely by new territory on which to settle the immigrants). This contest has two large and potentially cataclysmic foci: the potential challenge to Israel military hegemony of the nascent Iranian nuclear effort and the fate of the Palestinians and their claim to a West Bank state. Biden inherits these problems essentially unsolved from his predecessor; how he handles them will largely define the prospects the United States can more fully realize its interests in the region—particularly its goal of regional stability.

Constructing the problem in this manner is unconventional, and many will argue it is incorrect. Since 1979, the Iranian regime has been the whipping boy of American policy, and the Israelis have had reasonably free rein to pursue Greater Israel. The result has been mixed. The Israeli position, for as long as it can be maintained without devolving to territorial war over its occupied lands (e.g., Syrian Golan) and the slow-walk annexation of the West Bank, have enjoyed policy success—at the expense of others. Iranian success has been more measured in areas such as extending influence in the Shiite Crescent and harassing Israel from adjacent territory. Both are transitory accomplishments that manage but do not solve underlying dilemmas. Regional stabilization requires condominium on the two basic issues: nuclear balance and territorial adjustment. These represent the core items in the pursuit of Middle Eastern conflict.

This reality is the central core of a broad agenda of issues roiling Middle Eastern politics, and how it is resolved has direct implications for United States interests in the region. This situation is not entirely the fault of the departed regime, as most of the problems have been festering for some time: the Trump struggle to resolve them, after all, was in some ways a continuation of efforts of previous Democrat and Republican regimes. The Trump contribution was, in some ways, to refocus attention to a very unilateralist, thoroughly Likud-like Israeli orientation. The more multilateralist general Democrat predilection has been for a more even-handed approach to the region. The general purpose of both efforts has presumably been to produce peace and stability—the preferred American condition—in the region. The question is whether the Biden approach will produce a more effective result than has the Trump approach. Not every American or Middle Eastern source will agree on the most productive ways to attack the problem. The best that can be done is to look at the possibilities and render personal and national judgments. Using categories already established, laying out some of the challenges will occupy the remaining pages.

Israel. Reflecting the arguably unorthodox approach of this text, the menu begins with the continuing role of Israel as a regional power. Israel has considered its national security challenge to be existential since its independence in 1948 and the accompanying vows of the surrounding Islamic neighbors to destroy Israel and its inhabitants. Given the Holocaust experience, Israeli obsession with its existence and safety and the "never again" mantra it created in Israelis is understandable, and American regional policy has always started from the need to protect Israel and do whatever was necessary to ensure its continued existence and security.

While Israelis have appreciated that pledge and determination, there has always been the lingering fear that, if honoring the pledge to Israel physically imperiled the United States, the Americans might have second thoughts: Is honoring the commitment adequate justification for possibly causing the destruction of the United States? Such a consideration may seem abstract today, but it was a vow originally made in the context of the Cold War, the ultimate expression of which could have been an all-out nuclear war between the United States and the Soviet Union. The French, who aided in the development of the Israeli nuclear program and thus indirectly in its weaponization, asked themselves the same question in the 1960s, concluded that the Americans might have second thoughts, and responded by developing their own independent nuclear capability, the force frappe. The Israelis have always maintained their efforts were aimed at deterring the Soviets, adding credence to the connection.

The contemporary problem is that the Israelis may have prepared too well against their existential threat and taken actions which inadvertently imperil the security and tranquility of the contemporary balance. There are two obvious manifestations of the Israeli security policy that reflect this problem. The most obvious and troubling has been the Israeli nuclear capability. That capability and the veiled threat against its neighbors that they could be the targets of those weapons in the event they menace Israel has removed most of the bellicosity from Arab commentaries on Israel, and it has made Israel the military "king of the hill" in the region despite a relatively small population and vulnerable territory. Expansionism has similarly made military attacks against Israel more difficult. The efforts have unquestionably aided contemporary Israeli security, but implementing strategies including the Samson Option mean they have potentially made the security of Israel's neighbors more insecure. They also have created an adversarial relationship with other pretenders to regional status, notably the Iranians.

Particularly during the Trump administration, the United States was basically acquiescent in these thrusts of policy. Trump embraced the annexation of territory by Israel (e.g., Golan), and indirectly reinforced the nuclear monopoly by its opposition to Iran and even in the assassination of Iranian scientists and by continuing the policy of neither confirming nor denying Israel's possession of the weapons. Like all his predecessors, Trump simply ignored the existence of the Israeli nuclear weapons program while condemning Iranian nuclear research. The question is how that policy might change in the Biden administration. It may be of some instructive value that Biden's Secretary of State Antony (Tony) Blinken was one of the authors of policy toward Iranian nuclear activity during the Obama administration and a coauthor of the JCPOA.

Iran. The second major antagonist in Middle Eastern geopolitics has been Iran. As already noted, the relationship between Iran and the United States and Iran and Israel has been erratic, swinging from periods of cooperation and civility to periods of vitriol and conflict. This fluctuation has been particularly strong in the Iranian relationship with the United States. From the end of

World War II until the Iranian Revolution of 1979, the heart of the relationship rotated around relations with the Shah and was viewed as mutually beneficial. The United States provided much of the expertise and guidance for the White Revolution, and in return, the Shah's government spent generously on American weapons and enforced free passage for oil destined for the United States through the Persian Gulf. Most Americans (including their leaders) were oblivious to substantial domestic hatred of the Shah and opposition to his transformation of the country, making the façade of great friendship and common cause a false front that was exposed after the Shah was overthrown. There is a remaining level of respect for one another among some members of the elite in both countries, but it is latent and difficult to tap into because of sectarian opposition in Iran and intense negative propaganda (some driven by the Israelis) toward the Iranians.

Iranian interaction with Israel has similarly had significant ups and downs. During the period of the Arab-Israeli wars between 1848 and 1973, for instance, Iran was as close to a friend as Israel had among the Islamic states. The two countries proper relationship began to deteriorate with the success of the Iranian Revolution. At heart, their competition is grounded on two closely related factors: claims to security symbolized by conferral of pivotal state status for one or the other and the fact or prospect of nuclear weapons.

American policy toward the two countries during the Trump administration was, as noted, heavily tilted toward Israel, especially on the kinds of geopolitical questions that are central to their enmity. Trump supported expansion into the occupied territories, which Iran has opposed, and both parties are heavily committed to their positions. If Israel expansionism is security derived, the effort to expand Iranian influence has been driven by the desire to demonstrate that they are the obvious pivotal state. To Trump, Israeli actions were appropriate and to be rewarded; quite similar Iranian actions were viewed as aggressiveness to be condemned and punished, mostly through crippling sanctions. The nuclear program of Iran, at the same time, was condemned as provocative and dangerous; the operational Israeli nuclear arsenal was ignored as if it did not exist.

U.S. policy in the region under Biden will likely be much friendlier to Iran than Trump policy has been. Even before inauguration, Biden hinted he wanted to see modifications in the JCPOA that would allow an American re-entry into the arrangement, and the Iranians have incentives to cooperate with the Americans because of their dire need to have Iranian funds impounded in the United States released to them. Iranian need and American desires could open the possibility of dialogue that could become part of a wider regional dialogue, although one that will be strongly opposed in some quarters in the United States, Iran, and Israel.

SAUDI ARABIA AND THE GULF STATES

Saudi Arabia is undergoing the most difficult process of change of any of the Middle East states. Politically, it is an anachronism as one of the world's few remaining absolutist monarchies. This anomaly was reluctantly accepted by a world community that desperately needed the petroleum lying beneath Saudi territory, but that toleration has worn thinner as the world's energy system has moved away from petroleum and alternate sources have made countries less reliant on oil from the politically aberrant Gulf states.

Part of the dilemma for the Saudis is their extreme resistance to change. The House of Saud has ruled for well over two centuries and does not want to relinquish the power that absolutism provides them. Twenty-first-century politics threatens their privilege and is to be avoided to the extent possible without further eroding support for the Kingdom. The rise and actions of MBS symbolize this dilemma. When he was first anointed as successor to the Crown and responded with mild (by world if not Saudi) reforms like allowing women to drive, he was extolled as a modernist and source of change.

When he was found to have been complicit in the murder and dismemberment of a Saudi-born American journalist and as a vocal supporter of the Saudi genocide in Yemen, that impression changed. Further, the House of Saud relies critically on the extremely conservative Wahhabis for funds, and the price is religious conservatism that limits the government. This influence is foundational for the regime, but it is also profoundly antimodernist, and leads some to suspect Saudi motives and actions. Seventeen of the twenty-one attackers on 9/11 were, after all, Saudi citizens, and there were widespread suspicions that Saudi Wahhabis provided considerable monetary support for the Islamic State during its rampage. Saudi Arabia is also the site of the holiest sites of Islam at Mecca and Medina, adding to the conservatism that weighs on the regime.

The need for Saudi Arabia to modernize and become a more normal part of the international system arises from these kinds of forces. Saudi Arabia has been a major regional influence because it could hold the world hostage to its petroleum. It must find a different, and probably more conventional, way to assert itself as an important, even pivotal, regional actor. This effectively means it must compete with Iran for that position, and without the influence of oil wealth, it is not well positioned to do so. The recent condominium between Saudi Arabia and other Persian Gulf states with Israel thus serves as a double-edged geopolitical attempt both to contain Iranian interest expansion and to use its new relationship with the Israelis to enhance its geopolitical position. The initiative would have been impossible not long ago as the Saudis were leading advocates of the destruction of Israel, but Israeli nuclear weapons, which are quite capable of transforming the Saudi desert into an irradiated wasteland, have changed that relationship. The Israelis, of course, are acutely aware of this change and why it has occurred, and the result is to reinforce their attachment to their regional nuclear hegemony.

THE SPIN-OFFS

The central triangular competition between Israel, Iran, and Saudi Arabia also extends to other sources of regional conflict. Iran and Israel are the major contestants and have the most to gain or lose, but so do the participants themselves. The contest over the Shiite Crescent is the most obvious, especially in the western portion of the crescent. The Iranians have been active in Syria to support the Assad regime that shares Shiism with them. Southern Syria has been a staging ground for Iranian-sponsored raids into Israel to try to dislodge the Israelis from their Syrian Golan stronghold and to establish themselves as a major post–civil war influence in the region. A strong continuing Iranian presence allows them to gain additional strength among Lebanese Shiites and to help Iran try to champion Palestinian statehood. All these goals, of course, are opposed by the Israelis. This ongoing competition will be influenced by whether Syria survives the civil war intact or splits into several states, one of which would be headed by the Alawite Shiites who currently rule the country (the Assad family).

The impact of change in the Crescent reverberates even further. The Palestinian and Kurdish issues remain on the agenda, and the resolution of either or both would change the region's geopolitics or at least open new possibilities for changing the adversarial relationship among the actors. The Palestinian problem has been the longest standing, spanning most of the post-1948 period. It is both a moral and territorial issue. When Israel was created, both the Jews and the Arab Palestinians agreed they would cohabit the region amicably, including the implicit recognition that the Palestinians, like the Israelis, deserved a state of their own. Those intentions proved unattainable, as there was simply not enough desirable territory to satisfy the sovereign needs of both groups, and the West Bank (which was part of Jordan until 1967) became hotly contested territory, accelerated by the aggressive pursuit of further Jewish immigration as part of the Greater Israel policy. As Israeli power has grown and its population has increased, the Palestinian situation has grown worse, and advocacy of the Palestinian state has eroded in the shadow of Israel's mushroom-shaped cloud. Most of the international community remains rhetorically committed to a Palestinian state, but its practical attainment continues to fade and rarely makes the public spotlight in the Muslim world. At the moral and geopolitical levels, the march toward Israel annexation remains a major regional barrier to any kind of lasting, just regional solution.

The Kurdish desire for statehood has received far less attention internationally and within the United States. At one level, this is strange, because the Kurds have been useful allies for the Americans in places like Iraq and against the Islamic State (IS), whose forces were effectively contained and defeated by Kurdish militias. The Kurds feel they deserve American support and appreciation for what they have done to make the region less conflictual; they have received minimal assistance in their quest.

The dissolution of the Crescent's (and the region's) two most artificial states is also part of the problem. The breakup of Iraq would likely be into three states: a Shiite state in the south, a Sunni state in the middle (the so-called Sunni triangle), and the Kurdish Autonomous Region has been an independent state in fact if not name since 2003, along with Rojava (Syrian Kurdistan). Iraqi Kurdistan could easily form the critical mass for a more comprehensive Kurdistan, a prospect opposed most strongly by Turkey and Iran.

The other state that could dissolve is Syria. It has deep divisions between the Sunni majority and the minority Shiite (Alawite) government, but should the government prevail—as seems virtually certain—that outcome will be delayed for some time. In that case, Syria will likely turn its attention to regaining control of the Golan Heights and allow Rojava to remain a semi-independent entity like Kurdish Iraq. Given the massive need for rebuilding financing after the war and the likelihood adequate funds will be unavailable, Syria will likely remain a source of concern for the foreseeable future.

The problems of the region, particularly from a U.S. vantage point, end with the longest physical American involvements—Afghanistan and Iraq. Iraq is much more a part of the regional mix than Afghanistan. Iraq is part of the Shiite Crescent, it both borders upon Iran and its largest single population segment is Shiite. At the same time, Iraqi Shiites are Arab while the Iranians are Persian. Iran seeks primary influence in the country, a situation some say the U.S. invasion of 2003 inadvertently promoted. Iraqi Kurdistan is also part of the heart of what would be an independent Kurdistan.

Afghanistan does not fit neatly into any aspect of regional politics. It is a physical outlier located at the eastern periphery of the region, and its fiercely independent tribesmen simply want to be left alone by all outsiders, including the Middle Easterners discussed here. Afghanistan's blessing and curse is geography. It is a blessing because its location and forbidding topography take it outside the mainstream of the rest of the region. It is a curse because, as noted earlier, major east–west and north–south trade and invasion routes traverse it. The Afghans are difficult to defeat and conquer, but they also attract outsiders who do not leave willingly. A reasonable question can be raised about why the United States did not know about or recognize these dynamics in 2001 when it failed to capture Osama bin Laden but stayed in the country after bin Laden and his colleagues had left. Beyond preventing the possible return of Al Qaeda to the country, it is hard to discern a positive American interest in Afghanistan.

CHALLENGES FOR THE NEW ADMINISTRATION

Most of the extensive conflicts in the Middle East have deep roots that only change at the margins from one American administration to another, and how the United States has dealt with most matters in the area do not change a great deal if a Democrat or a Republican occupies the White House. The three major enduring American interests, a secure Israel, reliable and reasonably priced access to petroleum, and the absence of outside influence (other than American and some European) have dominated policy for over seventy years. Except for mostly Arab attempts to defeat Israel over the first quarter century of Israeli independence, these policy preferences have been realized with acceptable outcomes from an American viewpoint.

Most of the more apocalyptical prospects have declined since Israel established its effective military hegemony in the region. This means there have been essentially no major threats to the premier American interest of protecting Israel since 1973. This situation is clearly positive for the Israelis, for whom its major geopolitical challenges have been in the form of terroristic artillery attacks from across the border in places like Lebanon and Syria, actions for which the Israelis blame the Iranians for sponsorship and support. These attacks are, however, limited asymmetrical warfare annoyances, not qualitatively the kind the Arabs threatened in the immediate aftermath of Israel's declaration of statehood.

There is, however, a geopolitical double-edged sword of sorts that has accompanied the changed Israeli situation. Israel is admittedly much more secure physically than it has ever been, but the reasons for its security are the seeds for possible greater future instability. Particularly under the Trump administration, Israel was materially bolstered greatly by the United States. Trump endorsed territorial expansion into Syria and took actions that added momentum to Israeli annexation of the West Bank and denial of Palestinian statehood like accepting Jerusalem as the capital of Israel, while continuing the very generous subsidization of Israel with American aid (Israel receives more military aid from the United States than any other country). Trump and Netanyahu have been politically joined at the hip, and this is a reversal of more traditional U.S. policy that was closer to Israel than any other regional state but not to the point of offering Israel a geopolitical carte blanche. The effective abandonment of Palestine, whose self-determination had previously been an American goal, is an example that was swept aside by the Trump administration and the discredited "peace plan" for the West Bank offered by the administration in 2020.

The negative edge of the security sword arises from how Israel achieved its preeminence. Put simply and bluntly, the reason is nuclear weapons. Since 1973, when Israel secretly armed its nuclear arsenal and threatened to use it when it was in some danger of losing the Yom Kippur War, the threat that Israel makes to other regional actors is that if they menace, and especially if they threaten to defeat Israel in combat, those actors face the very real and sincere threat Israel will destroy the attacker with nuclear weapons. The possible (but impossible to predict) escalatory possibilities cannot be known in advance, and the question has always been whether any country would be crazy enough to use nuclear weapons when doing so could result in an escalation that could destroy the original attacker. Citing Masada and the Holocaust, the Israeli response of "never again" is based on the Samson Option of taking down the temple on itself as well as its enemies. They effectively warn their potential opponents that yes, they are crazy enough to initiate the end of days. Although it is a very debatable assertion, if one asks the question what nuclear power would be most likely (or least unlikely) to start a nuclear war, Israel is a candidate.

It is in this sense that Israeli nuclear weapons pose a geopolitical problem for everyone, including the United States. Israel is not the most powerful country in the world, but it may be the most dangerous. Nuclear weapons have made it the most powerful force in the Middle East, but that is part of a geopolitical dilemma as well. By any measure other than those weapons, Israel is not the primary state in the region. Iran is, and Iran wants to be recognized as not only the leading Shiite state in the region, but as the regional pivotal state. A quick look at the map and population statistics tells why. Iran has the largest population of any state in the region, for instance, and is wealthy if funds frozen by the United States are returned to it.

There is only one barrier to Iran's ambition, Israeli nuclear weapons, and both sides know it. If Israel did not have its bomb in the basement, it would, by virtue of its economy, highly trained and proficient Israeli Defense Force and its material and moral support by the United States, be one of the primary powers in the region but not a state that is so feared that nobody could even contemplate assaulting it. Knowing Israel could lob nuclear weapons onto a threatener's territory makes the contemplation of such a threat or action potentially suicidal and crazy: the calculation of the American-Soviet balance as MAD (for mutual assured destruction) was not a coincidence.

There are, of course, two rejoinders that make this arrangement potentially much less attractive than it must seem to Israel. The first is uncertainty. The world, after all, has exactly one experience with the use of atomic weapons, and the attack occurred when the attacking United States was the only nuclear possessor. When multiple states (including countries otherwise connected to Israel) have such weapons and a nuclear attack occurs, what happens next? The disturbing, but absolutely correct, answer is that no one knows. Given the grisly possibilities, no one wants to find out. To my knowledge only the Israelis have confronted this scenario and not answered it with an unqualified negative. "Never again" remains part of the calculus.

The other rejoinder is that Israeli nuclear weapons distort the geopolitics and allows Israel both to act as regional bully and arbiter of regional power. Nuclear weapons make Israel the effective pivotal state in the region, a claim they could not credibly make without them. That brings Iran into the mix. If both Israel and Iran had nuclear or weapons or neither of them did, there is little question that Iran would be the regional pivotal state. That shift in power would create a whole new set of questions and problems, but it would relieve others. Could, for instance, a nonhegemonic Israel continue to occupy disputed territories and resist the creation of a sovereign Palestinian entity? It would certainly be more difficult than it is, and especially how it has been for the past four years.

Nuclear imbalance has created the current balance in the region, and only the alteration of that balance can change it. The two most obvious possibilities are either the transformation of the region back to being nuclear weapons free or the Iranian acquisition of a nuclear capability. Israel opposes either solution. The Israelis see their arsenal as their ultimate source of safety and would be very reluctant to return to what they would view as a condition of weakness and vulnerability, even if the United States renewed or reinforced their pledge to protect them at all costs. The French force frappe lesson taught them that. Absolute opposition, including active, violent means, to the Iranian nuclear program, is a core part of Israeli security policy. The third possibility is a Middle East where both countries have nuclear weapons and they develop a relationship of mutual deterrence like the Cold War.

What changes will the Biden administration seek to implement to stabilize the situation? Cooling down Israeli-Iranian enmity will not solve all the region's many conflicts, but it is also likely that not much stabilization will progress as long as these two remain at one another's throats. For the last four years, virtually all American policy has been in support of Israel and in opposition to Iran, with an attempted minimization of American involvement in the rest of the region. That will certainly change. The Biden team brings a decidedly multilateralist philosophy to international relations, and most of the rest of the world was far less supportive of American policy under the Trump team. The Biden team is heavily made up of veteran multilateralists who helped craft pre-Trump policy. The Democrats have always favored the two-state solution on Palestine, and new Secretary of State Tony Blinken was one of the authors of the JCPOA. American return to multilateralism will likely be a high priority. There is little doubt that things will change. But how? What do you think?

BIBLIOGRAPHY

Alavi, Seyed Ali. *Iran and Palestine: Past, Present, Future.* New York: Routledge, 2019.

Allsop, Harriet. *The Kurds of Syria: Political Parties and Identity in the Middle East.* London: I. B. Tauris, 2015.

Anderson, Scott. *Lawrence in Arabia: War, Deceit, Imperial Folly, and the Making of the Modern Middle East.* New York: Anchor Books, 2013.

Axworthy, Michael. *A History of Iran: Empire of the Mind.* New York: Basic Books, 2016.

Bacevich, Andrew. *America's War for the Greater Middle East: A Military History.* New York: Random House, 2016.

Beaumont, Peter. "Trump's Middle East Plan: Key Points at a Glance." *Guardian* (online), January 28, 2020.

Benaim, Daniel, and Jake Sullivan. "America's Great Satan: The 40-Year Obsession with Iran." *Foreign Affairs* 98, 6 (November/December 2019), 56–66.

Beres, Louis Rene. *Surviving Amid Chaos: Israel's Nuclear Strategy.* Lanham, MD: Rowman & Littlefield, 2016.

Biden, Joseph R. Jr. "Why America Must Lead Again: Rescuing American Foreign Policy After Trump." *Foreign Affairs* 99, 2 (March/April 2020), 64–76.

Bregman, Ahron. *Cursed Victory: A History of Israel and the Occupied Territories, 1967 to the Present.* New York: Pegasus, 2015.

Cohen, Avner. *The Worst-Kept Secret: Israel's Bargain with the Bomb.* New York: Columbia.

Firro, Tarik. *Wahhabism and the Rise of the House of Saud.* Sussex, UK: Sussex Academic Press, 2018.

Fontaine, Richard. "The Nonintervention Delusion: What War Is Good For." *Foreign Affairs* 98, 6 (November/December 2019), 84–98.

Fromkin, David. *A Peace to End All Wars: The Fall of the Ottoman Empire and the Creation of the Modern Middle East* (Twentieth Anniversary Ed.). New York: Holt Paperbacks, 2010.

Ghattas, Kim. *Black Wave: Saudi Arabia, Iran, and the Forty-Year Rivalry That Unraveled the Culture, Religion, and Collective Memory in the Middle East.* New York: Henry Holt, 2019.

Gordon, Philip H. "The False Promise of Regime Change: Why Washington Keeps Failing in the Middle East." *Foreign Affairs* (online). October 7, 2020.

———. *Losing the Long Game: The False Promise of Regime Change in the Middle East.* New York: St. Martin's Press, 2020.

Gunter, Michael. *The Kurds: A Divided Nation in Search of an Identity.* Princeton, NJ: Markus Weiner, 2018.

Hersh, Seymour M. *The Samson Option: Israel's Nuclear Arsenal and American Foreign Policy.* With a New Afterword. New York: Vintage, 1992.

Hiro, Dilip. *Cold War in the Islamic World: Saudi Arabia, Iran, and the Struggle for Supremacy.* Oxford, UK: Oxford University Press, 2019.

Karpin, Michael. *The Bomb in the Basement: How Israel Went Nuclear and What That Means for the World.* New York: Simon & Schuster Reprints, 2006.

Katz, Yaakov, and Yoaz Hendel. *Israel vs. Iran: The Shadow War.* Washington, DC: Potomac Books, 2012.

Kerr, Robert M. (ed.). *Syrian Civil War: The Essential Reference Guide.* New York: ABC-CLIO, 2020.

Louer, Lawrence. Translated by Ethan Rundell. *Sunnis and Shi'a: A Political History.* Princeton, NJ: Princeton University Press, 2019.

Malley, Robert. "The Unwanted Wars: Why the Middle East Is More Combustible Than Ever." *Foreign Affairs* 98, 6 (November/December 2019), 38–47.

Maloney, Suzanne. "Dreams of Westphalia: Can a Grand Bargain Solve the Middle East Problem?" *Foreign Affairs* 99, 1 (January/February 2020), 143–158.

McGurk, Brett. "The Cost of an Incoherent Foreign Policy: Trump's Iran Imbroglio Undermines U.S. Priorities Everywhere." *Foreign Affairs* (online), January 20, 2020.

Mearsheimer, John J., and Stephen M. Walt. *The Israel Lobby and U.S. Foreign Policy.* New York: Farrar, Straus and Giroux, 2007.

Megsamen, Kelly. "How to Avoid Another War in the Middle East: De-Escalating after the Soleimani Strike." *Foreign Affairs* (online), January 4, 2020.

Melamed, Avi. *Inside the Middle East: Making Sense of the Most Dangerous and Complicated Region on Earth.* Washington, DC: Skyhorse, 2016.

Munayyer, Joshua. "There Will Be a One-State Solution: But What Kind of State Will It Be?" *Foreign Affairs* 98, 6 (November/December 2019), 30–36.

Parsi, Trita. *Treacherous Alliance: The Secret Dealings of Israel, Iran, and the United States.* New Haven, CT: Yale University Press, 2008.

Phillips. Christopher. *The Battle for Syria: International Rivalry in the New Middle East.* New Haven, CT: Yale University Press, 2016.

Power, Samantha. "The Can-Do Power: America's Advantage and Biden's Choice." *Foreign Affairs* 100, 1 (January/February 2021), 10–24.

Simon, Steven. *Iran and Israel: The Iran Primer.* Washington, DC: United States Institute for Peace Press, 2019.

Snow, Donald M. *Cases in International Relations: Principles and Applications.* Ninth Ed. Lanham, MD: Rowman & Littlefield, 2021.

———. *The Middle East, Oil, and the American National Security Policy: Intractable Conflicts, Impossible Solutions.* Lanham, MD: Rowman & Littlefield, 2016.

Van Creveld, Martin L. *The Land of Blood and Honey: The Rise of Modern Israel.* New York: Thomas Dunne, 2010.

Van Dam, Nikolaus. *Destroying a Nation: The Civil War in Syria.* London: I. B. Tauris, 2016.

Ward, Terence. *The Wahhabi Code: How the Saudis Spread Extremism Globally.* Baltimore, MD: Arcade Press, 2018.

Index

Abdal-Mahdi, Adil, 124
Abdullah II (King of Jordan), 122
Afghanistan, vii–viii, 2, 17, 32, 162, 164, 166–67
Afghan Persian Dari, 164
Afghans, 31, 163, 164, 168
Afghan War: cultural artifacts influencing, 164–65; as forever, xiv, 161–64; importance and attainability of objective, 166; lessons of, 166–68; sufficiency and salience of objectives, 164–66
Alawites of Syria, 21, 29, 103, 108, 126, 205
Alexander the Great, 163, 168
Algeria, 2
ammonium nitrate explosion, in Lebanon, 113
Anatolia, Turkey, 18, 88, 112
Anbar Awakening, AQI and, 108
Anglo-Iranian Oil Company, 26
animosities, tribal, 21, 81, 164, 190
AQ. *See* Al Qaeda
AQI. *See* Al Qaeda Iraq
Arabian Peninsula, 17, 21, 121, 144, 145, 151
Arabs, 21, 26, 65, 103, 164; Iraqi, 84, 87; Palestinian, 35, 62, 70; Sunni, 94, 108, 125. *See also* United Arab Emirates
Arab Spring, xi, 101, 104, 127–28
Arbatov, George, 3
arms, 22, 40, 113. *See also* nuclear weapons
al-Assad, Bashar: administration, viii, 27, 29, 86, 103, 104, 105, 125, 131, 134; criticism of, 110; opposition to, 107, 108, 109; support for, 114, 115, 117; war crimes and, 107
al-Assad, Hafiz, 103
asymmetrical warfare, 149, 156, 207; Iran and Palestine with, 30, 46, 66, 72; with Lebanon and Israel, 121; U.S. military with, viii, ix, 9, 31, 168, 171
Atoms for Peace program, 41

Bacevich, Andrew J., ix, 10, 31, 186
Bahrain, 21, 121, 123, 124, 128, 135
Balkans, ix, 10
Baloch, 164
Bantustans, 67
Bazzi, Mohamad, 113
Beaumon, Peter, 66–67
Ben-Gurion, David, 40
Benjamin, Daniel, 193

Beres, Louis Rene, 39, 40, 43–46, 50–51, 54, 62
BiBi. *See* Netanyahu, Benjamin
the Bible, 17, 83; David and Goliath, 29, 36, 48, 189
Biden, Joe: Afghanistan and, 166; challenges agenda, 200–203; challenges for, 197–200, 207–10; forever wars and, 162; on Middle East, 179; with Saudi Arabia and Gulf States, 204–5; spin-offs and, 205–7
Bill of Rights, U.S., 4
bin Laden, Osama, 11, 25, 92, 127, 170, 207
birth rates, 64
Blinken, Antony, 202, 210
Bolton, John, 129–30
Brunei, 79, 152
Bush, George H. W., 90, 129, 170
Bush, George W., 127, 173

Cable News Network (CNN), 90
Caliphate: AQI and, 105, 108, 128; establishing, 85, 86; ISIS and, 92–93, 118; in Kurdistan, 88; in Levant, 69; rebirth of, 10, 14; terrorism and, 173. *See also* Islamic State
Carter, Jimmy, 65
Cases in International Relations (Snow), 116
Cases in U.S. National Security (Snow), x
casualties: Afghanistan with U.S., vii; Kurdish territory and U.S., 92; Syrian Civil War, 10
cataclysm (nakbah), 35, 59
Central Intelligence Agency (CIA), 146, 183
chemical weapons, 83, 90–91, 108, 114, 127, 170, 171
China, 28, 144
Choosing Policy (CP), 51; assisting or impeding peace process, 73–75; endless wars avoided, 174–75;

impacts on U.S., 117–18, 135–38; with Israel and peace or resistance, 53–55; Kurdish state and, 96–97; U.S. interests and alternatives in Middle East, 11–14, 31–33
CIA. *See* Central Intelligence Agency
CIA World Factbook (2019–2020), 48, 124, 142
citizenship, 63, 80
climate change, 5
Clinton, Bill, 170
CNN. *See* Cable News Network
coal, 24
Cohen, 38
Cold War, Iran and Saudi Arabia: actor and anachronism, 151–53; comparison, 142–44; competition, xiv, 30, 141–42; conflict, 155–56; contemporary Saudi mix, 153–54; equation on Saudi side, 150–51; Iranian Revolution, 146–48; Iraq, Saudi Arabia, both or neither, 156–57; with relationship evolving, 144–45; revolutionary Iran and two great Satans, 149–50
colonialism, 23, 81
conflicts: DWICs, 175; with geopolitics and difficulties for U.S., xiv, 179–80; hot spots, 10–11; Iranian-Saudi Arabia, 155–56; Kurdistan and background of, 84–85; Middle East, 28–31; violent, 19. *See also* warfare; wars
Constitution, U.S., 4
convergence, Middle East and, 185–86
COVID-19 (coronavirus), 106, 109, 133, 153–54, 197
CP. *See* Choosing Policy
CRS. *See* Foreign Affairs Congressional Research Service
cultural artifacts, Afghan War and, 164–65
cyber warfare, 8
Cyrus the Great of Persia, 144, 182, 191

David (biblical character), 29, 36, 48, 189
Dayan, Moshe, 39, 44
demographics: Iran and Saudi Arabia, 143; Israel, 65; Muslims, 21; Palestine and time bomb, 64–67; populations and, 26, 86, *95*, *96*; security and, 72
desperation, in warfare, ix
developing world internal conflicts (DWICs), 175
Diab, Hasan, 124
Dimona EL 102, 41
disaster (nakbah), 35, 59
"Don't Pull Back" (Satloff), 23
Doran, Michael S., 63
Druze, 110, 131, 134
DWICs. *See* developing world internal conflicts

economy: GDP, 105, 124, 143; Muslims and, 22; Syria, 105–6, 109, 115; U.S. military costs, 31–32, 48, 73–74
Egypt, 20, 23, 128, 184; Israel and, 59, 182; peace, 49, 59, 182; population, 115; Russia and, 114; Six-Day War and, 38; Syria and, 103
electricity, for Turkey, 18
enclave state, 79
Erdogan, Recep Tayyip, 89, 112
Erlich, Reese, 114
ethnic divisions, 21

fanaticism, religious, 22
Federation of American Scientists (FAS), 40
Filkins, Dexter, 92, 93
Fishman, Louis, 21
Fontaine, Richard, 32
Foreign Affairs (magazine), ix, 23, 63, 162
Foreign Affairs Congressional Research Service (CRS), 32
forever wars, xiv, 161–64, 169–71. *See also* Afghan War; Iraq War

France, 2, 23, 37, 41, 91, 102, 202
Friedman, Thomas L., 7
fundamentalists, religious, 21

Gambia, 79
Gantz, Benny, 61
Gause, F. Gregory, III, 154, 188
Gaza, 50, 59, 63–66, 69–70, 75
GDP. *See* gross domestic product
genocide, 35, 36, 38, 107, 204
geopolitics, 1, 23, 36, 105; choices ahead, 189–94; between conflict sources and difficulties for U.S., xiv, 179–80; current balance, 180–86; future directions, 188–89; interests and responses with U.S. and Middle East, 186–87; Shiite Crescent and, xiv, 121–22, 130; summary today, 187–88
Germany, 24, 105, 116, 199
Gibson, Bryan R., 89
Golan Heights, xi, 49, 59, 61, 111, 182; as disputed territory, 50, 63, 68–69; expansion, 44–45, 50–51; population, 45, 48; Syria and, 29, 130–31, 198, 206; Syrian, 36, 103, 130, 200; tourism, 30, 45, 68
Goliath (biblical character), 29, 36, 48, 189
Gordon, Philip H., viii, 183
Grand Mosque, 126, 145
Great Britain, 23, 91, 102, 163
Great War. *See* World War I
gross domestic product (GDP): Israel, Iran, Lebanon, Iraq, 124; Saudi Arabia, 143; Syria, 105, 124
The Guardian (newspaper), 66–67
Gulf States, U.S. with Saudi Arabia and, 204–5
The Gun and the Olive Branch (Hirst), 42

Haass, Richard N., 2
Haiti, vii, ix, 186
Hamas, 22, 69, 74

Hazara, 164
heroin, 167
Hersh, Seymour M., 38, 40, 41, 42
Hezbollah, 22, 109, 113; Iran and, 69, 74, 111; Lebanon and, 104, 122, 126, 130, 131
Hirst, David, 42
Hitler, Adolf, 38
Holocaust, 24, 26, 35, 36, 62, 201, 208
hostage crisis, in Teheran, 126, 148
Houthis of Yemen, vii, 21, 28, 154, 184
human rights violations, 64, 180
Hussein, Saddam: AQ and, 127, 161; fall of, 87, 91–92; Iraq War and, 162, 169–70, 171–72; Kuwait and, 90; poison gas and, 83, 90; terrorism and, 31

Ibn Abd al-Wahhab, Muhammad, 151
Ibn Saud, Muhammad, 151
ICC. *See* International Criminal Court
IDF. *See* Israeli Defense Force
IISS. *See* International Institute for Strategy Studies
IISS Military Balance (2016), 149
imperialism, xii
India, 40, 43, 50, 123, 157
Indyk, Martin, xi, xii, 192
interests: control and priorities, 4; geopolitics with U.S. and Middle East, 186–87; intensity of, 5–7; international, 4–5, 26; Israel with U.S. influence, policy options and, 47–50; Kurdistan and competing, 86–89; level of, 4–5; LTV, 6–7, 13–14, 32; Middle East and U.S. with changing, 25; of Shiite Crescent and U.S., 129–31; U.S. and Kurdistan with conflicting, 89–93; vital, 6–7, 23, 32, 52–53, 93, 165, 173, 187, 189–90. *See also* national interests
International Criminal Court (ICC), 107, 114
International Institute for Strategy Studies (IISS), 143, 149
international interests, 4–5, 26
Iran, viii; Afghanistan and, 162; with asymmetrical warfare, 30, 46, 66, 72; conflicts in, 10; demographics, 143; GDP, 124; great Satans and revolutionary, 149–50; Hamas and, 69, 74; Hezbollah and, 69, 74, 111; influence, 27; Israel and, 28, 43, 47; Kurdistan and, 87, 94; Kurds, Syria post civil war and, 131–34; military, 143, 146, 149; Muslims in, 21; nuclear weapons, 41, 198; oil and, 146, 189; Palestine and, 30, 46, 66, 69, 72, 192; peace and, 191, 193–94; population, 94, 115, 208; Quds revolutionary militia, 9–10, 133, 149; SAVAK, 147; Shiite Crescent, 155; Shiite Muslims in, 116; Syria and, 109, 115–17; Turkey and, 84; U.S. and, 7, 8–10, 116–17, 141–42, 146, 182–83, 198–99, 202–3; White Revolution, 147, 203. *See also* Cold War, Iran and Saudi Arabia
Iranian Azerbaijan, 24, 146
Iranian Revolution (1979), 2, 90, 126, 145, 146–48, 188
Iranian-Saudi Arabia, 155–56
Iran-Iraq War (1980–1988), 10, 87, 143
Iraq: AQ and, 170–71; AQI, 105, 107–8, 128; Arabs, 84, 87; GDP, 124; Iran-Iraq War, 10, 87, 143; IS and, 88; Kurdish Autonomous Region of, 18, 86, 87, 206; Kurdistan and, 87–88, 94; Muslims in, 21; no-fly zone over, 91; oil and, 87; Operation Desert Storm and, viii–ix, xii, 9–10, 83, 90, 127, 186; partition and, 24; population of Kurds in, 87; Saudi Arabia and, 156–57; Shiite Muslims, 84; sovereignty of, 91; Sykes-Picot agreement and, 23–24, 101, 103, 110; Syria and, 20, 136–37; U.S. in, vii
Iraq War (Second Persian Gulf War) (2003–2011), xi, xii; as forever, xiv,

161–63, 169–71; importance and attainability of objective, 172–73; lessons of, 173–74; sufficiency and salience of objectives, 171–72

Iraq War, first (Persian Gulf War) (January–February 1991), 170, 187; Operation Desert Storm, viii–ix, xii, 9–10, 83, 90, 127, 186

irredentism, 20, 82, 84, 88

IS. *See* Islamic State

ISIS, viii, 19, 69, 107, 109, 122; Caliphate and, 92–93, 118; expansion of, 118, 172–73, 185; Syria and, 105–6

Islamic State (IS), xi, 18, 21–22, 66; AQ and, 107; Caliphate and, 10, 14, 69, 85, 86, 88, 92–93, 105, 108, 118, 128, 173; Kurds and, 93, 206; resurgence, 14, 166

Israel: arms, 40; birth rate, 64; catastrophic threats to, 45; challenges, 201–2; criticism of, xiv, 2; demographics, 65; Egypt and, 59, 182; France and, 202; GDP, 124; geopolitics and, 36; with impediments to U.S. policy, 50–52; Iran and, 28, 43, 47; Jews, 65; Lebanon and, 121; Likud Party, 39, 46, 61; mushroom-shaped cloud of, 205; with nationalism, 20; nuclear weapons, 29, 36, 37–41, 48, 50, 53, 71, 72, 155, 180, 182, 191–92, 193, 198–99, 204–5, 208; nuclear weapons, evolution of, 41–42; Palestine and, 26, 29, 46, 52–53, 64–68, 182, 205; peace and, 53–55, 191, 193–94; populations, 48, 65, 70–71; role of, xiii, xiv, 29, 35–39; Samson Option and, 40, 42, 43–44, 50, 52–53, 62, 66, 191, 202; Saudi Arabia and, 30, 141, 180; security, 27, 36, 38, 39, 70, 72; Six-Day War and, 38, 44, 126; Soleimani and, 10; sovereignty of, 59; as strategic liability, xiv; Syria and, 104, 109, 111; territorial expansion, 44–47, 49, 50–51, 63, 70; two-state solution, 38, 39, 46, 62–67, 71, 74, 180, 193, 210; UAE and, 141; U.S. and, vii, xi, xiv, 25–27, 36–39, 47–49, 51–54, 60, 62, 66–67, 71–72, 73, 130, 137, 138, 179–82, 190–91, 198–99, 200–201, 207–8; U.S. influence, interests and policy options, 47–50. *See also* Palestine

Israeli Defense Force (IDF), 67, 121, 208

Israeli-Palestinian reconciliation, xi

Italy, 23, 79, 82

JCPOA. *See* Joint Comprehensive Plan of Action

Jerusalem, 60–61, 63, 65–66, 74, 130, 198, 207

Jews: Holocaust and, 24, 26, 35, 36, 62, 201, 208; Israeli, 65; Masada and, 37, 40, 42, 208; population, 26. *See also* Israel

Joint Comprehensive Plan of Action (JCPOA), 199, 202, 203, 210

Jordan, 20, 38, 49, 122, 135

journalists, murder of, 154, 183–84, 199, 204

Karzai, Hamid, 165, 167

Kashmir, 17

Khamenei, Ali (Ayatollah), 149

Khashoggi, Jamal, 154, 184, 199, 204

Khomeini, Ruhollah (Ayatollah), 148, 149

Kim Jung Un, 8

Kosovo, vii, 10, 186

Kurdish Autonomous Region of Iraq, 18, 86, 87, 206

Kurdish Project (2016), 88, 95

Kurdish self-defense militia forces (pesh merga), 85, 87, 88, 93, 97, 128, 173

Kurdish state, CP and, 96–97

Kurdish Workers Party (PKK), 18

Kurdistan, viii, 186; with American conflicting interests, 89–93; with background of conflict, 84–85; Caliphate in, 88; free, 19, 24; Iran and, 87, 94; Iraq and, 87–88, 94; irredentism and, 82, 88; irredentism and case of, 84; oil and, 89–90, 94; policy options and consequences, 93–96; populations, *95, 96*; with statehood, 86–89, 96–97; statelessness and, 80–83; with stateless people, xiii–xiv, 29, 79–80; Syria and, 86, 94, 97; territory and U.S. casualties, 92; Turkey and, 88–89, 93, 94. *See also* Syrian Kurdistan

Kurds, viii, xiii, 194; with defeat of ISIS, 19; Iran, Syria post civil war and, 131–34; IS and, 93, 206; Palestinians and, 20–21; with partition, 110; populations, 80, 84, 86, 87, 88, 108; sovereignty and, 87; Sunni Muslims, 85; Syrian, 18, 110; territories, 85; Turks and ethnic, 18, 112; U.S. and, 83, 91, 93, 171; VIs of, 93

Kushner, Jared, 38, 67, 154, 179

Kuwait: Operation Desert Storm and, viii–ix, xii, 9–10, 83, 90, 127, 186; U.S. military in, 32, 171

land, 63, 70–71, 82. *See also* territories

Lebanon, vii, 38, 59, 121, 124; Hezbollah and, 104, 122, 126, 130, 131; Palestinian refugees in, 64, 113, 131; Sykes-Picot agreement and, 23–24, 101, 103, 110; Syria and, 102, 103–4, 109, 112–13, 122, 130; Syrian Civil War refugees in, 113, 131

Lesotho, 152

less-than-vital (LTV) interests, 6–7, 13–14, 32

Levant, 69, 121

Libya, 128

Liel, Alon, 67

Likud Party, Israel, 39, 46, 61

LTV interests. *See* less-than-vital interests

Lustick, Ian S., 48, 66

MAD (mutual assured destruction), 209

Malkasian, Carter, 164, 168

Malley, Robert, ix, x, 10, 157

Maloney, Suzanne, 18

Marines, U.S., vii, 2, 10

Masada (73 AD), 37, 40, 42, 208

MBS. *See* Mohammad bin Salman

McGurk, Brett, 27, 104, 105

Mearsheimer, John J., xiv, 73

Middle East: American policy and endless war in, 31–33; with Cold War priorities, 25–27; conflict, 28–31; in context, 20–21; convergence and, 185–86; CP and U.S. interests and alternatives in, 11–14, 31–33; current balance in, 180–86; geopolitics, interests and responses with U.S., 186–87; politics, 21–22; with post-Cold War priorities, 27–28; regional instabilities overview, xiii, 17–19; U.S. and, xii–xiii, 11, 19, 22–24, 66–68, 179–80; with U.S. interests changing, 25; U.S. national security policy in, vii, x–xi, 1, 20, 23, 32, 162, 169, 179; violence in, 17, 19–20, 83

The Middle East, Oil, and the U.S. National Security (Snow), 19

The Middle East, Oil, and the U.S. National Security Policy (Snow), x

military: Alawites of Syria and, 108, 126; IDF, 67, 121, 208; IISS Military Balance, 149; Iranian, 143, 146, 149; Russia, 146; Saudi Arabia, 143, 149

military, U.S.: with asymmetrical warfare, viii, ix, 9, 31, 168, 171; costs, 31–32, 48, 73–74; Operation Anaconda, 165, 168; Operation Desert Storm, viii–ix, xii, 9–10, 83,

90, 127, 186; troops deployed, 32, 136, 166, 171, 186–87, 189
Mohammad bin Salman (MBS), 145, 152, 156; human rights violations and, 180; with Khashoggi murder, 154, 184, 199, 204; Vision 2030 and, 188
Monaco, 79
Mongol Hordes, 163
Mossadegh, Muhammad, 26, 117, 146, 183, 193
Mubarak, Hosni, 128
Muhammad (Prophet), 141, 151
multilateralism, 197–98, 210
multinationalism, 20, 21, 81–82, 84, 188
mushroom-shaped cloud, xi, 113, 192, 205
Muslims, 21–22, 43, 84, 116. *See also* Sunni Muslims
mutual assured destruction. *See* MAD
mutual deterrence, nuclear warfare with, 43

nakbah (disaster, cataclysm), 35, 59
Nasser, Gamal Abdul, 170
nation, defined, 80–81
national interests: control and priorities, 4; CP with U.S. and alternatives in Middle East, 11–14, 31–33; in geopolitical, economic, political and historical context, 1; intensity of, 5–7; level of, 4–5; purpose, 1; in realm of endless war, 10–11; security and, 3; threats and responses, 7–10; U.S., 25–27
National Interest study (2015), 40
nationalism, 20, 21, 81–82, 84, 188
national security policies, 3, 19–20; Saudi Arabia, 153
national security policy, U.S.: in Middle East, vii, x–xi, 1, 20, 23, 32, 162, 169, 179; *The Middle East, Oil, and the U.S. National Security*, x, 19; multilateralism as, 197–98, 210; 9/11 influencing, 127

NATO, viii, xii, 89, 91, 97, 112
navies, 133, 146, 149
Navy, U.S., 2
NBC News, 122
Netanyahu, Benjamin (Bibi): administration, 29, 36, 63, 65, 125, 131, 135; Gantz and, 61; on Iran, 43; legacy, xiv, 37; Palestine and dream of, 67–68, 71; policies, 45–46, 200; territorial expansion and, 63; Trump and, 37–38, 39, 51, 53–54, 60, 66, 67–68, 73, 130, 137, 138, 181, 187, 189, 198, 207–8
Newsweek (magazine), 32
9/11: AQ and, 11, 126, 127, 161, 163, 164–65, 167; influence of, 28, 30–31, 127, 170, 179, 185, 186; national security policy influenced by, 127; Saudi Arabia and, 204; Wahhabi of Saudi Arabia and, 25, 204
Nixon, Richard, 12, 13, 54
no-fly zone, over Iraq, 91
Northern Watch. *See* Operation Provide Comfort
North Korea, 8, 43, 181
nuclear warfare, 37, 181, 208, 209; mushroom-shaped cloud and, xi, 113, 192, 205; with mutual deterrence, 43; Samson Option and, 40, 42, 43–44, 50, 52–53, 62, 66, 191, 202
nuclear weapons: Dimona EL 102 reactor, 41; Iran, 41, 198; Israel, 29, 36, 37–41, 48, 50, 53, 71, 72, 155, 180, 182, 191–92, 193, 198–99, 204–5, 208; Israel and evolution of, 41–42
Nuristani, 164

Obama, Barack: administration, vii, 2, 93, 103, 117, 130, 169, 202; Arab Spring and, 128
occupation: Afghans and resistance to, 164; territories, 82–83
oil: access to, 185; Anglo-Iranian Oil Company, 26; AQ and, 22; arms and,

22; Iran and, 146, 189; Iraq and, 87; Kurdistan and, 89–90, 94; Kuwait and, 90; *The Middle East, Oil, and the U.S. National Security*, x, 19; OPEC, 24; possession, 22; producers, 2, 22; Russia and, 24, 116–17; Saudi Arabia and, 90, 132, 144, 151, 154, 183, 188; Soviet Union and, 27; Turkey and, 86; U.S. and, 27–28, 189; as VI, 189–90; World War II and, 24

Old Testament, 17, 83

Oman, 32, 152

one-state, two-state solution and, 62–63

OPEC. *See* Organization of Petroleum Exporting Countries

Operation Anaconda, U.S. military and, 165, 168

Operation Desert Storm (January–February 1991), viii–ix, xii, 9–10, 83, 90, 127, 186

Operation Provide Comfort (Northern Watch), 83, 91, 171

Organization of Petroleum Exporting Countries (OPEC), 24

Oslo accords (1993), 67, 73

Ottoman Empire, 23, 79, 101, 132

Owen, John M., 17

Pahlavi, Mohammad Reza (Shah): fall of, 2, 126, 142; hostage crisis and, 126, 148; rule of, 117, 123, 141, 144, 145, 146, 147, 183, 203

Pakistan, 40, 115, 157, 167

Palestine: approaches to problem, 62–64; with asymmetrical warfare, 30, 46, 66, 72; barriers to accord, 70–71; BiBi's dream, 67–68, 71; Holocaust and, 24; Iran and, 30, 46, 66, 69, 72, 192; Israel and, 26, 29, 46, 52–53, 64–68, 182, 205; other parties influenced by, 68–69; parameters and options, 61–62; peace and, 70–71, 73–75; sovereignty of, 63, 67, 74; as stateless nation, xiii, xiv, 59–61,

73; Syria and, 68–69; time bomb demographic and, 64–67; treatment of, xiv, 2; two-state solution, 38, 39, 46, 62–67, 71, 74, 180, 193, 210; UNRWAPR, 59, 64, 71; U.S. and, 27, 71–73; with U.S. policy options and consequences, 69–70

Palestinians: Arabs, 35, 62, 70; Kurds and, 20–21; population, 64–67; refugees, 64, 113, 131

partition, 24, 110, 134

Pashto language, 164

Pashtuns, 163–65

peace: Atoms for Peace program, 41; CP and, 53–55, 73–75; Egypt, 49, 59, 182; Iran and, 191, 193–94; Israel and, 53–55, 191, 193–94; Jordan, 49; negotiations and land for, 63; Oslo accords, 67, 73; Palestine and, 70–71, 73–75; Samson Option and, 62; Saudi Arabia and, 191; SIPRI, 40; Versailles Peace Conference, 79, 80, 103; World War I and, 18

Peace of Westphalia, 18

Pergola, Della, 64

Persia, 20, 144, 182, 191

Persian Empire, 144

Persian Gulf War (January–February 1991). *See* Iraq War, first

Persians, 21

pesh merga (Kurdish self-defense militia forces), 85, 87, 88, 93, 97, 128, 173

Petraeus, David, 19

pirates, 2

PKK. *See* Kurdish Workers Party

poison gas, 83, 90, 114

policies, 3, 19–20, 45–46, 153, 200; Israel with impediments to U.S., 50–52; Israel with U.S. influence, interests and, 47–50; Kurdistan with options and consequences, 93–96; Middle East with endless war and American, 31–33; Palestine and U.S.,

69–70. *See also* Choosing Policy; national security policy
politics, 3, 21–22. *See also* geopolitics
Pompeo, Michael, 199
populations: Afghan, 163; Arabs, 65; Egypt, 115; Golan Heights, 45, 48; Iran, 94, 115, 208; Israel, 48, 65, 70–71; Jews, 26; for Kurdistan-affected states, 95; Kurds, 80, 84, 86, 87, 88, 108; land area including Kurdistan and regional, 96; Lebanon, 131; Muslims, 43; Pakistan, 115; Palestinians, 64–67; sizes and changes, 124; Sunni Muslims in Syria, 107; Syria, 107, 108; Turkey, 94
Putin, Vladimir, 106, 114, 115, 190

Al Qaeda (AQ): AQI and, 105; Iraq and, 170–71; IS and, 107; motivations, 66; 9/11 and, 11, 126, 127, 161, 163, 164–65, 167; oil and, 22; Operation Anaconda and, 165, 168; Taliban and, 163, 166, 167
Al Qaeda Iraq (AQI): Anbar Awakening and, 108; Caliphate and, 105, 108, 128; Sunni leaders and, 107–8
Qatar, 32, 152
Quds revolutionary militia, Iran, 9–10, 133, 149

Rabin, Yitzakh, 63
al-Rasheed, Madawi, 19
refugees: Palestinians, 64, 113, 131; Syrian Civil War, 113, 131; UNRWAPR, 59, 64, 71
religion, xii, 17, 21, 22, 25, 143
Republic of South Africa (RSA), 41, 67
resistance: Israel and CP with peace or, 53–55; to occupation by Afghans, 164
responses, to national interests, 7–10
Rhodes, Ben, 169
rights of people, UN Charter on, 88
Rohani, Hassan, 124, 149

Rojava. *See* Syrian Kurdistan
RSA. *See* Republic of South Africa
Rumsfeld, Donald, 173
Russia, viii, 49, 163; arms, 40; diminished, 188–89; Egypt and, 114; Iranian Azerbaijan and, 24; military, 133; oil and, 24, 116–17; Ottoman Empire and, 23; Syria and, 20, 25, 27, 86, 103, 107, 109, 114–15, 189; Turkey and, 86, 136. *See also* Soviet Union

Sadjadpour, Karim, 9
Salafists, 21–22, 105, 128, 129
Salman bin Abdulaziz al-Saud (King of Saudi Arabia), 153, 192
Samson Option: Israel and, 40, 42, 43–44, 50, 52–53, 62, 66, 191, 202; without peace possibility, 62; U.S. and, 74
Satans, two great, 149–50
Satloff, Robert, 23
Saudi Arabia: as actor and anachronism, 151–53; conflicts in, 11; contemporary mix, 153–54; demographics, 143; GDP, 143; Iran and view of, 150–51; Iranian-Saudi Arabia, 155–56; Iraq and, 156–57; Israel and, 30, 141, 180; with Khashoggi murder, 154, 184, 199, 204; military, 143, 149; with nationalism, 20; national security policy, 153; 9/11 and, 204; oil and, 90, 132, 144, 151, 154, 183, 188; peace and, 191; sovereignty of, 152, 153; with terrorism in Yemen, 28, 153, 180; UAE and, 141; U.S. and, vii, 142, 183–85, 199; U.S. with Gulf States and, 204–5; Wahhabi of, 21–22, 25, 144, 150, 151–52. *See also* Cold War, Iran and Saudi Arabia
SAVAK, 147
Second Persian Gulf War (2003–2011). *See* Iraq War

security: barriers to accord and physical, 70; demographics and, 72; Israeli, 27, 36, 38, 39, 70, 72; national interests and, 3
sharia law, 22, 145, 152
Shiite Crescent, 155, 185, 192, 205; characteristics of major states in, *123*; dissolution of, 206; geopolitical balance in, xiv, 121–22, 130; interests of U.S. and, 129–31; Iran, Kurds and Syria post civil war, 131–34; landmark events, 125–29; region and overview, 122–25; U.S. influenced by, 135–38. *See also* Iran; Iraq; Lebanon; Syria
Shiite Muslims, 21, 22, 84, 116
Shikaki, Khalil, 67
Shinkman, Paul D., 112
Simon, Steven, 193
SIPRI. *See* Stockholm International Peace Research Institute
Six-Day War (1967), 38, 44, 126
Sky, Emma, 172
Snow, Donald M., x, 19, 116
Soleimani, Qasem, 6–7, 8–10, 28, 133, 149
South Africa. *See* Republic of South Africa
sovereignty: defined, 7; Iraqi, 91; irredentists and, 82; Israeli, 59; Kurds and, 87; Kuwaiti, 10; Palestinian, 63, 67, 74; Saudi Arabian, 152, 153; state and, 81
Soviet Union, 25, 27, 32, 188
Spain, 23
state, 204–5; CP and Kurdish, 96–97; enclave, 79; sovereignty and, 81. *See also* Islamic State; two-state solution
statehood, Kurdistan, 86–89, 96–97
stateless nations, xiii, xiv, 59–61, 73. *See also* Palestine
statelessness, Kurdistan and, 80–83
stateless people, xiii–xiv, 29, 79–80. *See also* Kurdistan

Stockholm International Peace Research Institute (SIPRI), 40
suicide bombings, 22, 70
Sunni Arabs, 94, 108, 125
Sunni Islam, 19
Sunni leaders, AQI and, 107–8
Sunni Muslims, 84, 85, 107; with Anbar Awakening, 108; Wahhabi of Saudi Arabia, 21–22, 25, 144, 150, 151–52
Swaziland, 152
Sykes-Picot agreement, 23–24, 101, 103, 110
Syria, 2, 59; Alawites of, 21, 29, 103, 108, 126, 205; Arab Spring and, 101, 104; conflicts in, 10–11; economy, 105–6, 109, 115; Egypt and, 103; as eye of storm, 103–4; France and, 102; GDP, 105, 124; Golan Heights and, 29, 130–31, 198, 206; importance of, xiv, 101–3; international ramifications and, 109; Iran and, 109, 115–17; Iraq and, 20, 136–37; ISIS and, 105–6; Israel and, 104, 109, 111; Kurdistan and, 86, 94, 97; Lebanon and, 102, 103–4, 109, 112–13, 122, 130; with other affected/interested states, 110–17; Palestine and, 68–69; Palestinian refugees in, 64; partition and, 24, 134; population, 107, 108; with regional actors impacted, 109–10; Russia and, 20, 27, 86, 103, 107, 109, 114–15, 189; Six-Day War and, 38; Sykes-Picot agreement and, 23–24, 101, 103, 110; Syrian Kurdistan and, 86; Turkey and, 102, 111–12; U.S. and, vii–viii, 86, 104, 107–8, 117–18, 200
Syrian Civil War, 29, 104, 122; casualties, 10; cost to rebuild, 105, 109, 115; post-civil war, Kurds and Iran, 131–34; post-civil war prospects, 106–8; prospects post-, 106–8; refugees, 113, 131
Syrian Golan Heights, 36, 103, 130, 200

Syrian Kurdistan (Rojava), viii, 111, 113, 206; battle over, 20; independence for, 30; neutral zone and, 85; population of Kurds in, 86; role of, 97; Syria and, 86; Syrian Kurds in, 18, 110; Turkey in, 18, 93, 102–3; U.S. and, 23, 29

Tajiks, 164
Taliban, viii, 31–32, 161, 163–64, 166, 167
target-rich environments, 43
territories: disputed, 47–48, 50, 63, 64, 68–69, 83; with IS expansion, 86; Israel with expansion, 44–47, 49, 50–51, 63, 70; Kurdish, 85; with lack of inhabitable land, 70–71; land and, 63, 70–71, 82; occupation, 82–83; Shiite Crescent and region, 122–25, *123*; U.S. casualties in Kurdish, 92
terrorism, xiii, 2, 23, 27, 173; Saudi Arabia and, 28, 153, 180; U.S. and, 28, 93; with U.S. VIs, 32, 165. *See also* 9/11
Thirty Years' War, ix, 18, 128
Thomas-Greenfield, Linda, 197–98
Thompson, Elizabeth F., 101
threats, to national interests, 7–10
Time (magazine), 9, 43, 61
tourism, Golan Heights, 30, 45, 68
tribes: Afghan, 164, 168; animosities, 21, 81, 164, 190; AQI and leaders of Sunni, 107–8; Pashtuns, 163–65
Trump, Donald: administration, x, 2, 3, 23, 27, 29, 63, 64, 74, 102, 103, 117, 157, 162, 169, 185, 197, 199–200, 201, 202, 210; Afghanistan and, vii, 166; Bolton and, 129–30; Golan Heights and, 50–51; MBS and, 154; Middle East and, xii–xiii, 11, 66–67, 179–80; Netanyahu and, 37–38, 39, 51, 53–54, 60, 66, 67–68, 73, 130, 137, 138, 181, 187, 189, 198, 207–8; Putin and, 190; Soleimani and, 7, 8–9; Syria and, viii, 86

Tunisia, 104, 127, 128
Turkey, viii, 17, 30, 84; Anatolia, 18, 88, 112; Kurdistan and, 88–89, 93, 94; NATO and, xii, 91, 97; population of Kurds in, 88; Russia and, 86, 136; Syria and, 102, 111–12; in Syrian Kurdistan, 18, 93, 102–3
Turkmen, 164
Turks, 18, 21, 112
2020 World Almanac and Book of Facts, 108
two-state solution: one-state and, 62–63; resistance to, 64–65, 66, 67; support for, 38, 39, 46, 62–63, 64, 67, 71, 180, 193, 210; variations of, 63, 74. *See also* Israel; Palestine

UAE. *See* United Arab Emirates
UN. *See* United Nations
United Arab Emirates (UAE), 123, 141, 152, 157, 179
United Nations (UN), 47, 88
United Nations (UN) Relief and Works Agency for Palestinian Refugees (UNRWAPR), 59, 64, 71
United States (U.S.): arms, 40; Bill of Rights, 4; casualties in Afghanistan, vii; casualties in Kurdish territory, 92; challenges for, 200–205, 207–10; CIA, 146, 183; Constitution, 4; CP and Middle East with interests of, 11–14, 31–33; CP with impacts on, 117–18, 135–38; geopolitics, interests and responses with Middle East, 186–87; geopolitics between conflict sources and difficulties for, xiv, 179–80; Holocaust and, 36; with hostage crisis in Teheran, 126, 148; interests of Shiite Crescent and, 129–31; Iran and, 7, 8–10, 116–17, 141–42, 146, 182–83, 198–99, 202–3; in Iraq, vii; with Iraq, Saudi Arabia, both or neither, 156–57; Israel and, vii, xi, xiv, 25–27, 36–39, 47–49, 51–54, 60,

62, 66–68, 71–72, 73, 130, 137, 138, 179–82, 190–91, 198–99, 200–201, 207–8; Israel and influence, interests and policy options of, 47–50; with Kurdistan and conflicting interests, 89–93; Kurds and, 83, 93, 171, 191; in Lebanon, vii; Marines, vii, 2, 10; Middle East and, xii–xiii, 11, 19, 22–24, 66–67, 179–80; *The Middle East, Oil, and the U.S. National Security*, 19; national interests, 1, 25–27; Navy, 2; oil and, 27–28, 189; Palestine and, 27, 71–73; policy and endless war in Middle East, 31–33; policy impediments and Israel, 50–52; policy options and consequences with Palestine, 69–70; quandary and Israel, 52–53; Samson Option and, 74; Saudi Arabia and, vii, 142, 183–85, 199; with Saudi Arabia and Gulf States, 204–5; Shiite Crescent influencing, 135–38; Soviet Union and, 32, 188; spin-offs, 205–7; Syria and, vii–viii, 86, 104, 107–8, 117–18, 200; Syrian Kurdistan and, 23, 29; Taliban and, 161; terrorism and, 28, 93; Turkey and, viii; Vietnam War and, vii, ix, xii, 12–13, 175; VIs, 7, 23, 32, 52, 53, 165, 173, 175, 187, 189–90; warfare costs, 31–32, 48, 73–74; Yemen and, vii. *See also* Afghan War; Iraq War; military, U.S.; national security policy, U.S.; 9/11

UNRWAPR. *See* United Nations Relief and Works Agency for Palestinian Refugees

Uzbeks, 164

Van Creveld, Martin, 42
Vatican City, 79, 152
Versailles Peace Conference (1919), 79, 80, 103
Vietnam War, vii, ix, xii, 12–13, 175
violence: conflicts and, 19; Middle East and landscape of, 17, 19–20, 83; with murder of journalist, 154, 183–84, 199, 204; religion and, 17, 22; with statelessness, 83; suicide bombings, 22, 70

VIs. *See* vital interests
Vision 2030, 188
vital interests (VIs): defined, 6; of Kurds, 93; oil as, 189–90; qualifications, 6; role of, 7; U.S., 7, 23, 32, 52, 53, 165, 173, 175, 187, 189–90

Wahhabi of Saudi Arabia, 21–22, 25, 144, 150, 151–52, 204
Walt, Stephen M., xiv, 73
war crimes, 107
warfare: cyber, 8; desperation in, ix; nuclear, xi, 37, 113, 181, 192, 202, 205, 208; U.S. costs, 31–32, 48, 73–74; in World War II, viii, ix. *See also* asymmetrical warfare
wars. *See specific* wars
wars, endless, 23; CP and avoiding, 174–75; forever and, xiv, 161–64, 169–71; in Middle East and American policy, 31–33; national interests in realm of, 10–11. *See also* Afghan War; Iraq War
Waterbury, John, 101
weapons: chemical, 83, 90–91, 108, 114, 127, 170, 171; nuclear, 29, 36, 37–42, 48, 50, 53, 71, 72
weapons of mass destruction (WMD), 161, 170, 171
Welsh, David, 81
West Bank: as disputed territory, 47–48, 50, 63, 64; expansion, 44–45; with lack of inhabitable land, 70–71; Palestinian refugees in, 64; symbolic importance, 60
White Revolution, 147, 203
Wikipedia, 10
winners, viii, ix, 12, 114, 167–68
WMD. *See* weapons of mass destruction
women, 152, 154, 184, 204

World War I (Great War), 18, 23–24, 79, 101, 102, 103, 110
World War II, viii, ix, 10, 24, 101, 208

Yemen, 10, 128, 143; Houthis of, vii, 21, 28, 154, 184; Saudi terrorism in, 28, 153, 180; U.S. and, vii

Yemen Civil War, 154
Yom Kippur War (1973), 42, 54, 146, 180–81, 182, 208

Zarqawi, Abu Musab, 108
zero involvement option, 14
zero-sum games, 83, 185

About the Author

Donald M. Snow is professor emeritus at the University of Alabama, where he taught courses on international relations, American defense policy, and foreign policy. He is the author of numerous textbooks including *Cases in U.S. National Security*, *U.S. Foreign Policy*, *Back to the Water's Edge*, Fifth Edition, *Regional Cases in U.S. Foreign Policy*, Second Edition, and *National Security*, Seventh Edition.

www.ingramcontent.com/pod-product-compliance
Lightning Source LLC
Chambersburg PA
CBHW022011300426
44117CB00005B/134